To James MacGregor Burns,
whose work and friendship inspired me

A Time
of Paradox
America from
Awakening to Hiroshima,
1890–1945

GLEN JEANSONNE
WITH DAVID LUHRSSEN

ROWMAN & LITTLEFIELD PUBLISHERS, INC.
Lanham • Boulder • New York • Toronto • Plymouth, UK

ROWMAN & LITTLEFIELD PUBLISHERS, INC.

Acquiring Editor: Niels Aaboe
Developmental Editor: Ann Grogg
Production Editor: Terry Fischer
Photo Editor: Andrew Boney
Typesetter: Andrea Reider

Published in the United States of America
by Rowman & Littlefield Publishers, Inc.
A wholly owned subsidiary of The Rowman & Littlefield Publishing Group, Inc.
4501 Forbes Boulevard, Suite 200, Lanham, Maryland 20706
www.rowmanlittlefield.com

Estover Road
Plymouth PL6 7PY
United Kingdom

British Library Cataloguing in Publication Information Available

Library of Congress Cataloging-in-Publication Data

Jeansonne, Glen, 1946–
    Time of paradox : America from awakening to Hiroshima, 1890–1945 /
    Glen Jeansonne.
        p. cm.
    Includes bibliographical references and index.
    ISBN-13: 978-0-7425-3381-3 (pbk. : alk. paper)
    ISBN-10: 0-7425-3381-6 (pbk. : alk. paper)
    1. United States—History—20th century. 2. United States—History—
20th century—Biography. 3. United States—Civilization—20th century.
I. Title.
E741.J428 2006
973.91—dc22   2006035628

Printed in the United States of America

⊗™ The paper used in this publication meets the minimum requirements of
American National Standard for Information Sciences—Permanence of Paper
for Printed Library Materials, ANSI/NISO Z39.48-1992.

Contents

PART II
An Era of Trial and Triumph, 1920–1945

Preface

A Time of Paradox has both a theme and a message. The theme derives from the inconsistencies and anomalies, some frustrating, some wonderful, in the human condition. The period covered in the book was a time of contradiction and irony, which I term paradox. I employ the word "paradox" in a metaphorical rather than in a literal sense. It is not a dictionary definition but can mean, in this context, irony, contradiction, a thing that seems to be what it is not, an unlikely event, or an oxymoron.

Each age has its share of paradoxes, in the metaphorical sense. Some are inherent to the march of civilization, with its relapses, and some are specific to the particular age. In the time covered here, the human condition never seemed more poignant; much was accomplished and much was lost. The term seems especially appropriate to this time because of the scope and dimension of both our successes and our failures. We dared greatly, and like all who dare greatly, we sometimes failed greatly. Yet the period saw the unconquerable aspect of the human will emerge intact. What is even more striking is the acceleration of the pace of change, a term that combines speed and rate of increase in speed, finally producing a momentum that carries over unless it is blocked. While change is inevitable, it is neutral in itself, neither good nor evil. Change, even for good, can be painful, but what is more painful is resistance to change.

The message of A Time of Paradox is more complex and potentially more important. Yet it cannot be summed up in a byte and might resonate differently with individual readers. This is no attempt to deliberately obscure but rather to grant every reader the right to his or her own interpretation. Inherently, people will read the book for different reasons, and find some parts more appropriate to their personal interests than others. But while A Time of Paradox is factual, it is more than a compendium of facts and illustrations. It is deliberately more personal, speculative, and provocative than the most textbooks, more imaginative than derivative, and it departs from some orthodox interpretations. It is succinct and jargon-free, yet it includes the essential facts as well as broad generalizations and original metaphors and examples. Unlike some similar books, it represents, for the most part, a single viewpoint. Although vulnerable to error of interpretation, the viewpoint is consistent, though it contains surprises. The author chose, for example, to devote more attention to such aspects of history as spirituality, technology, and sexuality, than comparable books. I hope to have done so in a manner that is open-minded and non-judgmental, yet take no offence to those who disagree. Errors of fact or interpretation can be mitigated by discussion and corrected in later editions.

For clues to the author's overall viewpoint, and the book's message, read carefully the prologue and the epilogue and, to a lesser extent, the prologues to the individual eras and the conclusions to the chapters within those eras. In general, I believe that such human traits as love and hate are not opposite emotions, but opposite extremes of the same emotion. And they can be transmuted.

Whether one reads *A Time of Paradox* as a scholar, a student, or a general reader, I hope it brings them pleasure as well as knowledge. The facts might be forgotten within a few years or submerged in the subconscious. The message in the metaphors might stick longer. Further, I have proceeded on the premise that history is a story about people much like ourselves and that when we read or write it we hold up a mirror to ourselves. People feel as well as think and *A Time of Paradox* is meant to appeal to feelings as well as to the intellect. The residue of the feelings will probably outlast the residue of the facts.

In addition, I believe the best guide to understanding history lies not in elaborate paradigms but in experience and common sense. There are definite patterns in history, but their origins and the way they emerge results from a mixture of factors, some obvious, some obscure, and some beyond human understanding. Though I believe things happen for a reason—otherwise there would be little point in studying or remembering them—I do not claim to know each specific reason. At best, I am an experienced guesser. Scholars should be careful about assuming that we are wiser than others. I have worked with fellow Ph.D.s my entire career, yet I suspect there are beggars on the streets of Calcutta with a potentially higher I.Q. than anyone at my university.

Another premise is that everything is connected. Thus I have tried to incorporate many varieties of history without purporting to be an expert in all of them. But appreciation of history requires not only an appreciation of its diversity but an understanding of how that diversity is connected. Albert Einstein believed that imagination is more important than knowledge in the study of physics. That is true in the study of history as well. After all, history tells us only the story of paths chosen. We do not know the results of where those not chosen might have led.

In analyzing the characters in our history books, I believe it is important to strike a balance between imposing the standards of our time on them, and viewing them in terms of what they knew at their time, and the realistic options they had. One surmises, for example, that General George Armstrong Custer might have reacted differently at Little Bighorn had he known of the Indians over the hill.

The organization of *A Time of Paradox* is related to its philosophical design and facilitates its use as a teaching tool, and as an escort through the past. The book is divided into Eras, each with a theme. Each era is divided into six chapters that cover topically, within a rough chronological framework, the events of that era. The chapter themes relate to the theme of the Era, which in turn connect to the overall theme of paradox. Each Era includes three brief biographical profiles that illustrate a sub-theme of the period. The individuals are not selected for their significance, nor are they necessarily representative. In fact, most are secondary figures. Rather, they are chosen because of their illustration of the diversity of the era and the overall theme of paradox, as well as for their human interest.

The book includes a prologue and an epilogue, which interpret, summarize, and draw conclusions. Anyone wanting an overview might read these first. In addition, there is a separate prologue introducing each era, which provides an interpretive overview. There is a timeline for each era and a selective list of readings. The book is designed to be succinct, yet factually comprehensive and reasonably priced. Its relative brevity facilitates the use of complementary, more specialized studies. The provocative interpretations are intended to stimulate dialogue, whether in the classroom, in book clubs, or in the minds of individual readers.

In retrospect, what strikes me most about the *A Time of Paradox* is its evolution in the direction of diversity and the breadth and breathtaking speed of change. The interconnections mentioned earlier include not only the interconnections of events to one another, but the interconnections of America to other nations, perhaps, we will find, to other worlds. More important are the connections between individuals. All of these connections were necessary to arrive at the point we now stand.

We are mortal, in a narrow sense, yet each of us leaves behind an imprint on the planet earth. King Arthur is supposed to have told his aspiring knights that before he gave them a sword they must become a poet. The world needs poets and students, spiritual warriors and military warriors, scholars, and plumbers. It would not work if we were all one kind. I am proud to be a historian and consider it important. Yet I have never been summoned in the middle of the night to fix a history book that had suddenly burst open.

Acknowledgments

I embark upon the prospect of thanking those who contributed to *A Time of Paradox* with trepidation. Because the genesis of the book is distant, and my memory is fallible, I might omit someone who rendered me valuable service. On the other hand, the help of some might be so subtle they may be surprised to be mentioned.

Bruce Borland, formally of HarperCollins, was crucial in accepting my idea for the book and more than any single editor believed in its trade potential. Mary Carpenter was largely responsible for bringing the book to Rowman & Littlefield. Laura Roberts Gottlieb of Rowman & Littlefield, the book's chief editor, exercised patience and coaxed out of me the best I could do. Andrew Boney was essential to the book's completion. Niels Aaboe is the final editor.

Over the course of a decade, about seventy-five referees read portions of the manuscript. However, only Ronald Snyder read the entire book and he wrote the most complete and thoughtful analysis. Of the readers who signed their reports, the most helpful were Leo Ribuffo, who, as usual, was intellectually honest, and Kari Frederickson, a former student, now a prominent historian.

David Luhrssen worked closely with me, especially in the book's final stages. He did the research and wrote the first draft of two of the chapters on cultural history. In addition, he helped with photograph selection, captions, and indexed the manuscript. I turned to Herbert M. Levine whenever I encountered a problem. An old teacher, colleague, and friend, Herb helped with photo and map research. He used his computer skills and strategic location near the Library of Congress to iron out numerous difficulties. I am grateful for the assistance of Michael Gauger, although he did not agree with the final version of the book.

I had a superb copy editor, Ann Grogg, who edited my previous book, *Transformation and Reaction*. Like most writers I incline to believe that the best strategy to altering my prose is benign neglect. Yet Ann improved it, while adhering to the principle: "If it ain't broke, don't fix it." Ann's husband Bob, who fact-checked, is one of the most meticulous historians I know. Meredith Vnuk checked facts and updated, as did Nick Katers, and Sarah Lager. Stacey Smith aided with photographic research, as did Mary Manion. Jacqueline Kelnhofer was my chief proofreader. Other proofreaders included David Luhrssen, Lori Lasky, Joan Hoss. Bruce Fetter, Neal Pease, and Lex Renda.

I owe major personal and professional debts to Joan Hoss. She literally lived with the book, typed the final manuscript, and prepared it for submission while I was away researching my next book on Herbert Hoover. Joan and John Kiekhaefer were my chief computer gurus. Though she is not a historian, Joan understands the book's underlying message better than anyone who has read it.

Greg Hoag is a wonderful teacher of nonacademic truths and Sarah Sullivan, my personal trainer, kept my body intact. Milton Bates advised me on many aspects of the manuscript, including style, content, and publishing strategy, from its inception.

Some of my colleagues lent key support. Neal Pease, Jeffrey Merrick, Joe Rodriguez, and especially Lex Renda helped adjust my teaching schedule to my biorhythms. Among colleagues or former colleagues who suggested sources in their areas of expertise are Michael Gordon, Mark Bradley, Bruce Fetter, Victor Greene, David Hoeveler, and David Healy. No persons in the department were more essential to the book's completion than Louise Whitaker, Anita Cathey, and Teena Rawls.

The past and current directors of the Golda Meir Library provided access to its resources and all have been personal friends: Bill Roselle, Peter Watson-Boone, and Ewa Barczyk. My most important friend who navigated me through the labyrinths of library research is Ahmad Kramah, whose knowledge of recent American history is exceeded only by his generosity. Two of my colleagues on the University Library Committee, Winston Van Horne, and Mordecai Lee, have been particularly supportive.

There are several historians from whose work I have profited, some of whom are personal friends: Thomas C. Reeves, John Milton Cooper, William B. Pemberton, David Fromkin, James MacGregor Burns, Michael Beschloss, Dennis Dickerson, James W. Cortada, Thomas Schoonover, John Ehrman, and the late Stephen Ambrose.

I want to acknowledge some of the major influences in my life: my late father, Ryan J. Jeansonne, who knew the New Deal first-hand; the late William

A Time of Paradox: America from Awakening to Hiroshima 1890–1945

> "Some are born great, some achieve greatness, and some have greatness thrust upon 'em."
>
> —Shakespeare, *Twelfth Night*

THE AMERICAN epoch from 1890 to 1945 was a time of paradox, of struggle and accomplishment, of lives lost and victories won. The paradoxes, or ironies, were plentiful. Who would expect that a man in a wheelchair would be elected president—not once, but four times, and become the nation's greatest politician? Who would imagine that we would win two world wars and lose more persons to death in an influenza epidemic that followed the Great War than in combat during both world wars combined? Or that we would lose more workers to industrial accidents on the home front than to battle in World War II? That during the war, life expectancy in America would actually increase. Certainly, these events seem paradoxical.

Yet my use of the word "paradox" is metaphorical rather than a precise dictionary definition. Every period of history has its paradoxes, which are unique to that time. Use of the word is particularly appropriate to twentieth-century America, however, because the paradoxes were prolific and magnified. They exploded out of the barrel of a gun, the backfire of a Model T, or the detonation of an atomic bomb.

By the standards of the world's great civilizations—of China, India, Persia, Rome, Greece, and Egypt—the United States was an adolescent.

Few, such as Alexander the Great, are given the opportunity to lead at such an early age. Americans awakened near the dawn of the century to new roles in industry, culture, and diplomacy, and flexed their military muscles in the Spanish-American War and World War I.

Under two almost-great presidents in the Era of Awakening, America announced its place on the world's stage. Theodore Roosevelt brought a child's enthusiasm, and, some quipped, a child's maturity, to the presidency. An example of the latter is that, like some children, he enjoyed playing at war, and considered it humankind's most heroic enterprise. Yet as president he never fought a war. His successor, the generation's second near-great president, did fight one, much to the envy of Roosevelt. Woodrow Wilson, a great domestic leader, vowed to fight "a war to end all wars." Paradoxically, both presidents, who had inspired such promise, ended sadly. An embittered Roosevelt wrenched apart his party and made Wilson's victory certain in 1912. Wilson failed to achieve the reputation as peacemaker for which he yearned. Paradoxically, he is remembered more for the failed Treaty of Versailles than for his remarkable accomplishments.

Yet if politics and diplomacy engaged intellectuals, ordinary Americans awakened to other problems and delights. They entered the century on an upbeat tempo, pounding tinny pianos with the magic of ragtime composed by such prolific geniuses as Scott Joplin. Another genre, the blues, provided a somber, haunting quality, reflecting the experience of slaves. Americans thrilled to the athletic triumphs of Jim Thorpe, fretted over the "Black Sox" scandal of 1919, and increasingly enjoyed basketball, invented as an indoor alternative to football in 1891.

At the beginning of the nineteenth century no one could be certain that the newly established United States possessed a culture distinct from its British motherland. By the start of the twentieth century, however, the United States had produced writers and painters admired the world over, even if major figures such as Henry James and John Singer Sargent did much of their work in Europe. Although it would not prove easy to banish long-ingrained feelings of cultural inferiority and insecurity, Americans in the new century would take their place in the vanguard of culture.

The impact of American culture owed much to political and economic forces as the nation ascended to its role as the world's banker, industrial powerhouse and political arbiter. It also resulted from the changing character of the country's people as immigrants from many nations added new vitality to the American scene and black migrants from the rural South brought their music and oral traditions to the urban centers of the North. Without the input of ethnic minorities, many of them subject to prejudice, American culture would not have attained its sweeping scope and joyful emotional release.

Like politics and culture, gender and race relations were in flux. Women campaigned for suffrage, strived to uplift the poor, and to prevent war. African Americans joined the National Association for the Advancement of Colored People (NAACP) to advance their claims to political rights. W. E. B. Du Bois, a prolific and militant black intellectual, debated the more traditional black educator, Booker T. Washington, over priorities and tactics for African American progress.

If the first generation of twentieth-century Americans was astonished by the acceleration of change, the changes of the interwar era (1920–1945) were stunning. The nation's most prosperous decade was followed by its worst depression, topped by World War II, leaving Americans victorious, patriotic, and prosperous, yet drained and eager for the comfort of family and the security of a steady job.

Under two Republican presidents in the 1920s, Warren G. Harding and Calvin Coolidge, the government receded to the background amidst a technological and sexual revolution. A silver stake was driven through Harding's reputation by the scandals that emerged after his death in 1923. His successor, Coolidge, quiet and quaint, was popular because much of the nation was prosperous, though pockets of poverty remained.

The most important revolution of Americans during the era, arguably the most important of the century, did not occur in politics or economics but in sexuality. The sexual revolution began before the twentieth century and showed no signs of slackening in the third millennium. Technology accelerated the sexual revolution, and science and medicine complemented it. The automobile became a portable bedroom. Sexuality also blossomed in popular culture and ultimately came to dominate it.

Americans debated religious issues, such as the teaching of evolution in public schools. The debate did not end with the trial of John Thomas Scopes for teaching evolution in Tennessee in the 1920s, but continues with cultural wars over intelligent design in the twenty-first century.

Two practical inventions transformed American life: the automobile and the radio. Automobiles began chugging along dusty roads early in the century and in the 1920s Henry Ford put the nation on wheels. Americans could find new jobs, vacation, embark on unchaperoned dates, and work on auto assembly lines. They could also rob banks, kidnap children, get speeding tickets, breathe exhaust fumes, get rear-ended, and be knocked down at a crosswalk.

The radio transformed communications, entertainment, politics, and culture. We listened to jazz, then swing. We laughed at Amos 'n' Andy, unaware, at the time, that they were implicitly racist. Virtually every genre that appeared in silent films, talkies, and technicolor got its start on radio, which in turn had adopted many of them from Vaudeville. News reporting made the nation aware. Cultural homogeneity was accentuated. Tin Pan Alley, Broadway, and Louis Armstrong came to Main Street. Franklin Roosevelt gave us Fireside Chats and assured us that the only thing we had to fear was fear itself. Father Charles Coughlin warned us of conspiracies of international bankers and Jews who had foisted upon us the gold standard. In Europe, Hitler and Mussolini mesmerized the masses, as did Huey Long in America, showing that every technological marvel has its dark side.

When 1920s prosperity collapsed with a thud after the stock market crash of 1929, Herbert Hoover, a vaunted Progressive, became the most activist president in history. Hoover struggled valiantly yet vainly to heal the most intractable depression in modern history. A shy, quiet, modest Quaker, Hoover was nonetheless imaginative and energetic. Under the right conditions he could inspire, as he had done in saving Belgium from starvation during World War I.

Hoover addressed the psychological letdown by delivering about eighty speeches via radio, which he wrote himself, because he considered ghostwritten speeches intellectually dishonest. (He was the last president to write his own speeches.) While not as eloquent a radio speaker as FDR, he has been underestimated. He was better than Harding, Coolidge, presidential candidates Al Smith and Alf Landon, and on a par with Harry Truman. The chief problem was not Hoover's speeches but the fact that 25 percent of the work force was unemployed.

In his pre-presidential career Hoover had fed the starving, clothed the naked, inspired the hopeless. Now opinion turned against him with a vengeance. No president in the twentieth-century has been subjected to greater vilification. Paradoxically, Hoover's public image was almost totally the opposite of reality. Probably the tag "do-nothing" president applied less to Hoover than to any of his predecessors. Moreover, beneath his mask of Quaker stoicism, he was a caring, sensitive person, who did not visit soup kitchens because he feared he might cry in public.

Hoover helped save farms and homes from foreclosure, loaned money to failing banks and businesses through the Reconstruction Finance Corporation (RFC), supported labor unions, and exhorted states and private businesses to accelerate construction, hold the line on wages, and avoid dismissing workers. He tried to rally his nation at a time when only results would have been convincing and he did not have a crooked bone in his body. Most of his countrymen failed to appreciate his efforts, however, as unemployment spread its gloom across the land. They wanted an economic miracle and Hoover had none.

No Democrat could have won in 1928, during the sunshine of "Coolidge Prosperity," and no Republican could have won in 1932, during the downpour that followed the lightening bolt of the stock market crash in 1929. The Democratic candidate, Franklin Roosevelt, promised a vague New Deal, yet scolded Hoover for profligate spending and vowed to slash the budget and trim the bureaucracy. A paradox, indeed, if one could read tea leaves.

For students of American history, the chronology of the presidency from the early 1930s to the mid-1940s is simple. There was only one president: Franklin Delano Roosevelt. Roosevelt, like Hoover, was calm and courageous. He had battled polio and possessed an iron will that made him confident, tough, inspirational, and resilient. If Roosevelt was no economic mastermind, he was a political one. Altogether, the New Deal symphony he directed was a cacophony of intellectual dissonance. The bureaucracy swelled, public works rose, and reforms created the foundation for the modern welfare state. An army of bureaucrats and workers took up pencils and shovels to do battle with unemployment. Yet the depression did not end. Hoover had said that the solution to ending the depression lay not in creating new, temporary, government jobs but in restoring old, permanent jobs. This the New Deal never did.

But for American presidents, even in the worst of times, domestic policy is only one barrel of a two-barreled shotgun. Clearly, Adolf Hitler was the greatest threat to world peace in the first half of the twentieth century and had he not tried to gorge Germany with more conquests than it could digest, might have pulled Western civilization down with him. Yet the attack on America came from Japan, not Hitler, and Americans found themselves in a two-front war.

The victorious war also ended the depression, brought full employment, and prosperity greater than the 1920s. Hitler's holocaust discredited racism. For the first half of the twentieth-century, victory over the Axis Powers and the end of the Great Depression marked the apogee of American achievement. It solidified FDR's place in the pantheon of Great Presidents. Americans had traveled a long way since the frontier closed in 1890 and the new century beckoned them to unprecedented opportunities. The country had been toughened by depression and war had, seemingly, taken its place as the world's foremost power. Yet Americans were not permitted to rest upon their laurels. New perils, more complex paradoxes, lay ahead.

The 1890s:
Bridge to the
Twentieth Century

A MERICANS TRAVELED a narrow path to the twentieth century that widened into a highway as the century progressed and the velocity of change accelerated. When they traversed the bridge of the 1890s into the new century, they found not a paradise but a paradox. The prelude was filled with surprise and disappointment and ended with a roar and new responsibilities.

The End of the Century

The gala that previewed the twentieth century was the World's Columbian Exposition held at Chicago in 1893. There were new inventions galore, including a fabulous White City aglow with tens of thousands of lights when the sun set. Visitors rode the world's first Ferris wheel and watched magicians and the belly dancer "Little Egypt" perform her gyrations. The historian Frederick Jackson Turner warned that the American frontier was closed. The 1890 census, he said, revealed that there was no longer a continuous westward moving line of settlement. The frontier, with the abundance of free land, shaped the American character and Americans would be a different people without it, he forecast.

The decade was stressful, with industrialization, labor turmoil, massive immigration, and business consolidation. Some of America's political leaders straddled the centuries. Theodore Roosevelt, for example, blended the old and the new. He was at home in the city and on the open range, thirsting for adventure as America awakened to world power. William Jennings

THE GREAT WHITE CITY
Columbian Exposition in Chicago, 1893.
(Library of Congress)

Bryan championed rural interests, ran for president three times, and also was involved in the debates over world power.

The debate over world power was accompanied by a debate over economic power. Many of the industrial moguls overlapped the centuries, and they saw themselves hailed as industrial statesmen and condemned as "robber barons" who gouged the public and exploited labor. Partly, their status went up or down with the economy and the economy was, for the most part, an engine of prosperity, yet the Panic of 1893 inaugurated the most catastrophic depression to date. Politicians, too, saw their fates rise and fall as they tried to ride the winds of change. Political power shifted to states, regions, and cities, as well as ethnic concentrations. Yesterday's city boss was today's villain. Reform began below and crested just after the turn of the century when an assassin's bullet introduced an Era of Awakening.

From Farm to Factory

Between the Civil War and the turn of the century, everything—good and bad—grew. First was the economy. Second was the city. From a nation of billowing fields, America became a land of belching smokestacks. In the 1890s, for the first time, the value of industrial goods eclipsed the value of agricultural products. By 1890, 51.7 percent of the labor force worked outside agriculture, and by 1894, American industry was producing twice as much as British industry. Industry not only grew, but its range of products became broadened. By 1900 the chief industries, in order of value, were slaughtering and meatpacking, flour milling, lumbering, iron and steel, and machine-shop products. American agriculture, the chief exports, dominated world markets, and total exports exceeded imports.

Innovations in technology drove industrial production. Moreover, there were improvements in business management, in more efficient use of labor, and in industrial organization, as well as revolutions in transportation and communication. Especially important was the mass of relatively prosperous consumers on which industry thrived. The vast empire of the British, by contrast, had greater numbers but less purchasing power.

The stories of some of the industrial titans, whether one admired or loathed them, are the stuff of fantasy fiction. Within their stories are imbedded some of the paradoxes of the age. Andrew Carnegie, a poor immigrant from Scotland, is an archetypal example. Beginning as a telegrapher for the Pennsylvania Railroad, by age twenty-four, Carnegie became superintendent of its western division. Meanwhile, he invested his savings, surviving the downturn of 1873, and concentrated his money in the steel industry. Employing new technology he created a steel monopoly that also controlled iron mines and railroads. A ruthless businessman, he undersold rivals, bankrupting them. In 1901 he sold his empire to the United States Steel Corporation for $250 million, making him one of the richest men in the world. Carnegie spent the rest of his life as a philanthropist, endowing libraries, universities, charitable trusts, foundations, and Carnegie Hall in New York City. Some felt the gifts were tainted because of Carnegie's merciless business tactics. Figures such as Carnegie, hard-fisted at times, soft-hearted at others, are among the paradoxes of the era.

Similar to Carnegie, only richer and more ruthless, John D. Rockefeller did for oil what Carnegie did for steel. Ironically, he retired before widespread use of automobiles created an even greater demand for his product (used largely for lighting and medicine during his time). Like Carnegie, Rockefeller created a vertical monopoly including pipelines, refineries, and oilfields, forcing railroads to pay him rebates for his business. By 1880 Rockefeller's Standard Oil controlled 90 percent of the American oil industry. Staying just within the law, company attorneys devised a form of organization whereby stockholders held shares not in tangible assets, but in a trust composed of the assets of other companies. By 1897 Rockefeller largely retired from managing the company and devoted much of his time to philanthropy. Before his death in 1937, he gave away an estimated $550 million, establishing the Rockefeller Foundation and the General Education Board and endowing the University of Chicago.

For all the good works done with their money, the industrialists had more power than is healthy in a democracy. They wielded it to crush strikes—including the Homestead strike at a Carnegie Steel mill in 1892, a violent 1892 silver mine strike at Coeur d'Alene, Idaho, and the 1894 strike at the Pullman Palace Car Company near Chicago. Carnegie was not involved in the Homestead strike, having retired and left management of the mill to Henry Clay Frick; nevertheless, it tarnished his reputation. When contract negotiations deadlocked, Frick locked out the workers, hiring replacements and guards to protect the new employees. The strikers threatened the guards, and in response Frick employed some three hundred Pinkerton detectives, who engaged in a gun battle with the strikers, in which seven men died. After the detectives surrendered, the governor dispatched the militia to preserve order. Much of the public seemed to sympathize with the strikers until an anarchist not connected with the strike attempted to kill Frick, but Frick recovered from his wounds, and the strike was settled on company terms.

The Pullman strike occurred in the wake of the Panic of 1893. George Pullman, whose company manufactured railroad sleeping cars, slashed wages and laid off workers, claiming that the company's solvency depended on the cuts. Laborers complained that he refused to reduce rents and prices at his company town. Pullman would not negotiate with the American Railway Union, so Eugene V. Debs, president of the union, organized a strike against all lines handling Pullman cars. U.S. Attorney General Richard Olney obtained an injunction against the strike on the grounds that delay of the trains interfered with delivery of the mail. The union refused to obey the order, federal troops were sent in, and riots ensued, leaving thirteen dead, fifty-three wounded seriously, and seven hundred freight cars burned. The strike was lost and Debs served six months in prison for defying the injunction. The Supreme Court upheld his sentence and the use of injunctions against strikes, a practice that Congress did not outlaw until 1932.

Companies in the sugar, whiskey, copper, and lead industries abused their power by copying Rockefeller and forming trusts. As the public came to fear the trusts because of their unscrupulous conduct, huge profits, and monopolies, lawmakers investigated, condemned the trusts, and, on the federal level, passed the 1890 Sherman Antitrust Act to ban them. But there were few prosecutions under the vague law. Standard Oil circumvented it by reorganizing as a holding company, a corporation that held a controlling share of at least one other firm; and the Supreme Court adopted a probusiness

The Populists spoke for the rural poor who felt victimized by the industrial and agricultural revolutions. In the late nineteenth century, farmers increased production by introducing machinery, employing innovative methods of cultivation, and bringing millions of fertile acres in the West under cultivation. The most productive farmers in the world, their harvest exceeded demand and caused prices to plummet. Farmers paid dearly to get their products to market because railroads charged them exorbitantly. Banks extorted unreasonably high interest rates. Compounding their plight were cultural isolation, lack of access to city conveniences, and a decline in status. Once viewed as the backbone of democracy, farmers were now stereotyped as crude and ignorant. Some Populists blamed Jews and other scapegoats for their problems. Yet their movement addressed valid grievances, and many of their reform proposals later became law. Their most enduring legacy was their idea that the government was responsible for reforming the economy.

Farmers had created fraternal groups that became political ones, beginning with the Grange in 1867 and continuing with the Farmers' Alliances, the forerunners of the Populist Party. In 1890 the party was born at a convention in Topeka, Kansas, and some Populist candidates won election to Congress. The farmers who organized heeded Mary Lease of Kansas, who urged them to "raise less corn and more hell!" But not enough hell was raised in the 1892 presidential election, in which Cleveland polled 5.5 million popular votes and 277 electoral votes to Harrison's 5.18 million and 145. The Populist ticket won more than 1 million popular votes and 22 electoral votes, carrying Kansas, Colorado, Idaho, and Nevada. The elections were the first in which the Australian, or secret, ballot printed by the government rather than by the parties, was used nationally.

Shortly after Cleveland's inauguration, the Panic of 1893 struck, the stock market collapsed, and the nation plunged into depression. By the end of the year, some five hundred banks and almost sixteen thousand businesses failed. Railroad construction declined, consumer sales fell, and unemployment reached about 20 percent. In 1894 Jacob Coxey, in a widely imitated demonstration, led a march of unemployed workers called "Coxey's Army" on Washington. He wanted to protest the administration's refusal to inflate the currency in order to create jobs. The economy rebounded in 1895, only to bottom out the next year.

Cleveland blamed the Sherman Silver Purchase Act and bimetallism; he believed restoration of the gold standard was essential. Populists continued to argue that gold was the problem, not the solution. Cleveland persuaded Congress to repeal the act, but the drain of gold from the Treasury continued. When the reserves fell below $100 million, the level that economists considered essential to maintaining the standard, Cleveland floated four bond issues. These increased gold reserves, yet they were costly to the government and reaped lucrative profits for rich investment bankers such as J. P. Morgan. Moreover, they failed to end the depression. Cleveland also failed to provide the meaningful tariff reform he had promised in his campaign. The Wilson-Gorman Tariff enacted only marginal reductions; it was amended more than six hundred times in the Senate, mostly to protect special interests. The one progressive feature of the legislation, a small income tax, was rejected by the Supreme Court in 1895.

The economic dislocation cost the Democrats control of both the House and Senate in 1894. Southerners and westerners who sympathized with Populist demands for inflation rejected Cleveland. In 1896, the silver Democrats gained the upper hand and nominated William Jennings Bryan, who roused the convention with his speech in defense of the silver standard. At thirty-six, the Nebraskan was the youngest major party nominee in history. His nomination on a silver platform preempted the chief issue of the Populists, whose only realistic chance for victory was to endorse Bryan, though that would sacrifice their overall program in pursuit of a single plank. Nonetheless, they nominated Bryan.

Bryan was one of the more famous politicians never elected president. A great orator, if not a great intellect, he was an economic liberal and a religious fundamentalist. He considered becoming a minister before turning to law and politics. Moving from his native state of Illinois in 1887 in pursuit of a career, he was elected to Congress from Nebraska in 1890 and 1892. Defeated in his bid for the Senate in 1894, he became a journalist for a prosilver newspaper. In many respects, Bryan was a symbol of America about to enter the century of paradox, an amalgam of consistency and contradiction, of principle and pragmatism, confident in his faith, yet confused and appalled by some of the developments of his time. To oppose him, the Republicans nominated McKinley and endorsed the gold standard, the protective tariff, and the Monroe Doctrine forbidding encroachment in the Americas. McKinley, an ex-major in the Union Army, served as governor of Ohio and as a congressman. He won the nomination with the aid of his patron, millionaire Cleveland businessman Mark Hanna.

With Bryan popular in the South and West and McKinley commanding the East, the Midwest became the battleground. Bryan found it difficult to attract workers on fixed incomes who would not gain from inflation; their weekly wages, in a relative sense, would be worth less. Thus, workers and the urban poor were unwilling to join the rural poor and indebted

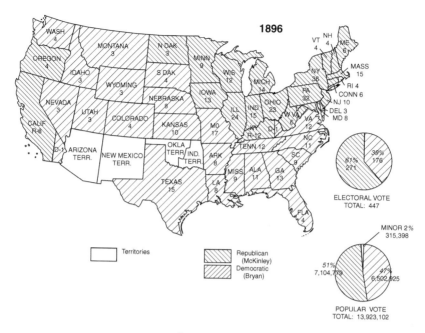

Election of 1896

farmers. Besides the currency issue, the election presented voters with a choice foreshadowing the cultural wars of the twentieth century. McKinley represented stability and the rising industrial nation, while Bryan represented a way of life based on rural values.

McKinley's lavishly financed campaign spent $3–$5 million. Directed by Hanna, it was the best-organized campaign to that point in American history. The candidate remained at his home in Canton, Ohio, where he spoke to visiting delegations while spokesmen saturated the Midwest with literature. They touted McKinley as "the advance agent of prosperity" and ridiculed Bryan as a country buffoon. Bryan, whose campaign spent just $25,000, made six hundred speeches to some 5 million people. In one of the watershed presidential elections of American history, McKinley polled 7.1 million votes to Bryan's 6.5 million and won in the Electoral College by 271 votes to 176.

True to the predictions of McKinley's partisans, his term heralded the return of prosperity, though it was not because of the president. McKinley supported, and Congress passed, the 1897 Dingley Tariff that increased duties. Congress also increased taxes on estates, corporations, tobacco, alcohol, and some luxury items. In addition, in 1900 lawmakers passed the Gold Standard Act, providing for currency backed solely by gold. Predating those moves, gold discoveries in Alaska, Australia, and South Africa and the introduction of new mining technology enabled world gold production to more than double between 1891 and 1896. The abundance spurred inflation, and by 1898, farm prosperity returned. Prosperity, ironically, nailed the coffin shut on the Populist Party. Farm-based protest would arise in the twentieth century as the economy collapsed in the greater depression of the 1930s.

Expansion and War with Spain

Of the events that initiated the Era of Awakening, the most important was the Spanish-American War that ended the nineteenth century. The war was vital in the shift from the old style of American diplomacy to the new. Before the 1890s, policy makers were often isolationist; their conduct of foreign policy was reactive; they gave little specific guidance to diplomats abroad; and the army and navy were not prepared for international warfare. But during the 1890s, the United States embarked upon a more aggressive and activist role in foreign affairs. Several factors inspired the change: the depression, which stimulated an unprecedented interest in foreign trade and new markets overseas, and the maturing of a post–Civil War generation that did not share its predecessor's distaste for military adventure. Also contributing to the awakening were greater knowledge of and contact with other countries through missionaries and journalists, and Alfred Thayer Mahan, whose *The Influence of Sea Power upon History, 1660–1783* (1890) prodded officials to modernize the navy.

Under Harrison and Cleveland, the United States had become increasingly involved in hemispheric affairs. The Harrison administration secured a three-part protectorate of the Samoan Islands, where America, Germany, and Britain wanted Pacific coaling stations, and stopped Canadian fishermen from slaughtering seals. Diplomacy settled a dispute with Italy over the lynching of eleven Italians in New Orleans, and preserved peace with Chile after two American sailors died in a brawl in Valparaiso. Cleveland compelled Britain to accept an American commission's settlement of a dispute between London and Venezuela over British Guiana's border, but he opposed Harrison's plan to annex Hawaii.

Cuba, just one hundred miles off the tip of Florida, was tied to the United States strategically, commercially, and emotionally. To many Americans, Spain's rule of the island seemed a violation of the Monroe

Doctrine, and Cubans rebelled for independence in the Ten Years War (1868–1878) and in 1899. Cuban exiles in New York helped finance the 1899 insurrection and furnished propaganda to provoke American involvement. William Randolph Hearst's *New York Journal* and Joseph Pulitzer's *New York World*, locked in a circulation war, exaggerated Spanish cruelty. Americans were particularly angered when Governor General Valeriano Weyler, soon to be known in the United States as "Butcher" Weyler, forced Cubans to move from the countryside to enclaves guarded by Spanish troops. Anyone outside the hamlets might be shot.

American outrage did not lead directly to war. The business community, still recovering from the depression, was not enthusiastic, and Cleveland announced that the United States would be neutral. Yet in 1896, both major party platforms called for Cuban freedom. McKinley sought Cuban autonomy within the Spanish Empire and humane rule of the island, preferring to pursue his goals through private negotiations. Much of the pressure for intervention arose in Congress and heated toward the boiling point, particularly after two incidents in February 1898. First, the Spanish minister in Washington, Depuy de Lome, wrote to a friend in Havana that McKinley was weak, cowardly, and opportunistic. A rebel sympathizer who noticed de Lome's return address opened the letter and sent it to insurgent supporters in New York, who published it in the *Journal* on February 9. In the United States, de Lome's letter was considered an insult indicating that Spain was not negotiating in good faith. Next, the battleship *Maine*, which McKinley had dispatched to Havana as a goodwill gesture and to evacuate Americans, exploded and sank on February 15, killing 260 sailors. Blaming the blast on a Spanish-laid mine, war became almost certain. (In 1976, after a thorough review of the evidence, investigators concluded that a fire in a coal-storage bunker triggered an ammunition explosion on the ship. Twenty-two years later, however, a *National Geographic* study found evidence suggesting that a mine could not be ruled out as a cause.)

Cubans rioted for independence, and the Hearst press carried the headline "Remember the *Maine* and To Hell with Spain!" Assistant Navy Secretary Theodore Roosevelt, eager for war, ordered the Hong Kong based Pacific squadron under Commodore George Dewey to prepare to attack the Philippines, a Spanish colony. Spain offered to arbitrate the *Maine* episode, accept American relief aid for the Cubans, and consider granting the island autonomy, but refused to accept American mediation over Cuba's status in the Spanish Empire. When the United States upped the ante by insisting on independence for Cuba, the Spanish refused, preferring war to diplomatic surrender. Finally, on April 11, McKinley delivered

THE ROUGH RIDERS
Theodore Roosevelt (Center) in the Spanish-American War.
(Library of Congress)

a war message to Congress. The House and Senate adopted a joint resolution recognizing Cuban independence and approving force to dislodge
Spain. The upper chamber attached an amendment by Colorado's Henry
M. Teller, stating that the United States would liberate Cuba rather than
annex it. In response, Spain declared war and Congress followed.

The war lasted slightly more than three months and appeared to confirm Mahan's theories about naval power. On May 1 at Manila Bay in the
Philippines, Dewey destroyed his opponent and lost just one American life.
Striking another decisive blow, the Atlantic fleet trapped the Spanish ships
in Santiago harbor and sank them with almost no U.S. casualties on July 3.
Four days later, in the afterglow of triumph, McKinley signed a joint resolution of Congress to annex Hawaii, which became an American territory.

On the ground, logistical problems and inexperienced leadership
plagued the American effort, but the ineptitude of the Spanish generals
compensated. Combat focused on the city of Santiago, where the
Americans placed 17,000 Spanish troops under siege. On July 1 the Army

took El Caney and San Juan Hill, gaining control of the high ground around Santiago and preventing the Spanish from escaping. The most glorified hero of the ground war was Roosevelt, who resigned his post to organize a volunteer cavalry unit, the Rough Riders, that included cowboys and Ivy League students. A contingent of black soldiers, like the Rough Riders, stormed up San Juan Hill.

Victory followed in the Philippines and Puerto Rico, and on July 17, Santiago surrendered, virtually ending the combat. The war stopped on August 1 when Spain surrendered. Cuba became independent; Puerto Rico became an American territory; and American troops occupied the Philippines pending a decision on their fate. Some 5,462 Americans had died in Cuba, only 379 in battle. Disease killed most, spread by unsanitary conditions in army camps, impure food, insects, and sweaty dress inappropriate to the tropics.

Making the peace proved more difficult than winning the war. Many Americans, opposing imperialism, wanted to liberate the Philippines. Bolstering their arguments, Emilio Aguinaldo, whose rebel forces helped American troops seize the islands, resisted U.S. control. McKinley believed that failure to accept the Philippines might mean their takeover by Japan or Germany, and that the islands were unprepared for independence. Congressional Democrats did not want to accept the islands as a colony, yet some changed their minds after Bryan, who wanted to make imperialism an issue in the 1900 presidential election, endorsed the treaty. On February 6, 1899, the Senate approved the treaty 57 to 27, just one vote more than the required two-thirds majority.

Even without the Philippines, the United States was destined to be a Pacific power because of its long western coastline, but acquisition of the islands gave the country a more tangible stake in the area. Many Americans embraced world power enthusiastically, as if invigorated by a rousing Sousa musical march. Others accepted it soberly, realizing that if their nation were to call the tune, they would have to pay the piper.

An Era of Awakening, 1900–1919

Prologue

A S THE TWENTIETH century dawned, America awakened to the world, seeking to seize the new century and possess it, with its industrial and military might, its innovative culture, and its spirit of adventure. Perhaps the optimism was exaggerated for a nation so young, yet it was unquenchable, soon to be stimulated by a new president whose energy and charisma were electric. If Thomas Edison had wired Theodore Roosevelt, it might have lighted a city.

Entering the Era of Awakening, Senator Albert J. Beveridge proclaimed: "The twentieth century will be American. American thought will dominate it. American progress will give it color and direction. American deeds will make it illustrious."

At the dawn of the century, the United States was primitive in many respects. Automobiles were rare; paved highways did not exist, nor did aviation. Women could vote in only four states; African Americans, who could not vote at all in most places, endured poverty, racism, and discrimination. But there were reasons for ebullience, due to the realization that the country's size, location, population, and natural and human resources would guarantee it a major place in the world. In 1900 the nation consisted of forty-five states, 76 million people, and thirty-eight cities of more than 100,000 inhabitants. The third largest country in the world in land area behind Russia and Canada, the United States boasted the most dynamic economy. It had the most productive farms, the most miles of railroads, the greatest steel production, the highest per capita income.

Furthermore, the progressive movement was overhauling the engine of democracy for a dash at the future. Over the next two decades, four amendments would be added to the Constitution, providing for the popular election of senators, a federal income tax, woman suffrage, and prohibition of alcohol. A host of other reforms were enacted on the federal, state, and local

RIDING INTO THE FUTURE
Carriages fill New York City's 5th Avenue, 1900.
(National Archives)

levels. And under Theodore Roosevelt and Woodrow Wilson, the presidency experienced a renaissance. Seldom have two luminaries so ignited the public mind within a single generation. The most significant chief executives between the end of the Civil War and the start of the New Deal, they contrasted in styles and temperaments and exploited each other as a foil. Each possessed an iron will that would not permit him to give up (although fate might have been kinder to them if sometimes they had given up).

Roosevelt, who took office in 1901, awakened the country like a fire bell in the night. He thrilled, confounded, and polarized Americans. The first to recognize and exploit the press, he created a mystique around his job and curiosity about him and the first family. With TR work and play, joy and conviction, commitment and passion were fused. In the three-ring circus of American politics, Roosevelt was the uncaged lion in the center ring, and when he roared the world applauded.

Where Roosevelt was fire, Wilson was ice. Roosevelt's rhetoric was inflamed by the power of his delivery, but Wilson's was inspired by the

Time Line

An Era of Awakening, 1900–1919

March 20, 1900 Open Door in China declared approved.

September 6, 1901 Anarchist shoots President William McKinley, who dies September 14. Vice President Theodore Roosevelt succeeds him.

July 15, 1903 Henry Ford sells first car.

November 18, 1903 United States signs treaty to acquire Panama Canal Zone.

December 17, 1903 Orville and Wilbur Wright make first airplane flight.

December 6, 1904 Roosevelt announces Roosevelt Corollary to Monroe Doctrine.

February 12, 1909 National Association for the Advancement of Colored People founded.

November 5, 1912 Democrat Woodrow Wilson defeats Republican incumbent William Howard Taft and Progressive candidate Theodore Roosevelt in presidential election.

February 25, 1913 Sixteenth Amendment authorizing a federal income tax ratified.

May 31, 1913 Seventeenth Amendment providing for direct election of senators ratified.

December 23, 1913 Wilson signs Federal Reserve Act.

April 6, 1917 United States enters World War I.

January 8, 1918 Wilson outlines "Fourteen Points" for peace terms.

March 11, 1918 First U.S. case of influenza that would kill more people than World War I, including 686,000 in America.

November 11, 1918 Armistice ends World War I.

January 29, 1919 Eighteenth Amendment, Prohibition, ratified.

November 19, 1919 Senate rejects Treaty of Versailles.

CHAPTER ONE

TR, Taft, and the Progressive Impulse

THE 1900 presidential election saw William McKinley once again defeat William Jennings Bryan for the presidency. The new vice president was Theodore Roosevelt, the hero of the Rough Riders of the Spanish-American War. TR replaced Vice President Garret A. Hobart, who had died before the campaign. During the campaign, Roosevelt opened the Era of Awakening with a jolt. Vibrant, ambitious, he had a child's delight in politics. With Roosevelt and Bryan jousting on the stump, and McKinley remaining in the White House above the fray, the Republican ticket trounced the Democrats, gaining more than 7.2 million popular votes and 292 electoral votes to the Democrats' 6.35 million and 155. Bryan not only failed to expand his southern and western base; he lost his home state of Nebraska.

Six months later, McKinley traveled to Buffalo, New York, for the Pan-American Exposition, a celebration of hemispheric scientific and artistic progress. At a public reception, Leon Czolgosz, an anarchist angered over the president's taking of the Philippines, shot McKinley twice. Eight days later, one of the bullets killed him. Mark Hanna, McKinley's patron, exclaimed: "My God, that damned cowboy is in the White House!"

Theodore Roosevelt

A cowboy Roosevelt was—and much more. He was also a conservationist; a zoologist; a hunter; an athlete; an amateur historian; an author who would write thirty-six books remarkable for their intellectual range and quality; and an assistant navy secretary. He spent time as a federal civil service commissioner; a police commissioner; and a state legislator, as well as an acclaimed war veteran and governor. The youngest man ever to assume

STRIKING AT THE PRESIDENCY
A depiction of the assassination of William McKinley
at the Pan-American Exposition, 1901.
(Library of Congress)

the office of president, at forty-two, he was to institutionalize the strong presidency and become one of the greatest men ever to occupy the White House. Reflecting the Time of Paradox, he had a zest for living but was burdened with great sorrow; he would leave the country a great deal but he felt that he had not left enough.

Born in Manhattan to Martha "Mittie" and Theodore Sr., a noted philanthropist, this exceptional American was a sickly child, suffering from asthma, nervousness, stomach problems, a skinny body and eyes requiring thick spectacles. Roosevelt overcame his physical obstacles and anxiety, however, with a regimen of discipline, boxing, weight lifting, hiking, swimming, rowing, and tennis. He improved his mind, reading prodigiously, killing and stuffing birds and animals, collecting and cataloging plant specimens, and aspiring to a career in zoology. Military service also figured in Roosevelt's plans. His mother came from a wealthy southern family, and because her relatives fought for the Confederacy in the Civil War, her husband did not serve in the Union Army, hiring a substitute. Young Theodore considered this a stain on his family's record and yearned for action.

In 1876 Roosevelt entered Harvard University, where he boxed, wrestled, wrote two pamphlets on the birds of New York, and graduated with honors. Over the next few years, his personal life reached other turning points. First, halfway through his college studies, his father died and left Roosevelt $125,000, making it unnecessary for him to earn a living. Next, Roosevelt's interests shifted from zoology to the humanities. Finally, after planning to marry his childhood sweetheart, Edith Carow, Roosevelt was introduced to the beautiful Alice Hathaway Lee by a classmate, fell in love, and asked Alice to marry him. After some hesitation, she accepted, and in 1880 they wed.

Roosevelt built a large home on Long Island, began to study law at Columbia University, and started to work on the first of ten books he was to write before entering the White House. When he was just twenty-three, he published the well-received *Naval War of 1812*, which argued that the United States nearly lost the war because it had not built a powerful navy. He also entered politics as a Republican state assemblyman. His naiveté and uninhibited campaign style made party regulars wince, yet his incandescent energy impressed them. In office, the aggressive Roosevelt attacked boss rule, patronage politics, and special interests. He appeared to strike a balance between independence and party loyalty. Critics thought the Harvard boy with a squeaky voice was effeminate, a notion Roosevelt shattered by punching a Democratic colleague.

But in February 1884, Roosevelt's life grew dark. Two days after Alice gave birth to a girl, his mother died of typhoid fever. Hours later, his wife succumbed to kidney failure. He named his daughter after her mother and wrote of his wife in his diary, "And when my heart's dearest died, the light went from my life forever." It was too painful for Roosevelt to mention his wife Alice afterward; he never wrote about her, nor did he speak of her to his daughter. Followed by what he called "black despair," he left the baby with his sister, Bamie, and headed for the Dakota Badlands, where he became a rancher and cowboy. His brief sojourn was one of the formative experiences of his life. He rode the range, camped, hunted, pursued outlaws, and won the admiration of fellow cowboys. No political opponent would ever again credibly charge that Roosevelt was an effete intellectual. The austere surroundings, the arduous physical work, and the long hours toughened Roosevelt's body and healed his soul. Ranching in Dakota territory also inspired him to write the four-volume *Winning of the West*, one of the most popular histories of its time.

Returning east in the fall of 1884, Roosevelt resumed his relationship with Edith Carow. The couple became secretly engaged and married quietly in 1886. Shortly before the wedding, TR ran for office and finished third in a three-man race for New York mayor. In 1889, though, he went to Washington to serve as a civil service commissioner under Benjamin

Harrison. Roosevelt was a controversial commissioner, exposing corruption in the administration that appointed him.

Six years later he resigned to accept appointment as a New York police commissioner. Again, Roosevelt was incorrigible. He roamed the city in the early morning, seeking crime and corruption and observing the underside of life among the impoverished. Often reporters, such as Jacob Riis, accompanied Roosevelt, and the press helped build his legend. Perhaps worst of all, as far as his bosses were concerned, he fired the police chief and enforced Sunday closing laws against taverns, making him a political liability for the Republican mayor.

His support of McKinley's candidacy earned Roosevelt another tour of duty in Washington in 1897, this time as assistant navy secretary. He was determined to see the nation build a superior navy, necessary for a great country. A potent fleet was needed for the United States to approach the level of the British, Germans, and Japanese. War was noble and romantic, TR thought, and the country needed one. Hence when the sinking of the *Maine* heightened tension with Spain, Roosevelt urged McKinley to drive the Spaniards from the New World. When war arrived, Roosevelt could not wait to dive into it. Resigning his post, he was commissioned a lieutenant colonel and authorized to assemble the Rough Riders. From some twenty thousand applicants, including cowboys, Indians, Ivy League scholars, and football, tennis, and polo players, he selected one thousand who embodied his ideal of masculinity, trained them, and transported them to Cuba. In what he described as his "crowded hour," Roosevelt showed courage under fire and inspired his troops. He said it was the most important event in his life.

Victory on the battlefield helped lead to victory in politics. Roosevelt ran for governor of New York in 1898 at political boss Thomas Platt's request. He agreed to consult with Platt on patronage. As a campaigner, the Rough Rider was more show than substance, but the show was important. Roosevelt won narrowly and once more proved willing to work with reformers and bosses. He obtained passage of a civil service law, a raise for teachers, a tax on utilities, an eight-hour day for state employees, and a ban on racial segregation in schools. He supported unions, only to anger them when he called out the National Guard to keep order. Platt, too, grew disillusioned, fearing Roosevelt as a rival for control of patronage. Thus Platt engineered placing his rival on the McKinley ticket in the presidential contest of 1900.

The Spirit of Reform

Roosevelt became president when the progressive impulse was beginning to inspire measures to alleviate the social problems of expanding capitalism. Spanning the early decades of the 1900s, progressivism was a spirit of reform among intellectuals and local reformers that percolated to the federal government. Unlike farm-based populism, progressivism took root in cities and towns. Progressives wanted to save capitalism, not destroy it, and they advocated moderate change. Much hardship, progressives believed, arose from social ills, and reformers, with the help of social scientists, might improve society. "Those who have studied the causes of poverty and social evils have discovered that nine-tenths of the world's misery is preventable," Toledo Mayor Samuel Jones said.

Progressivism overlapped with the feminist movement, which strived to enact reforms related to women, children, families, and politics. Foremost among their objectives was woman suffrage, a cause that united most women. Other aims were the abolition of child labor, the establishment of juvenile courts, mandatory school attendance, limits on hours for working women, prohibition of alcohol, and the direct election of senators by voters instead of by legislatures. Because of respect for motherhood, women were considered uniquely qualified as advocates of reforms affecting families. Perhaps the most eminent progressive woman's leader was Jane Addams, a social worker who established Hull House in Chicago, one of many settlement houses providing social services to the underprivileged. One of Hull House's residents was Florence Kelley, leader of the National Consumers' League, which lobbied for protective labor laws that would limit what employers could require of women and children. Chicago was also the birthplace of the General Federation of Women's Clubs. Started in 1890 with ten thousand members, it grew to more than 1 million by 1910 and provided a voice for progressive reform.

Some women and other reformers, were motivated in part by the Social Gospel, a link between political progressivism and liberal Protestantism. Frequently called Christian Socialism, the Social Gospel emphasized the duty of the able, the wealthy, and the state to help the masses. This creed clashed with Social Darwinism, the application of Charles Darwin's theories of evolution in nature to human society. Social Darwinists held that the survival of the fittest in the marketplace led to progress, an idea that rationalized the status quo and opposed government attempts to regulate business or uplift the poor.

Progressives gave the first serious attention to urban poverty. Crowded, tenements were breeding grounds for crime, disease, and alcoholism. Social scientists, reporters, and politicians questioned the assumption that the poor were victims of their own flaws, suggesting they might be victims of society's flaws. Private charity, offering services rather than money, had long served the poor. Now people asserted that government should deal with poverty. This idea was championed among organizations such as the Socialist Party and by moderate reformers, including Roosevelt. The wealthy ignored the poor at the risk of revolutionary upheavals that might abolish capitalism, TR believed.

Urban vice often was connected with machine politics and bosses. The bosses of Democratic machines on the East Coast and Midwest often proved too formidable for the reformers, however. Their constituents were loyal because the machines provided rudimentary services and interceded with authorities. Held in a relationship of dependency, city dwellers considered bosses their friends, and opposed attempts to end boss rule. But there was no denying the extent of corruption, as journalist Lincoln Steffens documented in his 1904 book *The Shame of the Cities*. In nearly every city he studied, Steffens found bosses who took bribes for favoring businesses in granting utility franchises, contracts for public services, and construction of municipal buildings; these businesses, in turn, charged exorbitant prices. Bosses also stole from the public by padding city payrolls with "deadhead" employees who did little for their paychecks.

Steffens's revelations provoked some cities to invent forms of government that applied business efficiencies to government and removed administration from politics. Galveston, Texas, introduced the commission government, whereby each elected commissioner was responsible for a specific facet of government. By 1912 some two hundred cities and towns had adopted this approach. Other communities hired professional managers to run municipal affairs. The mayor-council system did not disappear. Many progressives used it to improve their cities, to bring politics closer to the people. Samuel Jones had rented an empty factory and hired unemployed workers to run it according to the Golden Rule, a principle that he tried to apply to politics by establishing an eight-hour day for city employees and reforming the police. Mayor Tom Johnson, who made Cleveland a model city, introduced public ownership of utilities, reduced trolley fares, humanized prisons, and created parks, playgrounds, and public baths. He demonstrated not only the potential of municipal reform but also the difficulty of sustaining it, because some of his improvements were abolished after his term ended.

From the cities, Progressivism leaped to the states. Most impressive were the reforms created by governors such as Robert M. "Fighting Bob" La Follette of Wisconsin. La Follette served three terms in the U.S. House of Representatives as a Republican Party regular before his defeat in 1890. Rebelling against the party bosses, he welded a coalition of insurgent followers and won the governorship on his third attempt, in 1900. Under La Follette, Wisconsin embarked on reforms that he said made the state a "lab-

THE FIGHTING
REFORMER
Wisconsin's Robert M.
La Follette.
(Library of Congress)

oratory of democracy." "Fighting Bob" tightened regulation of corporations, taxed railroads on the full value of their assets, taxed inheritances,
compensated injured workers, required primary elections for state offices,
and conserved water and forest resources. Also, La Follette was one of the
first politicians to use university professors to help draft legislation to alleviate social problems, a process he called the "Wisconsin Idea." From the governor's mansion, La Follette moved to the U.S. Senate in 1906 where he
served until his death in 1925. La Follette was a more radical reformer than
Roosevelt, whom he considered overly cautious. TR dismissed La Follette
as an impractical, uncompromising idealist.

The Midwest produced the most progressive governors, including
La Follette and Albert B. Cummins of Iowa. The Northeast boasted Charles
Evans Hughes of New York; on the West Coast there was Hiram Johnson of
California. In the South, James K. Vardaman of Mississippi was a rabid seg-
regationist, yet he ended the convict lease system, regulated corporations,

improved social welfare and educational services, and helped pass the nation's first direct primary law, whereby candidates were nominated directly by primaries rather than by conventions. One of the ironies of progressivism was its coexistence with white racism in the South. Moreover, some progressives nationwide supported immigration restrictions on the grounds that immigrants were the offspring of inferior races, an idea based on the pseudo science of eugenics, the ranking of races by intelligence. Eugenecists also advocated "scientific" breeding of humans to produce a superior race. It led to sterilization of criminals and of the mentally handicapped in some states.

Invigorating the Presidency

Roosevelt's robust approach to politics gave some the impression that he was more liberal than he was. In fact, Roosevelt's chief motive for reforming capitalism was to preserve it. Before he could move the nation forward, he must educate the people by exhortation. A rousing orator, he described the office as a "bully pulpit" from which he could do so, though he moved ahead of public opinion. Despite his aristocratic background, he seemed closer to the people than his predecessors.

Roosevelt strengthened the presidency by challenging the supremacy of business. When he became president, huge business combinations—the trusts pioneered by Standard Oil—were beginning to dominate markets, and despite the Sherman Antitrust Act, they seemed to be immune from government regulation. Roosevelt startled the nation in 1902 by filing suit against one of the largest, the Northern Securities Company, a combination of three major railroads, and compelling it to dissolve. One of the company's magnates, investment banker J. P. Morgan, considering himself an equal of the president, wanted the two to settle the affair privately. Roosevelt achieved his purpose of demonstrating that the authority of government surpassed that of business. The administration filed forty-three additional antitrust suits during Roosevelt's tenure, earning him a reputation as a "trustbuster." Later, Roosevelt somewhat relented, concluding that size alone was an insufficient reason to attack business combinations; only those that violated the public interest need be broken up.

Although some considered Roosevelt an enemy of business, an assumption that was misleading, it did not follow that he always sided with labor. A 1902 coal strike in Pennsylvania, which dragged on and threatened to deny part of the country coal during the winter, was settled by intimidation. When the sides could not agree, the president prepared the army to take over the mines, denying wages to the miners and profits to the owners. Under this splash of cold reality, both sides relented and the strike was settled by a mediation commission appointed by the president. The commission granted the miners a 10 percent wage increase but denied the union recognition. Roosevelt believed he had given both sides a "Square Deal," a phrase that became associated with his administration.

Advancing on all fronts, Roosevelt tightened business regulation in 1903 by helping engineer the Elkins Act that prohibited railroads from paying secret rebates to large shippers in return for their business. The president proposed, and ushered through Congress, a bill creating a Department of Commerce and Labor. The measure included a Bureau of Corporations armed with subpoena power to investigate interstate business and expose illegal activities.

Other successes came in conservation. Roosevelt was the first president to focus public attention on natural resources. Emphasizing the overdevelopment of grazing, lumber, and water projects on public lands in the West, he withdrew about 120–160 million acres from development, increasing reserves by nearly one-half during his first term. Additionally, he supported the Newlands Reclamation Act of 1902, which set aside almost the entire

THE PRESIDENT
AND THE
ENVIRONMENTALIST
Theodore Roosevelt and
conservation pioneer
John Muir on Glacier
Point, Yosemite Valley,
circa 1906.
(Library of Congress)

proceeds from western land sales for construction and maintenance of irrigation projects in arid regions.

A ringmaster in the arena of governing, Roosevelt craved, and attracted, attention. He was the first president to hold press conferences, the first to be known by his initials, and the first to allow the press to cover the life of the first family. Family picnics and beeline hikes were the subjects of stories and Edith distributed family photos. Preferring simplicity, Roosevelt changed the name of the first family's residence from the Executive Mansion to the White House.

In 1904 Roosevelt became president in his own right by defeating the Democratic nominee, Judge Alton B. Parker, an obscure conservative from New York. William Jennings Bryan, a liberal who had lost twice, withdrew from consideration, stating that it was time for the party to try a conservative. Although Parker was an ineffective campaigner, one charge did strike the president in a vulnerable spot. He pointed out that the very corporations Roosevelt was boasting of taming had contributed to his campaign to protect themselves from antitrust prosecutions. Still, Roosevelt rolled over the Democrats, winning more than 7.6 million votes (57 percent) and 336 electoral votes to the Democrats' more than 5 million and 140.

As much as he loved power, Roosevelt revered tradition. He believed that he should preserve the two-term precedent set by George Washington and that his completion of McKinley's term represented nearly a full term. He did not want to appear power hungry. Thus, on the evening of his reelection, he announced he would not be a candidate for another term. He hoped this promise would remove political expediency from his policy making and allow him to do the right thing for the country. Yet expediency is the currency of politics, and the promise weakened TR politically. Further, he did love power and would leave the presidency still a young man, bored, with unfinished business, and an ego that would not allow any successor to fill his shoes.

Raking the Muck

In his second administration, TR resumed his reform agenda. In his first term he had concentrated largely on dismantling the trusts. Now he turned his attention to the railroads, considering strengthened transportation regulation and enhanced powers for the Interstate Commerce Commission (ICC) top priorities. TR thought about tariff reductions as well, yet believed they would divide the GOP. Consequently, he dodged the tariff issue, leaving it to his successor. But in collaboration with the president, Republican Representative William P. Hepburn of Iowa drafted a bill allowing the ICC to fix maximum railroad rates, audit railroad records, and require uniform bookkeeping methods. It could also regulate pipelines, terminals, and sleeping cars, and force railroads to sell steamship and coal properties to eliminate transportation monopolies. After the House adopted the measure, Roosevelt compromised to win Senate consent, amending the bill to give courts more discretion in determining rate changes. La Follette broke with him, claiming that the weakened bill betrayed the cause of reform. However altered, the law was the most significant regulatory measure enacted during Roosevelt's presidency.

Investigative journalists fed the demands for reform, exposing railroad practices, political corruption, adulterated drugs, and impure meat. Even though the journalists' aims resembled Roosevelt's, he denounced them as "muckrakers" after a character in Paul Bunyon's *Pilgrim's Progress* who would only look down and rake muck rather than look up to contemplate nobler matters. During the Senate debate over the Hepburn Act, TR condemned David Graham Phillips's book *The Treason of the Senate* (1906) as excessive in its criticism. Yet, although the influence of journalistic exposes declined after 1906, Roosevelt continued to seize upon the issues they raised. He introduced bills to regulate food and drugs and require meat inspections, the latter aided by Upton Sinclair's muckraking novel *The Jungle* (1906). The book tells the story of exploited workers at a meat-packing plant, where tubercular beef and poisoned rats are ground up into meat and workers who fall into the vats emerge as lard. Roosevelt signed the Meat Inspection Act and the Pure Food and Drug Act on the same day in 1906. The first law established standards and federal inspection for the slaughtering, processing, and labeling of meat. The second created the Food and Drug Administration with authority to test and approve drugs before they could be sold and to remove impure or fraudulently labeled drugs from interstate commerce. With the Hepburn Act, these measures constituted the high tide of TR's domestic reforms.

When it came to conservation, Roosevelt used executive orders to create national forests, monuments, parks, and wildlife reserves. This aggressive use of power irritated Congress. If Roosevelt annoyed some, he engaged the press and the public. On a hunting trip he refused to shoot a bear cub, and manufacturers created a toy "Teddy bear"; it became a favorite with children. Only the catastrophe of the 1906 earthquake and fires that devastated San Francisco could push Roosevelt off the front page momentarily.

Through much of Roosevelt's tenure, the nation was prosperous: the gross national product (the value of all goods and services produced in the country), income, and consumption grew. Farmers enjoyed one of their most prosperous decades in history, but in October 1907 a banking panic struck New York. Two financiers attempted to corner the copper market, and, when their scheme failed, investors began a run on companies that had financed it. The stock market tumbled, interest rates soared, and the unsound banking system was unable to control the crash born of reckless speculation.

Banker J. P. Morgan stepped in, helping pool funds of strong banks to sustain unsound ones in order to avert a total collapse. Treasury Secretary George Cortelyou issued $150 million in government bonds and certificates at favorable rates; by purchasing them, banks could bolster their collateral, shore up investor confidence, and avoid panic withdrawals. Morgan also acted to avert panic among brokerage firms by arranging the United States Steel Corporation's purchase of the Tennessee Coal and Iron Company. Roosevelt accepted the deal despite concerns over antitrust violations. The economy soon recovered, but the president's reputation among congressional Republicans never rebounded. As conservatives, they blamed his anti-big business rhetoric for the depression.

The courts too, slowed Roosevelt's pace of reform. The Supreme Court was a special source of bitterness, even though TR had appointed three justices, including Oliver Wendell Holmes Jr., who would be one of the greatest in history. In *Lochner v. New York* (1905), a ruling that infuriated TR, the court nullified a New York state law limiting bakers to ten working hours per day on the ground that the statute interfered with the freedom of contract. Yet three years later, in *Muller v. Oregon*, the court upheld an Oregon law that limited women laundry workers to ten hours per day. The justices accepted attorney Louis Brandeis's presentation of sociological and scientific data in favor of protective legislation for women.

TR and Taft: From Friends to Foes

In his final years as president, Roosevelt grew frustrated by his promise not to run again. He had been a good chief executive, he knew, but he felt he had fallen short of greatness because fate had not presented the opportunity to overcome a major crisis. Roosevelt, nonetheless, would not break his promise against running. Wishing to leave the nation a capable replacement, he turned to his close friend William Howard Taft.

Genial, intelligent, and humane, Taft had impressive administrative credentials. He had served as solicitor general, governor general of the Philippines, and secretary of war. He was, moreover, loyal to Roosevelt and a moderate progressive. Yet Taft had never run for office and hated campaigning. He did not like public speaking and lacked Roosevelt's fire; the public considered him bland in contrast to TR. But Roosevelt promoted Taft and the Ohioan easily won the Republican nomination. Then he

IN THE COMPANY
OF MILLIONAIRES
William Howard Taft
on the golf course.
(Library of Congress)

defeated Bryan, running futilely for the third time. Taft's victory was immense for a novice. He collected almost 7.7 million popular votes and 321 electoral votes to the Nebraskan's 6.4 million and 162.

Roosevelt sailed to Africa for a big-game safari, leaving Taft to run the country. Still, TR feared his successor was malleable and might be molded by stronger men while the Rough Rider was slaughtering lions. As Roosevelt feared, Taft moved to the right. Still, it would be wrong to conclude that Taft was not a progressive; his biggest flaw was that he was not Roosevelt. He lacked confidence and Roosevelt's aggressive spirit. A huge man, who overate and appeared passive, he was more suited for the judiciary. He could stand on principle, yet be indecisive. He did not like making political deals and failed to bedazzle the press. His only outdoor activity was golf, which he sometimes played in the company of millionaires. Most embarrassing, the obese president once got stuck in the White House bathtub and needed the Secret Service to pry him out.

Taft addressed the tariff issue and found out why TR had avoided it. It split the party. In 1909 he summoned a special session of Congress that produced a House bill with moderate cuts. Yet Senator Nelson Aldrich added nearly 850 special interest amendments. The resulting law did lower tariffs to an average of 38 percent from 57 percent in 1897, though a reciprocal rate provision allowed the president to raise or lower rates consistent with acts of other nations. The president alienated progressives by siding with their foe, arch-conservative House Speaker Joseph Cannon, in a power struggle. Congress also adopted the Sixteenth Amendment, allowing an income tax, which was ratified in 1913. Taft's record on these issues appeared more conservative to Roosevelt than it actually was. The Republicans were splintering, nonetheless, and Taft was unable to enforce party unity.

In 1910 the president entered another crossfire, this one between Interior Secretary Richard A. Ballinger and Chief Forester Gifford Pinchot. With Taft's approval, Ballinger sold millions of public acres that Pinchot had closed under TR's administration. Striking back, Pinchot accused Ballinger of facilitating the sale of public coal deposits in Alaska to a banking syndicate that included J. P. Morgan. Finding no basis for the charge, Taft ordered Pinchot to desist. Pinchot persisted and Taft fired him for insubordination. A congressional panel exonerated Ballinger, but that did not end the affair. Pinchot went to Italy to tell TR, just emerged from Africa, that Taft had betrayed the cause of conservation. In truth, Taft was committed to conservation and in a single term removed nearly as many acres from development as had Roosevelt in nearly two terms.

Even when Taft, identified with corporate interests, tried to regulate businesses, he fell short. In 1910 he engineered passage of the Mann-Elkins Act prohibiting railroads from charging more for short hauls than long hauls, a discriminatory practice used to gouge small shippers. Yet progressives considered the bill weak. Taft was more active than Roosevelt in filing antitrust suits, instigating more in four years than TR had in seven. Still, he angered TR in October 1911, when the Justice Department sued United States Steel over the acquisition of the Tennessee Coal and Iron Company. The suit made Roosevelt look dishonest or inept, perhaps duped by clever monopolists in his approval of the merger. TR complained that Taft had not objected to the deal at the time.

"We Stand at Armageddon"

In June 1910 Roosevelt returned from Europe to a hero's welcome in New York. Two months later, he delivered a series of speeches in support of progressive GOP congressional candidates in the fall elections. Using rhetoric that appalled Taft, TR declared that the rights of workers superseded the rights of capital and outlined reforms more leftist than any he had supported, including public review of state judges' decisions. Taft, believing the judiciary sacrosanct, thought Roosevelt had become power mad, yet neither could claim satisfaction in the election results. Roosevelt's progressives defeated Taft's conservatives in the primaries, yet lost to Democrats in the general election.

In February 1912, Roosevelt broke with Taft, entering the campaign for the Republican presidential nomination. He won most of the primaries (yet there were only a handful of primaries at that time), but Taft ingratiated himself with the party bosses and won the nomination. Roosevelt supporters walked out after being denied disputed delegates, muttering "Thou shalt not steal." The next day Roosevelt urged his followers to back him as a third party candidate in a speech with biblical gravity, concluding, "We stand at Armageddon and we battle for the Lord." Seven weeks later the new Progressive Party nominated its hero, singing "Onward, Christian Soldiers" and "The Battle Hymn of the Republic." Roosevelt said he felt as strong as a bull moose and the party acquired a nickname: "the Bull Moose Party." The party nominated Hiram Johnson for vice president.

TR hoped the Democrats would nominate a conservative, yet they turned instead to New Jersey's progressive governor, Woodrow Wilson. A political scientist, the president of Princeton before his election as governor, Wilson excelled Roosevelt in cold eloquence if not in demonstrative display. Wilson urged regulation of business by controlled marketplace competition, a program he called the "New Freedom." Roosevelt stuck to tougher direct government regulation, a plan known as the "New Nationalism." In truth, the differences were chiefly semantic. Yet the dialogue started one of the fundamental debates of the Time of Paradox, an argument over the degree to which the federal government should intervene in the economy.

In Milwaukee, on October 14, a would-be assassin wounded Roosevelt, who declined medical help and completed his speech. In fact, the Rough Rider seemed to enjoy the suspense. TR won his battle with mortality, but he, like Taft, realized he had little chance to win the election. The Republican fratricide had wrecked the party and carved a canyon between one of the closest political friendships of the era. A reporter found Taft sobbing, head in hands, on his campaign train, "Roosevelt was my closest friend." More than an election had been lost. Roosevelt wandered in the political wilderness, an outsider to the party he had helped rejuvenate, for the rest of his life. In time he resumed his friendship with Taft but became a shrill critic of Wilson.

Wilson's victory was a watershed, yet it was unclear whether voters had rejected the Republican party in favor of the Democrats or simply, exasperated, asked, "Which Republican party?" Wilson polled almost 6.3 million votes and won with just 43 percent of the popular vote in the three-way race. Roosevelt won 4.1 million popular votes and Taft drew 3.5 million. In the Electoral College, however, it was a Democratic landslide: Wilson, 435; Roosevelt, 88; and Taft, 8. Socialist Party candidate Eugene V. Debs received 900,000 votes, almost 6 percent.

Taft took the defeat much better than Roosevelt. He had never wanted to be president, preferring a place on the Supreme Court. Taft was neither

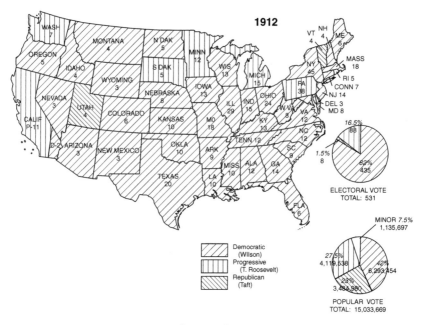

Election of 1912

a great nor an incompetent president. Temperamentally, he lacked the imagination and vision to inspire the masses, and he followed a man who excelled at leadership. Yet his accomplishments are sometimes underestimated. By no means dull or unintelligent, he left as his legacy the Mann-Elkins Act, conservationist activities, trustbusting, and the income tax amendment which Taft submitted in 1909 and the states ratified in 1913. The income tax levy started at 1 percent on incomes over $3,000 for single people and over $4,000 for married people, peaking at 6 percent on incomes over $500,000. Under his administration, Congress passed a constitutional amendment that placed the election of U.S. senators in the hands of the people (rather than state legislatures); it was ratified as the Seventeenth Amendment in 1913. Legislation also created postal savings banks as an alternative to commercial banks, a Federal Children's Bureau to supervise child welfare matters, and a commission to investigate labor conditions; established a Commerce Department separate from the Labor Department; and limited work on federal projects to eight hours a day. Moreover, as president, Taft appointed 45 percent of the federal judiciary, including six justices to the Supreme Court, the tribunal to which he aspired. In 1921 President Warren G. Harding made Taft chief justice and gave him a place in history as the only man to lead the high court and serve as president.

CHAPTER TWO

America Looks Outward, 1900–1912

A S THE NINETEENTH century ended, America had dived into the treacherous waters of international diplomacy. The century ended with a splash. The coldness of the water was invigorating and sobering. It was to be an Era of Awakening.

Theodore Roosevelt was fond of citing a west African proverb, "Speak softly and carry a big stick, you will go far." In reality, the proverb described TR's policies in reverse. He bellowed yet rarely inflicted force. He initiated no combat by American troops during his presidency. The only place where Americans died in battle was in the Philippines, where fighting began before he took office. But if Roosevelt was restrained in the use of force, he was not reluctant to threaten it. He took pride in presiding over a buildup of the navy from fifth largest on the planet to second, behind Britain's. Roosevelt welcomed the opportunity to be at the center of action. An assertive foreign policy, he believed, would help provide Americans with a sense of purpose and define their place in the world. His romance with war aside, he did not desire it while president, but sought a Pax Americana or, perhaps, a Pax Roosevelt.

The Roosevelt Corollary

Roosevelt's foremost concern was the Western Hemisphere. After the Cuban Revolution, the United States insisted on an amendment to the new Cuban constitution making it a virtual protectorate of the United States. The United States used the Platt Amendment in 1906, dispatching troops to maintain order on the island, where they remained until 1909.

Roosevelt was annoyed by European nations' attempts to employ their military to collect debts from Latin American countries. He particularly

VISIONS OF AMERICAN POWER
President Theodore Roosevelt speaking in South Lawrence,
Massachusetts, circa 1902.
(Library of Congress)

disliked Germany. TR believed Kaiser Wilhelm II was the most aggressive imperialist in the world. Early in his presidency, Venezuela refused to pay more than $70 million it owed to Germany. The European powers, joined by Venezuela's other creditors, Britain and Italy, hoped to compel payment by declaring a blockade of the coast in November 1902. The coalition sank Venezuelan vessels and the Germans landed troops. Roosevelt became involved when the Venezuelan dictator, who initially refused to negotiate, asked him to arbitrate. The president proposed that the claims be submitted to the International Court of Justice at The Hague. The coalition agreed, but maintained the blockade as the court deliberated. In 1904 the tribunal ruled in favor of the creditors.

The bankrupt Dominican Republic was another source of turmoil. To keep Germany and fellow creditors from collecting debts there, and to establish a rationale for American intervention in other Caribbean crises, the president and Secretary of State John Hay devised the Roosevelt Corollary to the Monroe Doctrine. The corollary, announced by TR in December 1904, declared that the United States would police the hemisphere to rectify "chronic wrongdoing" in Latin America. Under the corollary, from 1905 to 1907, U.S. Marines occupied the Dominican Republic, supervised customs collections, and used them to pay off debts.

Roosevelt and the Panama Canal

Of Roosevelt's foreign initiatives, the boldest and most controversial was his virtual seizure of a zone in Panama to construct an interoceanic canal. Americans had dreamed of a canal that would eliminate the voyage around South America. Plans were set in motion in 1850, when the United States and Britain signed the Clayton-Bulwer Treaty providing for joint construction. Fifty-two years later, in the 1902 Hay-Pauncefote pact, Britain yielded its rights to joint construction and was promised equal access and equal tolls. At the time Roosevelt became president, the canal remained just an idea. As a champion of a strong navy with an interest in the Pacific, he was in a hurry to build a canal.

Two options were proposed: a sea-level canal through Nicaragua, and a canal through Panama requiring locks. For the second, the United States had to buy the rights from a French company whose ten-year attempt to construct a canal ended unsuccessfully in 1889. The bankrupt company demanded $109 million for the rights, which were to expire in September 1904. On the recommendation of a government commission, the House voted for the cheaper Nicaraguan route. Nevertheless, the company prodded the Senate into endorsing the Panama route, publicizing a volcanic eruption in a Nicaraguan lake through which the canal was to be built and reducing its price for its rights to $40 million.

In 1902 Congress directed TR to accept the company's offer and to negotiate terms for operating the canal with Colombia, of which Panama was a province. The 1903 Hay-Herran Treaty met these aims. It guaranteed the company $40 million and Colombia $10 million plus $250,000 annually for a ninety-nine-year renewable lease on a six-mile-wide canal zone. The U.S. Senate approved the arrangement but the Colombian Senate deferred action, hoping for a better deal after the company's rights expired. Outraged, Roosevelt considered the rejection a national insult. He offered Colombia the treaty on a take-it-or-leave-it basis and exhibited

a contempt for the South Americans bordering on racism. Then a representative of the French company, Philippe Bunau-Varilla, traveled to
Washington to tell him a revolution was brewing in Panama and asked how
America would respond. TR was noncommittal but did not discourage the
uprising.

Panamanian business interests supported revolution, afraid that
Colombia's repudiation of the treaty might persuade the United States to
turn to Nicaragua. Moreover, if Panama became independent it might
receive the money to be paid to Colombia. Panama had a long revolutionary tradition, including numerous rebellions against Colombia. A nearly
bloodless revolution occurred on November 3, 1903. Bunau-Varilla, author
of a declaration of independence and constitution for the new country, had
bribed Colombian soldiers in Panama not to suppress the revolt. An
American gunboat offshore intimidated Colombia from landing soldiers.

Events raced to a climax. On November 6 the United States diplo-
matically recognized the Republic of Panama. A week later Secretary of
State John Hay accepted a visit from Bunau-Varilla, and the Hay–Bunau-
Varilla Treaty was negotiated. In exchange for a ten-mile-wide canal zone,
the company received $40 million and Panama received essentially the same
financial terms that Colombia would have received. Both countries con-
sented to the treaty early in 1904 and construction began in midyear. In
the United States the canal was wildly popular and embellished TR's glam-
our at election time. In Latin America, Roosevelt's tactics were resented.
Still, he never expressed regret for bullying smaller nations in the hemisphere. Not until 1921 did the United States pay an indemnity to Columbia
for helping strip it of a province.

One of the great engineering feats of the first half of the twentieth century, construction of the canal took ten years and cost more than $365 mil-
lion. The project also led to a medical breakthrough when Colonel William C.
Gorgas developed methods to eradicate the mosquito carrying yellow fever,
which had decimated construction workers. Although it did not open until
August 1914, years after he left the White House, the Panama Canal always
has been identified with Theodore Roosevelt. "I took the canal zone, and
let Congress debate, and while the debate goes on, the canal does also,"
he boasted.

TR believed Central American stability was essential to the security of
the canal, but he preferred not to intervene militarily in the region. The
outbreak of several wars made some action imperative, though, so the U.S.
summoned a Central American peace conference to meet in the fall of 1908
in Washington. The Central American nations reached eight agreements
designed to preserve the peace.

LINKING THE ATLANTIC AND PACIFIC OCEANS
The Panama Canal under construction.
(Library of Congress)

America as a Pacific Power

The United States sent missionaries to China, tried to develop trade there, and wanted to prevent Japan from conquering its larger, weaker neighbor. Because the major European nations and Japan had carved out spheres of influence in which they monopolized trade, the United States sought to maintain an "Open Door" in which nations shared trade in areas they dominated. America also owned Hawaii and occupied the Philippines, which it developed economically, although the Filipinos wanted independence and fought a costly war against America to obtain it. Competition between Russia and Japan in the Far East provoked the Russo-Japanese War. It began when the Japanese, in a surprise attack, sank the Russian fleet at Port Arthur in February 1904. Japan gained the upper hand in the war, yet Roosevelt preferred a compromise peace that would prevent either nation from becoming overly powerful. When the Japanese asked Roosevelt to mediate the war, he agreed, and Russia, experiencing internal turmoil, agreed as well. The parties met in August 1905 in Portsmouth, New Hampshire, where, after much frustrating haggling, the combatants reached terms. Russia accepted Japanese domination of Korea, and Roosevelt received the Nobel Peace Prize for his efforts.

Japanese pride and American prejudice clashed in California. In 1906, San Francisco officials segregated Asian children in public schools. Roosevelt informed the Japanese that he opposed the system, yet he was worried about alienating voters in California, who wanted to curtail Japanese immigration. An informal "Gentlemen's Agreement" was worked out. The Japanese voluntarily restricted immigration and the segregated system was ended.

Roosevelt feared that perhaps he had spoken too softly to the Japanese and not brandished a big enough stick. To impress them, and other nations, he dispatched all of America's battleships, painted gleaming white, on a global tour. Though billed as a goodwill tour, Roosevelt intended to intimidate. In fact, it heightened the naval arms race. Nonetheless, in 1908 Japan and America concluded the Root-Takahira Agreement whereby the United States recognized Japan's interest in Manchuria, and both countries agreed to observe China's territorial integrity and the Pacific status quo. When Congress threatened to withhold funds from the fleet, which Roosevelt high-handedly had dispatched without congressional approval, Roosevelt countered that he would leave the fleet, penniless, in the distant East. The funds flowed and the fleet returned on February 22, 1909, providing a going away party for the former president as he set out for Africa.

European Diplomacy

The United States shared the longest undefended border in the world with Canada, a British dominion. In the twentieth century Britain became America's closest informal ally. Yet, good neighbors occasionally quarrel. In 1902 Canada claimed lands in Alaska that cut off gold mines from the sea. The issue was settled in favor of the United States by a trilateral commission including representatives from the United States, Britain, and Canada. The British voted with the United States, feeling that friendly relations with America outweighed the interests of their own dominion.

Britain was willing to forsake ambitions in the Western Hemisphere and sought American support for its interests in the Middle East, Africa, and Asia. Britain also agreed with Roosevelt that Germany was the chief menace to world peace and that Wilhelm's designs in North Africa had to be stopped. The issues arose in the early 1900s when Wilhelm, resenting French domination of Morocco, part of the Ottoman Empire, implied that

and identified lawbreakers. Locally, vice commissions and special courts attempted to eradicate prostitution. At the national level, Congress passed laws prohibiting the importation of prostitutes, authorizing the deportation of immigrant prostitutes, and outlawing the transportation of women across state lines for immoral purposes. Drugs—morphine, heroin, and cocaine—had been sold legally in the nineteenth century. Reaction set in shortly after 1900, when Coca-Cola removed cocaine from its beverage after it was learned the drug could cause hyperactivity and paranoia. Despite the U.S. approval of the 1912 Hague Opium Treaty curtailing international trade of opium and cocaine, the federal government did little to control narcotic sales until 1919, although there were some state and local restrictions.

Immigrants

Cities attracted more residents who made up a greater share of the national population. From 1900 to 1910 more than 8 million immigrants settled in the United States, the greatest number in any decade before or since. In 1907, the record year, 1,285,349 arrived. Immigrants constituted more than 10 percent of the population and more than one-third the population of the twelve largest cities. By 1910 New York had more Italians than Naples, more Germans than Hamburg, twice as many Irish as Dublin, and more Jews than all of Western Europe.

Looking to America for democracy, religious freedom, and economic opportunity, the immigrants, most of them Catholics, found their best hope of employment in factories. Without immigrant workers, the industrial revolution of the late nineteenth and early twentieth centuries would have been impossible despite technology. Immigrants contributed skills, muscle, and a work ethic, taking dangerous, low-paying jobs in mines, mills, construction, canning, and meatpacking. Sixty to eighty percent of immigrants, excluding Jews, came to America to make money and take it back to their native lands.

Jews, while retaining their ancient cultural identity, were one of the most successful immigrant groups. Most immigrated from Russia and Eastern Europe, constituting more than half the immigrants from Russia between 1900 and 1920. About 45 percent lived in New York City, where they constituted one-quarter of the population. Many worked in the garment district, cigar factories, and printing plants. Some 75 percent of the first generation of Jewish immigrants' children rose to the middle class, the highest ratio of any group. Some Jews became socialists and leaders in the radical labor movement. Jews also thirsted for education. A higher percentage of Eastern European Jews obtained college educations than any other immigrant group during the Progressive Era.

THE CHANGING FACE OF AMERICA
Immigrants landing at Ellis Island, 1912.
(Library of Congress)

Some groups, such as Italians, French Canadians, and Mexicans, placed greater emphasis on family loyalty and proximity. Helping the family earn an income and taking care of children was more important than learning English or going away to college. Cultural assimilation was discouraged. Mexicans moved north in large numbers early in the new century to work in the irrigated fields of the Southwest; others fled the Mexican Revolution of 1910. Before 1924 there were no border guards and no laws prohibited immigration from the Western Hemisphere. By 1925, Los Angeles had a larger Spanish-speaking population than any North American city except Mexico City. Other immigrants included Filipinos and some 450,000 from the Middle East.

Immigrants changed, and were changed, by America. They intermarried and introduced new lifestyles, talents, and religious observances. Partly because they differed from the dominant Nordic Protestant culture, some feared them and considered them economic competitors. Discrimination, born of exploitation and a distaste of differences, was often their lot. Some believed the newcomers, especially Jews and Catholics, conspired to overthrow the government and monopolize the economy. In 1915, Leo Frank, a Georgia Jewish factory owner convicted of murdering a young Caucasian girl on dubious evidence, was dragged from his jail cell and lynched. Racial and religious prejudice were not the only elements in discrimination against foreigners. Some feared foreign ideologies, such as communism, socialism, and anarchism, and believed America could be saved by cleansing the nation of immigrants carrying the infection of such beliefs.

Women's Suffrage and New Possibilities

The twentieth century was a time of accelerated feminist consciousness that had germinated since the abolitionist crusade. Feminism, a movement for women's equality, made substantial progress during the Progressive Era, winning the vote in some states and accomplishing its chief objective in 1920, a constitutional amendment giving women the vote across the nation. The White House was of little help for much of the period. Roosevelt, for example, said, "Personally I believe in women's suffrage, but I am not an enthusiastic advocate of it because I do not consider it a very important matter." Feminists grew more militant, staging marches and protests and starting to break out of their narrow organizational base of upper-middle-class, educated white women. Also on the feminist agenda were equal educational opportunities and property rights, access to the professions, and liberalized divorce laws.

Women gained opportunities in education and employment and dominated new fields such as social work. Jane Addams, Florence Kelley, Lillian Wald, and Julia Lathrop pioneered in serving the urban poor. Lathrop, appointed to head the Children's Bureau in 1910, became the first woman to head a federal agency. Women entered the workforce in large numbers as stenographers, typists, and salesclerks. Women's image changed. Charles Dana Gibson created the prototypical "Gibson Girl" in his sketches, especially for magazine covers. The Gibson Girl was young, thin, and uninhibited and flaunted her sexuality by smoking, drinking, and wearing casual clothes. The sexual revolution advanced on other fronts as city environments made chaperoned dates more difficult to arrange and prostitutes available. Margaret Sanger, a New York nurse, promoted birth control, even though it was illegal in some states, and her activities got her arrested. Also, women began talking more frankly about sex, often in mixed company. The pressure for an explosion of sexuality in American culture gathered momentum throughout the era, which was an era of awakening for sexual change.

An Expanding Economy

The first two decades of the twentieth century were dominated by prosperity, interrupted by brief recessions that began in 1907 and 1914. Good times spared the era some of the turmoil and demand for radical change of the 1890s. Most people accepted the need for some government regulation of corporations. Total production nearly doubled between 1900 and 1910, then tripled by 1920. Farm prosperity complemented business and industrial prosperity. Pockets of poverty nonetheless persisted, especially in the South and the West, among rural people, minorities, and debtors. Railroad expansion slowed with the increasing competition from automobiles. Car registration climbed from 8,000 in 1900 to 458,000 ten years later. Power shifted from magnates such as John D. Rockefeller and Andrew Carnegie to investment bankers such as J. P. Morgan. Capital, not tangible national resources, was the lifeblood of capitalism. Expansion was the key to capitalism's success. In 1901 Morgan helped organize the world's largest corporation, United States Steel, capitalized at $1.4 billion. Like Rockefeller and Carnegie, Morgan was a ruthless business competitor and a philanthropist. He left much of his vast art collection to New York's Metropolitan Museum of Art.

The economy had a place for entrepreneurs such as Henry Ford, producer of the first practical mass-produced car. After building his first car in 1896, he applied the first movable assembly line to the automobile industry and introduced the Model T in 1908. Ford changed America fundamentally, as did the Wright brothers, Orville and Wilbur, inventors of the first practical heavier-than-air manned aircraft. Financing their work with profits from their bicycle company, they made their initial flight on December 17, 1903, at Kitty Hawk, North Carolina. By the close of 1905, they founded a company to build and sell airplanes and license European manufacturers. Glenn Hammond Curtiss, a motorcycle builder, also emerged as a major figure in aviation. In 1909 he won a race in France with a plane that averaged forty-seven miles per hour. By midcentury the leading producers of airliners were Boeing, McDonald Douglas, and Lockheed.

Growth of Organized Labor

Organized labor awakened to new leadership during the era. Its ranks swelled by immigrants and city workers, the number of union workers stood at 1.4 million by 1901, of which 1 million belonged to the American Federation of Labor (AFL). Just three years later, the AFL's membership had doubled. The efforts of Samuel Gompers, the president and cofounder, were largely responsible for the increase. A Jewish immigrant from London, Gompers became a cigar maker and organizer for the Cigar Makers International. As leader of the AFL, he pursued a pragmatic program: higher wages, shorter hours, and better working conditions. He collaborated with Marxists, yet was not a socialist and opposed violent strikes.

Gompers believed in a strong central organization that admitted unions based on the skills, or crafts, of their workers. He opposed the idea of industrial unions whereby all workers who made a single product belonged to the same union. He supported immigration restrictions, though an immigrant himself, on the grounds they depressed wages, and opposed the eight-hour day. Gompers supported Woodrow Wilson for president in 1912 and 1916, gaining influence within the councils of government. By 1900, the AFL had no durable rival. A small, temporary challenge emerged in the Western Federation of Miners. After several unsuccessful strikes among Colorado miners from 1903 to 1905, they created the stronger Industrial Workers of the World (IWW), led by William "Big Bill" Haywood. The IWW practiced class warfare, sabotage, and violence, claiming the AFL was insufficiently militant. The "Wobblies," as they were known, hoped to organize smaller industrial unions into "one big union" and stage a general strike to destroy capitalism.

The American Socialist Party, led by Eugene V. Debs, was more militant than the AFL, and, like the IWW, hoped to overturn capitalism. However, the Socialist Party expelled Haywood because he espoused violence, counter to its ideology. Unlike the AFL in another way, the Socialist Party ran candidates for office. Debs ran for president five times from 1900 to 1920. In 1910 the party elected its first big city mayor, Victor Berger of Milwaukee.

Women, too, were prominent in the ranks of radical labor, the most colorful of whom was Mary Harris "Mother" Jones. A heroine to miners, Jones was a participant in every major coal strike of her time. Belying her grandmotherly looks, she was militant, witty, tough—urging wives of miners to disrupt strikebreakers by parading through the mountains banging tin pans. During the second wave of feminism a radical magazine was named *Mother Jones* in her honor.

Elizabeth Gurley Flynn had a long career as a revolutionary and organizer for the IWW and the Communist Party. In the first two decades of the century, her celebrity was comparable to a movie star's. A charismatic orator, she welcomed court trials as forums to attract public sympathy for labor. Flynn was elected chair of the IWW in 1906 while Haywood lectured in Europe to celebrate his acquittal on charges of murdering the Idaho governor, who had called out the National Guard to suppress a strike.

Emma Goldman, a labor radical, anarchist, peace activist, and birth-control advocate, was an early backer of the Bolshevik Revolution. She helped her lover, Alexander Berkman, plot to assassinate Henry Clay Frick during the Homestead strike. Goldman also spent prison terms for urging workers to steal to eat, for espousing birth control, for distributing contraceptives, and for organizing a campaign against conscription during World War I. In 1919 Goldman and other radicals were deported to the Soviet Union. There, she became disillusioned with regimented rule and wrote one of the early internal critiques of the Soviet State. Leaving the U.S.S.R., she spent the rest of her life in Europe and Canada.

Less notorious than Goldman, but influential as a labor organizer, was Rose Schneiderman, a Jewish immigrant from Poland. One of the most effective labor orators, she helped organize successful strikes of New York shirtwaist makers (tailors) in 1909 and 1910. Those workers became martyrs for reform in 1911, when a fire at the Triangle Shirtwaist Factory killed 146 women. The owners had locked the fire escape doors to prevent union organizers from entering and employees from taking breaks. The building was a deadly trap for those who worked for a pittance in dangerously crowded conditions. Schneiderman encountered opposition in the New York Women's Trade Union League (NYWTUL), in part due to her efforts to organize immigrants, especially Jews. Resigning in protest, she joined the International Ladies Garment Workers Union, became frustrated with its lack of support for her efforts, and returned to the NYWTUL as president. In the meantime, Schneiderman had become convinced that suffrage was critical to women's progress and that the movement had to reach beyond its elitist roots to working-class women. She helped found the Wage Earner's League for Woman Suffrage, the first suffrage organization made up largely of industrial women workers, in 1911. Her advocacy was rewarded in 1917, when New York women won the vote. Many of Schneiderman's attempts to obtain safer work conditions, higher wages, and union recognition succeeded as well.

Crystal Eastman's investigations of labor conditions in New York led her to write *Work Accidents and the Law* (1910), a study in the new field of worker's compensation law. She helped draft such a law for New York State. During Wilson's presidency, Eastman served as an attorney for the U.S. Commission on Industrial Relations. Radicalized by her failure to obtain women's suffrage in Wisconsin, she joined Alice Paul in helping found the Congressional Union, a forerunner of the militant National Woman's Party. She also worked against militarism and war and was instrumental in creating the Women's Peace Party. Renamed the Women's International League for Peace and Freedom in 1921, it became the longest-lasting women's peace organization. Finally, Eastman helped form the National Civil Liberties Union, an early version of the American Civil Liberties Union, to protect the rights of conscientious objectors and defend freedom of speech.

Labor was caught in a paradox: militance sometimes gained concessions, yet it also frightened away recruits. By World War I, the IWW had only 60,000–100,000 members. The conviction of two radical union leaders in a bomb blast that destroyed the Los Angeles Times building and killed twenty nonunion men was a stigma for the IWW cause. Another setback came when a firm of hatters in Danbury, Connecticut, sued the hatters' union for $240,000 for a boycott under the Sherman Act. The United States Supreme Court upheld the judgment, saying the boycott was an illegal combination in restraint of trade. The IWW received a mixed decision in 1912, when tens of thousands of textile workers in Lawrence, Massachusetts, struck to protest wage cuts. With the AFL standing aloof, the Wobblies sent Haywood, Flynn, Mother Jones, and Sanger. Within six weeks the company yielded to many of the strikers' demands for higher pay, shorter hours, overtime, and no discrimination against strikers. Victory for the workers nonetheless proved temporary; the owners reversed most of their concessions within a year. Soon textile workers struck again, at Paterson, New Jersey, and Haywood and the Wobblies intervened again, but the strike was broken by May 1913.

Another strike in 1913 occurred at the Rockefeller family mines in Ludlow, Colorado. The state militia was summoned and several miners were killed in a skirmish known as the "Ludlow Massacre." Despite exhortations by Goldman, the exhausted strikers gave up. A commission investigating the strike caught John D. Rockefeller in a lie and tarnished his image. Though he claimed no knowledge of atrocious conditions in the mines, correspondence proved that he had known. Still, the Wobblies lost most. Their fiery rhetoric produced few tangible gains, and members defected to more pragmatic unions. Haywood was convicted of organizing strikes during wartime under the Sedition and Espionage Acts and fled to the Soviet Union to escape imprisonment. Like Goldman, he became disillusioned with Soviet communism, declined into alcoholism, and died in 1928. Yet, he was still revered in the U.S.S.R. and in some radical circles in America. His ashes were divided: some were buried within the Kremlin Walls and some in a Chicago cemetery.

Progressive Era presidents clearly disliked radical labor unions and placed a premium on maintaining order. Theodore Roosevelt supported union objectives such as the eight-hour day for federal workers and the elimination of convict labor. William Howard Taft shared some of TR's views, yet inclined in the direction of capital and, unlike Roosevelt, never invoked presidential power to settle strikes. At Taft's request, Congress created the Industrial Relations Commission to investigate working conditions, yet refused to confirm some of Taft's conservative nominees. Woodrow Wilson replaced some of Taft's selections with liberals and reappointed others. The commission's report to Wilson in 1915 confirmed the existence of harsh conditions, yet differed over remedial measures. Because he had benefited from AFL support in 1912, Wilson became the first president to recognize labor as a legitimate interest group, and he met often with Gompers. Union leaders were gratified by the president's appointment of liberals Louis D. Brandeis and John Hessin Clarke to the Supreme Court and by prolabor laws enacted during his administration.

Most critical was the Clayton Antitrust Act of 1914, decreeing that unions were not to be considered combinations in restraint of trade. Gompers compared the law with the ancient English charter, the Magna Carta, which defined the rights of Englishmen, but courts limited its impact. The La Follette Seaman's Act of 1915 limited penalties that could be imposed upon seamen under contract and set federal standards for living and working conditions aboard ships. The Adamson Act of 1916 gave railroad workers the eight-hour day. States joined the progressive parade by enacting a host of reform laws. These included child labor restrictions, compulsory school attendance, limits on the number of hours women could be required to work, and worker's compensation.

World War I stimulated the economy and strengthened the hand of labor. Strikes increased, despite a federal ban and Gompers's order forbidding AFL members to participate. Workers sought to keep pace with the rising cost of living and exploit the high demand for labor. The government, interested in maximizing production for the war effort, tightened its control over industry, allowing generous profits that facilitated higher wages. Profits and productivity, however, rose more rapidly than wages, and most unions did not win mandatory recognition by their employers.

Progress and Problems for African Americans and Native Americans

The progressive movement was nearly oblivious to the problems of minorities, as were most labor unions. African Americans, for example, benefited little from government regulations of working conditions or improvements in union contracts. Indeed, sometimes employers hired them as strike breakers. About three-quarters of African Americans lived in the rural South in 1900. They were less an urban people than were white Americans during

Better known to the general public than Du Bois or Washington was Jack Johnson, the world heavyweight boxing champion. Near-invincible, he frustrated white people by demolishing many a "white hope"—and marrying a white woman. Johnson was one of the first African Americans in a highly publicized field to hold the spotlight for years. Other blacks achieved scholarly and literary recognition. Carter Woodson, the only black person born of a slave to receive a Ph.D. in history, from Harvard, pioneered in social history. Devoting his life to the study of African Americans, he depicted them as major participants, not victims. Black journalists, with William Monroe Trotter and Ida Barnett Wells in the vanguard, crusaded for racial equality and against lynching, the vigilante violence used against black men.

Race riots broke out across the nation, the most serious of the southern violence occurring in Atlanta in 1906. White people attacked blacks after newspapers reported that black men had assaulted white women. Blacks retaliated, and looting and arson followed, turmoil that killed eleven blacks and injured sixty. Two riots erupted in Springfield, Illinois, the home of the Great Emancipator, Abraham Lincoln, during the first decade of the century. In 1919 more than twenty riots scarred the country, the worst in Chicago, where fifteen white people and three black people died in thirteen days.

Race flared intermittently as a national political problem during the Roosevelt administration. TR appointed William D. Crum, a black Republican, as collector of customs in Charleston, South Carolina, angering whites. A bitter debate ensued over confirmation and the Senate did not approve the nomination until 1905. Another controversy arose when the African American postmistress in Indianola, Mississippi, who had served since the 1880s, resigned under pressure from white people. The Post Office refused to accept her resignation, and during the impasse the Indianola branch was closed for months, finally reopening under a white postmaster. Roosevelt appointed fewer African Americans to patronage positions than previous GOP presidents and tried to court southern whites by ignoring black political interests. TR and his successor expediently thought that the GOP, as the party of Lincoln, could take black votes for granted. Roosevelt avoided public race baiting. He believed African Americans could be uplifted by education. Nonetheless, he shared the belief, common in his time, that they were genetically inferior to white people and that social reforms could never make the races intellectually comparable.

The most controversial racial dispute involving TR occurred in 1906. White residents of Brownsville, Texas, accused black soldiers from a nearby army base of shooting up the town, killing one white man and wounding a white police officer. None of the men in a battalion of all-black 25th Infantry Regiment would admit to guilt or identify guilty parties. Roosevelt had every battalion member dishonorably discharged and barred them from federal employment. His action inspired protests in the North and among blacks and some white Republicans. Ultimately the president admitted that he did not have the authority to prevent future employment and allowed reenlistment for those who swore they had not participated in or witnessed the incident. In 1972 the army changed the discharges to honorable ones.

Taft, who was secretary of war when the dishonorable discharges were issued, shared the belief in genetic inferiority of African Americans. He told a southern audience during the 1908 presidential campaign that he did not object to their disenfranchisement because the votes of the illiterates debased elections. Such questions, he believed, were best handled by state and local governments.

Wilson probably shared the beliefs of Roosevelt and Taft about black inferiority. He was not a crusader for civil rights, yet he was chiefly neutral on the subject. It simply was not a priority for him, and he dealt with most racial issues as matters of political expediency. For example, he helped individual African Americans, yet allowed his Treasury secretary and postmaster general to segregate their departments to appease congressmen.

Dealing with Native Americans, Roosevelt, Taft, and Wilson were assimilationists. Indians could learn to compete in the capitalist order by leaving their reservations and obtaining an education. TR wanted Indians to rise or fall on their own, separated from their tribal connections. Indian problems would disappear along with tribal cultures, he believed. Reflecting his intentions, the Burke Act of 1906 allowed Indians to sell land granted to them individually, so they could move to cities and take jobs or start businesses. Under this "Americanization" drive, rooted in the 1870s, some Indians prospered, but for the great majority, the program was ruinous. White people eager to exploit natural resources such as timber, oil, and minerals cheated Indians of their lands, cut their important tribal ties, and sent their standard of living spiraling further downward. By the end of Wilson's second term, Native Americans had lost two-thirds of their land and most of them were destitute, ravaged physically by alcoholism and other diseases. What was for white Americans an Era of Awakening was for Indians an epoch of misery.

CHAPTER FOUR

A Culture Awakening, 1900–1919

A S THE ERA OF Awakening jarred politics, the economy, and foreign policy, so did it stimulate culture. Cultural blossoming, initially, was less important in producing art and entertainment than consuming it. In popular culture, America offered the most lucrative mass markets in the world. When Americans turned to the fine arts, they preferred the work of Europeans. But the culture reflected social changes as well. The federal government assisted by allowing income tax deductions for contributions to the arts, which over time contributed more to artistic development than the direct subsidies of European governments. Under these conditions, it was likely that good art would emerge, and some did.

Americans began to export culture, including technology, political criticism, and science. Their research universities acquired resources and status. A U.S. resident who told a Frenchman that he reveled in the coffee shops of Paris was surprised when the Frenchman replied that he was more interested in the skyscrapers of New York. If the budding culture demonstrated that America was becoming more sophisticated, it also showed how the country was losing its innocence before World War I. Cultural criticism helped Americans understand there was a dark side to their nation—even before the war drove the point home.

Reading for the Masses

Before there can be art, there must be a demand for it. For writers, the way was paved in the 1900s and 1910s, a period of mass readership in which people devoured pulp and serious literature (mostly the former), magazines, newspapers, and specialized journals. The popular book market had been established earlier, as volumes written, printed, and published by

Americans began to outsell those of Europeans by the mid-1890s. Public schools produced an audience of readers. Developments in printing technology, including the linotype machine, rotary press, and cheap pulp paper, along with a national distribution system by rail, aided mass publishing. These improvements helped reduce magazine prices, making the publications affordable for a wide public and appealing to advertisers.

Readers found fiction and poetry, once sources of cultural continuity, converted into sources of rebellion, much like muckrakers altered journalism. Writers applauded revolution in foreign lands and called for it in their own. Novels described graphic sex, violence, and the seamy aspects of capitalism. Authors presented female characters who had sexual appetites, who were not gratified in traditional marriages, and who disliked being treated as porcelain dolls in high society. Poets evoked sadness and bleakness.

In the late nineteenth century, realism supplanted romanticism in fiction, and early in the twentieth, naturalist authors emerged to depict a harsher reality. Naturalists thought that realists underestimated the caprices in the universe that cast humans into tempests as mere objects, not as actors. Taking their cues from some of the intellectual trends that Sigmund Freud, Karl Marx, Charles Darwin, and Friedrich Nietzsche popularized, they described a world that was more turbulent than the world of the realists. To some degree, though, the naturalists mellowed with age, the women more gracefully than the men. Most concluded that the inhospitable environments that frustrated them in youth were not so bad after all, and that the ideals they pursued elsewhere were not as sublime; one could not escape one's roots, and one should not try to do so. Never completely recovering from bitterness, some naturalists nevertheless learned to place their suffering in context. They cultivated irony and concluded that the most mundane values are the most human, a lesson as important as the message that humans inhabit a world that is frequently impersonal and cruel.

Jack London's tales were widely read for their apparent romanticism when, in truth, he wanted to show the Darwinian struggle in nature that spun beyond human control. His stories of miners and animals in the Yukon, where he tried to strike it rich in the gold rush of 1897–1898, have been his most enduring works, including *The Call of the Wild* (1903), *The Sea Wolf* (1904), and *White Fang* (1906). A fine craftsman with a vivid narrative style, London was one of the better-known and higher-paid writers in America from 1900 to 1910. Then, burned out physically and emotionally, he died of a drug overdose in 1916.

Some considered Theodore Dreiser crude and immoral, and critics called his prose ponderous and his storytelling skills mediocre. But he became the most influential naturalist, writing prolifically and, as an edi-

Henry Adams, whose great-grandfather was the second American president and whose grandfather was the sixth president, used the *North American Review*, which he edited, to crusade against political corruption and economic abuse. Adams found the Era of Awakening a jarring time, an alarm that many intellectuals shared, as his most influential book, *The Education of Henry Adams* (1907), indicated. Technology would drive the century, he predicted, and men of his generation were unprepared for it, having received classical educations at the best schools. First printed in a small, private edition, the book did not become available to the public until 1918, after Adams's death, and the next year it won a Pulitzer Prize.

Whereas Adams feared that education could not address the problems of the unfolding century, John Dewey proposed changes to improve education. The teacher, psychologist, and philosopher was largely responsible for the proliferation of progressive education in elementary and secondary schools during the period. At the University of Chicago, he directed the laboratory school that experimented with teaching methods, deemphasizing memorization and discipline in favor of imagination. In psychology Dewey introduced the idea of functionalism, holding that intelligence is constantly changing as a result of interaction between individuals and their environment.

The emergence of Dewey's progressive education coincided with an enrollment boom in schools. Only 4.5 percent of children ages fifteen to nineteen were enrolled in secondary schools in 1890, but 41.6 percent were attending by 1930. A kindergarten movement that began in the early 1900s got children into school when they were young, and attendance laws kept them there longer. Other school reforms rose from political progressivism. Progressives tried to apply the scientific methods of the social sciences to education and to make teaching a profession by offering college degrees in education. A division of labor evolved between teachers and administrators. In the South, progressive education, paradoxically, coexisted with segregated schools.

More people sought a college education. Undergraduate enrollment rose from 1.8 percent of the college age population in 1890 to 4.7 percent in 1920; college ranks doubled by World War I. Income, race, religion, and gender limited opportunities to attend college. Women continued to enroll in the elite women's colleges founded after the Civil War, yet most matriculated at coeducational land grant universities in the Midwest and Southwest. Female college graduates wed in lower percentages than noncollege women, married later, and had fewer children. Some women made careers in academia, constituting one-fifth of college faculty by 1910.

Dewey's concepts were less important in higher education, a field that came to involve more graduate study and specialized research. Departing from its Protestant orientation, it became overwhelmingly secular. Scholars began to write mainly for other academics. Graduate study likewise encouraged specialization. Basic curricula included classes in sociology, social work, political science, and natural science.

Those fortunate enough to win admission to Harvard at the right time could study under William James, older brother of the novelist Henry James and a professor for decades until his retirement in the 1900s. A medical doctor and a teacher of philosophy, psychology, physiology, and anatomy, he was also interested in religion, psychic phenomena, psychotherapy, and education. *Principles of Psychology* (1890), James's major work in the field, became a widely used text for its concrete examples and humorous, colloquial, and metaphorical style. His most popular work, *The Varieties of Religious Experience* (1902), included studies of people whose lives were changed by mystical experiences. His chief contribution to philosophy was *Pragmatism* (1907), in which he introduced the idea that truth comes from daily experience, not from universal laws or theories. One had to "live today by what truth he can get, be ready tomorrow to call it a falsehood," James said.

Realms of Religious Belief

At the grass roots, affiliation with religious groups increased; by 1900 some 35.7 percent of Americans belonged to churches or synagogues, up from 15.5 percent in 1850. Religions that embraced urban values—Catholicism, Judaism, Quakerism, and Unitarianism—thrived naturally in cities; mainline Protestant denominations began to retreat to the outskirts of cities and retained their rural preponderance. Numerically the leading churches were, in order, Catholic, Methodist, Baptist, and Presbyterian. Among immigrants—Italians, Poles, Hungarians, Austrians, and Mexicans—the vast majority were Catholics, who founded schools and recreational organizations as options to public schools whose students were heavily Protestant.

Immigrant Jews adjusted to their new land, in part, by creating a big city network of cultural and philanthropic organizations, including the Young Men's Hebrew Associations and B'nai B'rith, and the branches of Reform Judaism and Conservative Judaism. Reform Jews rejected the idea that all Jews were exiles awaiting return to Israel, and used English prayers and organ music in services. Conservative Jews, choosing a middle ground between the changes of liberal Reform congregations and Orthodox synagogues, adapted to American culture but kept elements of ritual. They were especially involved in raising money to realize the Zionist goal of creating a Jewish state in Palestine. Other Jewish fund-raising was directed toward fighting anti-Semitism.

Much of the growth in religious membership, particularly in Christian denominations, was the result of loosened requirements for adherents. This was encouraged by evaluating preachers by the number of their recruits. The practice not only alienated traditionalists but left religious institutions less stringent in enforcing behavior. Families, churches, and synagogues passed on moral responsibility to government and secular officials. In foreign affairs religion retained an ambiguous role, a justification for dominance and a rationale for humanitarianism. William McKinley and Theodore Roosevelt cited Christianity to explain intervention and expansion overseas. Woodrow Wilson invoked religion in an effort to validate neutrality in World War I, then to justify the American entry into war, and, finally, membership in the League of Nations.

Challenges to religion also came from science, politics, and philosophy. The ideas of Charles Darwin, Sigmund Freud, and Karl Marx were controversial, especially Darwin's theory of evolution, for it contradicted the biblical story of creation. Modernists believed that the Bible could be reconciled with Darwin, that one umbrella could cover both religion and science, yet fundamentalists claimed that the umbrella favored science. To modernists, fundamentalists who interpreted the Scriptures literally were simpletons; to fundamentalists, modernists were at best lukewarm Christians. "Fundamentalism" had not been used frequently to define a set of religious beliefs until 1909, when a group of Protestants formed the World's Christian Fundamentalist League. The movement crystallized, in part, because women, immigrants, and changing sexual standards diluted tradition.

Protestants were divided over the concept of millennialism. Premillennialists, most of whom were religious conservatives, said the Second Coming of Jesus Christ would precede the thousand years of peace and bounty predicted in the Book of Revelation. Human attempts to reform the world were futile because redemption had to await the return of the messiah. One facet of premillennialism was dispensationalism, a doctrine that divided history into periods, ending with the Second Coming. Modernists were skeptical of premillennialism and dispensationalism, perceiving them as disincentives to engage in God's work on earth, that is, to improve the world. Critics responded that the modernists' Social Gospel elevated ephemeral concerns over eternal truths. Catholics had their own disputes, debating whether scientific theories and progress were compatible with church custom. Were the pronouncements of popes open to change by subsequent generations, priests, and theologians? Finally, could the laity interpret Scripture? Among Jews, the major question concerned the extent of assimilation permissible, evidenced in the split between Reform and Conservative Judaism.

Ash Cans and Architects

Around 1900 American painting threw a gauntlet at gentility with the advent of a group known as the Ash Can school because its disciples depicted tenements, dirty laundry, and trash cans on city streets, hoping to capture the vital and robust instead of the dainty. Some of its painters, especially the Ash Can leader, Robert Henri, and George Luks, were attracted to athletics. Luks's paintings of prizefighters became famous. Victorian sensibilities got another jolt from the New York Armory Show of 1913, which exposed some three hundred thousand visitors to the most recent European abstract art. Creating sensations at subsequent stops in Boston and Chicago, the exhibition shocked provincial Americans and propelled the transition from representational art to abstract art that projected the painter's feelings onto canvas. It took a long time before abstract art reached beyond the avant garde, but since 1913 modernism has dominated American painting.

Alfred Stieglitz promoted photography as a fine art, persuading museums to stage exhibits and maintain permanent collections. He gained recognition with a group self-styled the "Photo Secessionists." Stieglitz emphasized "straight" photos as opposed to doctored ones. Not surprisingly, the group took photos like those of the amateurs, only better, revealing trained eyes, discipline, and timing. Stieglitz's protégé, Edward Steichen, tested all facets of photography, including color. He became a brilliant portrait photographer and a pioneer of aerial photography. Another trailblazer, the documentary photographer Paul Strand, employed series of photos without captions to tell a story.

In architecture, the most pronounced trend was eclecticism. The Beaux Arts style, which sacrificed function to embellishment and comfort to decoration, reigned until the 1930s, but the midwestern practitioners Louis W. Sullivan and Frank Lloyd Wright were more significant. With his lean and spare designs, Sullivan broke with Beaux Arts and purportedly coined the phrase "Form follows function." He thought a building should reflect its purpose, originate in the architect's imagination, and be constructed from the inside out. Sullivan also helped popularize the building of skyscrapers, made possible by steel frames that supported walls hung like curtains. These tall office buildings materialized from the enterprise of architects, engineers, and businessmen rebuilding downtown Chicago after the devastating fire of 1871.

Wright surpassed his teacher Sullivan, becoming the most renowned— and likely the most controversial—American architect ever, designing more than eight hundred buildings, of which four hundred were constructed.

Even more than Sullivan's designs, Wright's welled up within him and overflowed to become reality. He combined imagination with technical competence and the vision to integrate structures into their natural settings. Wright synthesized the functional and ornamental prairie school house, whose long, low, horizontal lines harmonized with the landscape.

Innovations in Music

The major American musical style, jazz, emerged after World War I, although its roots, ragtime and the blues, appeared during the Era of Awakening. A mix of West African syncopated rhythms and the refinements of American slaves, ragtime spread among southern blacks who listened to touring minstrels and "professors" of music, often pianists, who entertained customers in houses of prostitution (practically the only places where they could find work) in New Orleans and Memphis. In the 1890s it moved up the Mississippi River and became a national obsession, but began to wane

LEADING THE WAY FOR RAGTIME
The fascinating lure of ragtime dance.
(Library of Congress)

by wartime. Scott Joplin, the top ragtime composer and performer, made his mark in 1899 with "Maple Leaf Rag," the first piece of American-composed sheet music to sell 2 million copies. He failed to realize fully his dream of merging ragtime with classical music and died at age forty-eight, insufficiently mourned for decades. Still, the form that Joplin helped create began the century on an upbeat tempo, spawned hundreds of compositions, and made possible a big mainstream hit, "Alexander's Ragtime Band," a 1911 work by white composer Irving Berlin. Berlin, the most accomplished popular composer in American history, published more than fifteen hundred songs, including "God Bless America," "White Christmas," and "Easter Parade," for Broadway, musical revues, and motion pictures. He was the king of Tin Pan Alley, the legendary mecca of popular melodic music in New York, a section of restaurants, clubs, ballrooms, and composing studios where the banging of tinny upright pianos sounded like a person striking pans.

Blues also entered the musical mainstream after whites popularized it. Originating from spirituals and work songs, blues preserved the memory of slavery and injustice, not to deny them, but to transcend them. W. C. Handy, a white coronetist, was instrumental in promoting blues and moving them north. His 1914 hit, "St. Louis Blues," provided a bridge to jazz.

Serious music continued to operate in the shadow of Europe, a supplier of symphonies, operas, instrumentalists, and conductors to the United States. Charles Ives tried to create a truly American symphony imbued with the spirit of his native New England, composing music that was original, if difficult to perform or appreciate. His most productive period occurred before he suffered a serious heart attack in 1918, yet in 1947, long after his retirement from writing music, Ives received a Pulitzer Prize for his Third Symphony, composed during 1901–1904.

But Europe did not dominate popular dance. Here the United States led, and popular dance enjoyed a considerable following throughout the twentieth century. Before 1900, many dances started in rural areas and then came to cities, a path reversed in the century. Once again blacks were in the forefront, initiating a series of fads incorporating aspects of African dances mimicking animal movements, among them the Turkey Trot, the Kangaroo Hop, and the Grizzly Bear.

Another pioneer, Ruth St. Denis, introduced a form of artistic dance derived from the French Delsarte form that blended rhythmic gymnastics with gestures conveying intense emotions. She helped to found the Denishawn school to teach her interpretive style, which integrated the spiritual and the exotic. St. Denis, however, did not make as much of an impression as did Isadora Duncan, a designer of solo performances who forged a genre of modern dance distinct from ballet. Duncan also conceived a system for training children to dance in a natural style.

Stage and Screen

Theater, particularly melodrama and musical comedy, flourished between 1890 and 1910. Few serious dramatists enjoyed wide recognition, although works of William Shakespeare, Henrik Ibsen, George Bernard Shaw, and August Strindberg had audiences in America. Drama centered on Broadway, but in 1915 the Washington Square Players were founded in New York to perform experimental drama, followed the next year by the Provincetown (Massachusetts) Players, organized to stage less slickly commercial plays, including ones by their own members, such as Eugene O'Neill.

In melodrama, the master was William Clyde Fitch, producer of numerous Broadway hits before his death in 1909 at forty-four. Fitch showcased the royal family of American stage, Ethel, John, and Lionel Barrymore. Fitch's plays were comedies of manners stemming from superficial episodes in the lives of the upper class, performed with exaggerated gestures. Musical comedies were another Broadway staple, a derivation of the European operetta, or comic opera, and the musical revue. *The Ziegfeld Follies*, a production that ran from 1907 to 1932, was the most lavish. It relied on lively songs, dance, jokes, flashy costumes, and beautiful women. Equally invigorating, singer, dancer, songwriter, playwright, and promoter George M. Cohan brought excitement to Broadway for two decades. "Mr. Broadway" wrote the songs "Give My Regards to Broadway" and "Over There" and produced shows bubbling with patriotism.

Vaudeville shows began in New York cabarets and toured the nation from the late 1800s to the Great Depression. Comedians, acrobats, jugglers, dancers, singers, musicians, ventriloquists, magicians, and animal acts performed for family audiences in "palaces" in towns and cities. The fame of many of the artists outlasted vaudeville: singer and comedian Eddie Cantor, magician and escape artist Harry Houdini, cowboy humorist Will Rogers, and comics W. C. Fields, the Marx brothers, and Fanny Brice.

Technology contributed new forms of urban entertainment, starting with the "talking machine," or phonograph, that Thomas Edison and others devised. Edison developed the first machines for business and abandoned the effort when he found no market. He resumed research after competitors found a market for phonographs to play music for saloon customers who deposited a nickel in a slot. Later, "penny arcades" were established, housing machines that dispensed gum, candy, and patent medicine, as well as music. Traveling lecturers carried "concert horns" with recorded entertainment to attract crowds.

★ JIM THORPE: VICTORY AND DEFEAT ★

None of the strong men of history could have competed successfully with him. They had great strength, we may infer, but they lacked his speed, his agility, his skill. A wonder, a marvel, is the only way to describe him.
—JAMES E. SULLIVAN, AMATEUR ATHLETIC UNION PRESIDENT

A STAR ATHLETE
Champion Jim Thorpe in the uniform of the Carlisle Indian School football team, 1909.
(National Archives)

COACH GLENN "Pop" Warner had had enough of the young man who was begging to play football. He was Warner's top track athlete, too valuable for a contact sport that might injure him. Finally, the coach handed him a ball and told him to give the defense some tackling practice. Jim Thorpe did no such thing; he ran around, past, and through them, not once but twice. "Nobody is going to tackle Jim," he said, flipping the ball to an astonished Warner.

With that display, Thorpe won a place on the team at Carlisle Indian School in Pennsylvania and went on to amazing performances. In 1911 he kicked four field goals and ran for a touchdown, giving his unheralded squad all of its points in a stunning 18-15 victory over powerful Harvard. In 1912 he returned kickoffs ninety and ninety-five yards for touchdowns on successive plays (the first was nullified by a penalty) in a 27-6 victory over an Army team led by Cadet Dwight D. Eisenhower. College football, however, was only one game in which Thorpe excelled. He was an Olympic track champion; he played hockey, professional football, and baseball; he golfed, swam, bowled, and wrestled—a record of remarkable versatility. Sportswriters recognized his achievements in 1950, naming Thorpe the greatest athlete and the greatest football player of the half century.

Thorpe's most memorable triumph came at the 1912 Olympic track and field competition in Stockholm, Sweden. He won the pentathlon, finishing first in four of the five events, then easily won the ten-event decathlon even though he had never competed in it. "Sir, you are the greatest athlete in the world," Swedish King Gustav V said. Thorpe meekly replied, "Thanks, King."

Alas, the glory soon disappeared. In 1913, after investigating reports that Thorpe played semiprofessional baseball in 1909 and 1910, the Amateur Athletic Union declared him a professional and ruled that he had been ineligible to compete at Stockholm. His feats were purged from the record books and he was ordered to return his Olympic medals and trophies. Thorpe had played professionally, but without realizing that he was jeopardizing his amateur standing. Moreover, as his defenders pointed out, the AAU did not challenge his eligibility within the time limits allowed by Olympic rules. It was a setback from which Thorpe never recovered. "Rules are like steam rollers," he wrote. "There is nothing they won't do to flatten the man who stands in their way."

The years after sports were difficult: Thorpe worked at several jobs without much success, he was troubled by poverty and alcoholism, and he lost much of his once-formidable physique. He went to his grave in 1953, without the vindication he sought. It took nearly forty years for the campaign on his behalf to bear fruit, but in 1982 the International Olympic Committee decided to lift the ban against Thorpe, reinstate his records, and present new medals to his children. Two years later, his grandson, Bill Jr., honored his memory by running in the first leg of the relay that carried the Olympic torch to the Los Angeles games.

Sources: Perhaps the best extended treatment of Jim Thorpe's life is Robert W. Wheeler, *Jim Thorpe: World's Greatest Athlete* (1975). For helpful short essays on Thorpe's life, see Robert Lipsyte and Peter Levine, *Idols of the Game: A Sporting History of the American Century* (1995); Associated Press sports staff, *The Sports Immortals* (1972); *Dictionary of American Biography, Supplement Five* (1977); and David Wallechinsky, *The Complete Book of the Olympics* (1984). Jack Newcombe, *The Best of the Athletic Boys: The White Man's Impact on Jim Thorpe* (1975), is also useful.

The greatest potential lay in the silent motion pictures introduced in the late nineteenth century and perfected in the twentieth. Again, Edison and his associates contributed to the progress of this medium, although Edison did not perfect it. Early movies using the kinetoscope were peep shows watched by one customer at a time. Next came the vitascope, projecting short films on a screen for a larger audience. This device gave way to nickelodeons, where people could see movies for a nickel and hear organ accompaniment. Some four thousand to five thousand nickelodeons were operating nationwide by 1907, but the market became saturated. One director, D. W. Griffith, grew tired of making short films. Determined to direct an epic, he adapted for the screen southern writer Thomas Dixon's novel of the Civil War and Reconstruction, *The Clansman*. The extravaganza glamorized the Ku Klux Klan and showcased racial stereotypes. At the time, though, *Birth of a Nation* (1915) was a financial and aesthetic triumph. Using multiple cameras that swept a broad field and showing hundreds of actors in battle scenes, Griffith demonstrated the power and potential of the young medium.

Competition in the once-chaotic industry was rationalized before and during World War I. Hollywood, California, possessing favorable weather and topography, became the center of the business. Stars such as the comic genius Charlie Chaplin, the demure Mary Pickford, and the heartthrobs

Theda Bara, Greta Garbo, Lillian Gish, Gloria Swanson, Rudolph Valentino, and John Barrymore commanded huge salaries. Genres of films arose, such as Westerns, romances, comedies, and adventures. Amid outrage over cinematic values, a code was enacted, limiting passionate embraces and sexual innuendo, and ensuring that good would prevail over evil. The code, of course, only temporarily slowed the tides of sexuality and violence that resisted attempts to ban them. African Americans presumably ran little if almost no risk of being corrupted by immoral portrayals, for they were not permitted to attend many theaters. When they could enter the establishments, they sat in segregated sections and watched white performers sing as blackface minstrels. Other racial and ethnic stereotypes, such as the penurious Jew, appeared on stage and screen.

Spectator Sports

Athletic competition was a frontier of entertainment, giving people liberty to participate in physical activity or to experience it as spectators. Initially recreation focused on hunting, fishing, and swimming. But as the economy grew centralized and urbanized, the organization of time became essential, and the spontaneity of rural activity diminished. In cities there was not much space for doing sports, but there were large audiences ready to watch them.

Parents and religious leaders who once considered sports unwholesome now deemed it character building, a cornerstone of Christian education. Teams were sponsored by the Young Men's Christian Association (YMCA) and the Young Women's Christian Association (YWCA). Americans loved sports heroes and contests because winners and losers were clearly defined, more clearly than in the increasingly complex industrial world.

By 1900 baseball was so popular that it was called the national pastime. The National League, established in 1876, appealed to the middle class by charging 50-cent admission to games, prohibiting alcohol sales in ballparks, and avoiding Sunday play. The American League, created in 1901, appealed to immigrants and the working class by charging 25 cents and allowing alcohol sales and Sunday games. Owners controlled the professional game by reserving the power to grant franchises. Players were contractually bound to their teams unless released or traded. Rival leagues for white players occasionally surfaced, signing a few marquee players from the major leagues before being driven out of business. African Americans, to whom the major leagues were closed, formed their own touring teams, the springboard for the Negro Leagues organized in the 1920s.

The so-called dead ball of this age made for low-scoring games featuring pitching and defense. Dead baseballs did not mean deadly dull play, as the period had many exciting players. The greatest was Ty Cobb, a master of offense and defense who compiled a .367 lifetime batting average and set records for stolen bases and hits that stood for decades. All the fame that the game gained because of Cobb and others was seriously threatened because of the "Black Sox" scandal. Eight Chicago White Sox players were accused of taking $80,000 in bribes from gamblers to deliberately lose the 1919 World Series to the underdog Cincinnati Reds. Seven were acquitted in court, and charges against the eighth were dismissed for lack of evidence. But Kenesaw Mountain Landis, the autocrat whom owners brought in as commissioner to handle the matter, banned all eight from the Major Leagues for life.

Although baseball dominated professional sports, the big men on college campuses were the football stars. By the end of the nineteenth century, football had become the most popular collegiate sport, a defining element in campus life and a major revenue producer from ticket sales and alumni donations. Professors and university administrators objected to the detrimental by-products: a win-at-all-costs mentality, an emphasis on athletic victories over academic objectives, the use of "ringers" on teams, and the violence of the game that resulted in injuries and even deaths. To rescue the sport, Roosevelt summoned leading football powers to a 1905 White House conference to "persuade them to play football honestly." From the meeting came rules that made the game safer, more credible, and more exciting, measures championed by Walter Camp of Yale University, the greatest coach of the period. Camp's rules helped keep college football far more popular than professional football, whose foundation was shaky. The inception of the American Professional Football Association, the forerunner of the National Football League, in 1920 stabilized the ranks somewhat, but the league would not truly capture public attention until the mid-1920s.

A third major sport, basketball, proved easily adaptable to urban and rural environments, middle classes and lower classes, men and women, amateurs and professionals. Seeking a safe, indoor alternative to football during the winter, James Naismith invented the game in 1891, nailing peach baskets to the gymnasium balconies at the YMCA training school in Springfield, Massachusetts. Basketball quickly pervaded city playgrounds, settlement houses, YMCAs, YWCAs, and schools.

Culture in the era was memorable for the variety of its offerings, the innovations and quality of artists, and the curiosity and open pocketbooks of its admirers. There were, nonetheless, limitations, as Americans were still largely conventional and imitative, more important as collectors and consumers than as creators. The period was one of rebellion, not quite revolution. That would come after 1919.

CHAPTER FIVE

Wilson, Reform, and the Coming of War

L IKE THEODORE Roosevelt, Woodrow Wilson brought intellect and emotion to the White House, swaying Americans with his eloquence and profound thought, and urging them to be the world's peacemaker, with him as peacemaker-in-chief. He was pious, yet competitive, a reluctant, yet spirited, combatant Historian. John Cooper, in his comparative biography of the two presidents, *The Warrior and the Priest*, leaves appropriate ambiguity as to which was the warrior and which was the priest. Like characters in a Shakespeare play they shared greatness and flaws. From a seemingly auspicious destiny, they both ended badly, surely a paradox.

Woodrow Wilson

A southerner, born in Virginia and raised in Georgia and South Carolina, Wilson was shaped by the Presbyterian faith of his father, a love of scholarship, and an ambition to become a great orator. Honing his oratorical gifts from solitary tree stumps, tempering his competitive streak to accommodate his frail body, and developing the patience of a scholar, he briefly practiced law, earned a Ph.D. in political science in 1886, and launched an academic career that brought him fame. Teaching at elite schools— Bryn Mawr, Wesleyan, and Princeton, he wrote well-received scholarly monographs such as *Congressional Government: A Study in American Politics* (1885) and a five-volume popular study, *A History of the American People* (1902). In 1902 Wilson became president of Princeton. After early success, he suffered frustrating defeats in academic politics and turned to a career in a presumably less frustrating field—state and national politics. He was invited to run for governor of New Jersey in 1910. Some of his backers doubted that he lacked the internal fortitude. "After dealing with university men, the men I am striving with appear as amateurs," said Wilson.

Wilson won the election comfortably and enacted a progressive agenda in his first term. The legislature passed laws for party primaries, limits on campaign spending, a worker's compensation law, a state board to regulate utilities, and authorized commission forms of local government. Elected to a second term, Wilson did not equal the achievements of his first term, but spent much time campaigning for president. The initial leader at the convention, House Speaker Champ Clark, with Alabama Representative Oscar W. Underwood in the race, could not muster the necessary two-thirds majority. Finally, Wilson prevailed, thanks to the support of William Jennings Bryan. Wilson was a compromise choice who appealed to his party's regional loyalties and was satisfactory to the rural and urban factions. In the general election, he was the strongest candidate in a field that included the shrill Theodore Roosevelt and the phlegmatic William Howard Taft. Ironically, the race featured three of the finest intellects ever to challenge one another.

Domestic Reform under Wilson

Wilson, like TR, used the forum of the presidency to educate not only the public but Congress. He delivered his State of the Union messages to Congress in person, breaking Jefferson's tradition of sending them in writing. In his first congressional session, Wilson helped enact a more comprehensive program of domestic reform than any previous president. The former academic went on to compile one of the most impressive records of domestic legislation of any chief executive.

Almost immediately, Wilson summoned Congress into special session and fulfilled his campaign promise to lower the tariff. The Underwood Tariff, signed by Wilson in 1913, reduced duties by almost 33 percent. Wilson's most enduring achievement was currency reform. The country badly needed more paper currency in circulation to support the expanding economy. Currency should, Wilson believed, be expanded or reduced to counteract trends in the economy that led to boom and bust cycles, such as the Panics of 1893 and 1907. Because conservatives favored private control and progressives wanted strong federal authority, the Federal Reserve Act of 1913 provided for a mix. It created a Federal Reserve Board of seven members, appointed by the president, and twelve regional federal reserve banks. The system was empowered to regulate the currency supply by raising or lowering the rate that it charged private banks to borrow from it or by buying or selling government bonds on the open market. In addition, the system issued new currency, Federal Reserve notes.

FROM ACADEMIA
TO THE WHITE
HOUSE
Woodrow Wilson
pushes for reform.
(Library of Congress)

To improve business regulation, Wilson submitted to Congress a pair of proposals adopted in 1914 as the Federal Trade Commission Act and the Clayton Antitrust Act. Superseding the weaker Bureau of Corporations, the new commission was authorized to collect data on monopolies, publish information to expose unfair practices, provide statistics for economic planning, issue injunctions, and file lawsuits to end practices restraining trade. The Clayton Act exempted labor boycotts and strikes from prosecution under the Sherman Act (although court interpretations would undermine the value of the law to unions) and prohibited firms from conspiring in price agreements that restricted trade. In supporting the laws, Wilson moved toward TR's advocacy of regulating, rather than busting trusts, but he did not fully accept TR's premise of the New Nationalism that espoused regulated monopoly. Wilson believed monopoly would crush competition and discourage entrepreneurs from starting businesses. Attorney General James McReynolds, a future Supreme Court justice, filed lawsuits to dismantle corporations that controlled more than 50 percent of the production, raw materials, and distribution of a commodity. The government won 70 percent of the cases, including suits against United States Steel, International Harvester,

Quaker Oats, National Cash Register, and the American Can Company. These companies were not "bad" monopolies in terms of conduct; their size induced the administration to dismantle them.

When it came to aid for farmers, Wilson was hesitant, but Bryan's partisans in the West and South insisted on assistance. Two noteworthy bills were passed in 1914. The Smith-Lever Act provided federal funds for experimental farming methods to increase production. The Cotton Futures Act limited speculation and required grading and labeling of cotton according to federal standards.

Personal tragedy struck Wilson on August 6, 1914, when his wife died of kidney disease. Throughout most of her months in the White House, Ellen Wilson was seriously ill and taxed by the stress of serving as first lady. Shortly before her death, Congress paid her tribute, passing a housing and slum clearance bill for which she had campaigned and naming it for her. In promoting legislation, Ellen Wilson set a precedent for her successors. Seven months after her death, in March 1915, Wilson met Edith Bolling Galt, an attractive widow, and they fell in love. Courting in the glare of White House cameras, though less newsworthy because of the war in Europe, the couple wed in December 1915.

Despite Wilson's legislative achievements, the 1914 congressional elections were a disaster for the Democrats, shrinking their majorities to narrow margins in both houses. Wilson began to tilt from the New Freedom to the New Nationalism, to measures that would not match those of 1913 and 1914 but still would be impressive. He helped create a Tariff Commission to recommend rate changes; a Shipping Commission to regulate and stimulate the dormant merchant marine industry; a prohibition on child labor in interstate commerce. In addition, Congress passed laws providing worker's compensation for federal employees; higher income and inheritance taxes on the wealthy; and the Adamson Act mandating an eight-hour day for railroad workers. Wilson also made his most important appointment, selecting his adviser, Louis Brandeis, for the Supreme Court. The first Jew to serve on the tribunal, Brandeis became one of the most distinguished justices ever.

Although Wilson is usually remembered for his foreign policy, his legacy in domestic matters deserves recognition. He and Theodore Roosevelt posed questions that would be debated for a century: At what points did the interest of the state and the interest of the individual clash? At what points did they complement each other? No one doubted the needs for self-interest, toward which Wilson shaded, and national interest, toward which TR shaded, but doubt persisted over the blend that carried the best hope for happiness. The two presidents offered vision, not a solution. The desire for both freedom and security is as old as humanity, and as evasive as the phantom of ultimate wisdom.

Wilson and the World

Just before becoming president, Wilson confided to a Princeton friend, "It would be an irony of fate if my administration had to deal with foreign problems, for all my preparation has been in domestic matters." In fact, Wilson was interested in foreign policy, but it was not his academic specialty. His only political experience was on the state level.

Latin America tested Wilson's resolve. Like his secretary of state, Bryan, he believed dark-skinned people were inferior. The administration established protectorates in Haiti and the Dominican Republic and continued Taft's protectorate in Nicaragua. Haiti was in tumult. A mob seized the president and the commander of the army and hacked them to death. A period of French military intervention and British occupation caused Wilson to send four hundred Marines in July 1915. Under a 1915 treaty, drafted chiefly by Americans, they remained in the country nineteen years, an occupation that some 3,250 Haitians died resisting. Under a constitution that also was drawn up mainly by Americans and adopted by Haiti in 1918, the United States managed the country's finances, elections, and internal improvements for a decade.

In the Dominican Republic, conditions were deteriorating at the end of the Taft administration. The assassination of the president in 1911 created a power vacuum that was not filled until Juan Isidro Jimenez won a U.S.-supervised election in December 1914. But Jimenez, caught between factions, resigned in May 1916, and America stepped in, taking charge of the government to prevent a civil war.

The administration attempted to improve its standing in Latin America succeeding in Puerto Rico because of the Jones Act of 1917, also known as the Organic Act. This law made the island a U.S. territory and gave its residents American citizenship and nearly all rights guaranteed in the U.S. Constitution. Many Puerto Ricans came to America in search of economic opportunity. The upper house of the legislature was made elective, as the lower house had been, and revenues that the United States helped collect were earmarked for the island treasury.

Relations with Mexico were turbulent. A 1911 revolution overthrew longtime dictator Porfirio Diaz, who was succeeded by Francisco Madero, overthrown in turn by one of Diaz's generals, Victoriano Huerta. Wilson encouraged General Venustiano Carranza, another aspirant to the presidency, refusing to recognize Huerta because he had seized power illegally. Meanwhile, the U.S. president pursued a policy of "watchful waiting." Relations with Huerta deteriorated further when American Marines clashed with Huerta's troops at Tampico Bay. The skirmish provoked resentment against Americans by all Mexican factions.

The Mexican president's seat seemed the object of a game of musical chairs. Carranza assumed power but split with one of his generals, Pancho Villa. The United States initially favored Villa, believing him pro-American. The administration switched sides, however, after Carranza's troops routed Villa, who retreated toward the United States. Feeling Carranza had popular support; America gave de facto recognition to his regime on October 19, 1915. This act alienated Villa. He looted a train and killed American passengers. In March 1916, he attacked towns in New Mexico and Texas, murdering Americans. Wilson federalized 100,000 troops from the Texas National Guard to protect the border. The president also assigned 12,000 soldiers under General John J. "Black Jack" Pershing (so called because he had commanded a regiment of black cavalrymen) to invade Mexico and capture Villa. The incursion failed, embarrassing the United States and angering Carranza, whose men fought with Pershing's. A joint commission stabilized the situation. Finally, in January 1917, Wilson, concerned about war with Germany, began withdrawing U.S. troops from Mexico. On March 11, Carranza was confirmed as president, and two days later Washington recognized his government.

If Wilson was tempted to intervene again, World War I smothered it. Villa died fighting Mexican troops. In 1919 Carranza codified anti-foreign practices. Foreigners were denied a dominant place in Mexican affairs, Mexican natural resources were to be controlled by Mexicans, and Mexico rejected the Monroe Doctrine.

Secondary to the focus on Latin America and Europe, involvement in the Pacific under Wilson focused on China, Japan, and the Philippines. On May 2, 1913, the United States became the first major nation to recognize the new republic of China. But America's belief in its mission to Christianize and Westernize China and to preserve Chinese territorial integrity brought conflict with Tokyo. Japan considered its huge, weak neighbor ripe for economic penetration.

To a lesser extent, Japan coveted the Philippines. With the 1916 Jones Act, America attempted to give the Philippines partial self-rule. The law conferred Filipino citizenship on former Spanish subjects, provided for male suffrage, established an elected senate, and vested authority in a governor general appointed by the U.S. president.

The Trials of Neutrality

The world plunged into "an abyss of blood and darkness," Henry James said, after a Serbian nationalist assassinated Archduke Franz Ferdinand, heir to the throne of Austria-Hungary, in the Bosnian town of Sarajevo on June 28, 1914. For decades Europeans had engaged in an arms race; alliances ensured that any war would spread. The late nineteenth and early twentieth centuries were fervently nationalistic. Ethnic groups yearned to become nations. Major nations competed to become dominant economic and military powers, acquiring colonies or seeking to preserve empires. The chief rivals were the British and French on one hand and Germany on the other. The decrepit empire of the czars in Russia was allied with the smaller Slavic nations, portions of their territory ruled by the Habsburg monarchy (Austria). Now those developments moved to a rendezvous with the apocalypse.

In the wake of the archduke's assassination by Gavrilo Princip, who wanted to unite the Serbian enclaves of the Habsburg Empire in an independent state, Germany gave a "blank check" to Austria. Kaiser Wilhelm offered to support any steps Vienna took to crush Serbia, including war with Serbia's Slavic protector, Russia. The Serbs complied partially to a stiff ultimatum from Austria, apologizing for the slaying but denying Austria a role in the investigation. Austria mobilized. Russia mobilized against Austria-Hungary, followed by mobilizations of the French and German armies. On August 1 Russia and the Habsburg monarchy declared war, drawing their respective allies, France and Germany, into combat. The Germans, seeking to outflank French defenses, invaded via neutral Belgium. Britain, bound to Belgium by treaty and hoping to protect France, declared war on Germany. World War I, then called the "Great War," commenced.

Since the time of George Washington, America's tradition had been to avoid European intrigues and wars, limiting interventions to the Western Hemisphere. In adhering to this precedent, on August 4, 1914, Wilson proclaimed neutrality. Most Americans sympathized with the Triple Entente powers—Britain, France, and Russia, bound by ties of language, culture, and trade—over the autocratic Central Powers, Germany and Austria-Hungary. Wilson hoped the United States could serve as a model of principled neutrality. But he also wanted a British victory due to his lifelong admiration of Britain.

The British blockade of German ports disrupted American trade, which annoyed Wilson, but German submarine warfare threatened lives, not merely cargoes. Submarines, the strength of the German Navy, could not fight by the existing rules of war. These required the searching and unloading of passengers before a nonmilitary ship could be sunk. Yet these rules assumed warships operated on the surface, as they had in previous wars. Now technology made the rules outdated. A surfaced submarine was too vulnerable to fire to be an ineffective weapon. Something had to give. It would not be Woodrow Wilson, who considered submarines immoral.

In February 1915 Germany said that its submarines would sink, without warning, ships entering a war zone around Britain. Wilson warned that he would hold Berlin to "strict accountability" for American losses. His resolve was tested on May 7, when a U-boat sank the British passenger liner *Lusitania*, killing 1,198, including 128 Americans. Wilson wrote three sharply worded notes to Germany implying that more sinkings would mean war. Bryan objected to the second, refused to sign it, and resigned. Bryan's pro-British successor, Robert Lansing, urged the president to stand firm against Germany. Outside the government, some of Wilson's critics, notably Theodore Roosevelt, demanded tougher measures.

On August 19, 1915, the Germans sank the British passenger ship *Arabic*. Forty-four, including two Americans, died. Privately, Wilson threatened to break diplomatic ties, hinting that Washington would go to war if Germany continued its sinkings. Berlin agreed not to sink liners without warning, yet on March 24, 1916, a U-boat torpedoed a foreign steamer, *Sussex*, injuring Americans. This time Wilson threatened to sever relations. Germany pledged to observe the rule mandating warning and evacuation of ships, provided Britain honor it as well. The president accepted the *Sussex* pledge and ignored the condition. He knew London could not comply because it would nullify the advantages of the British blockade. The American people were distraught about the sinkings, yet divided over whether to go to war. Business favored stability; it could make money by selling to the belligerents without war. Ethnic groups supported their mother country. Yet most Americans believed a German victory would be hostile to their interests.

Meanwhile, the president sent his adviser, Colonel Edward House, as an emissary to Europe in early 1916. House and his friend, British Foreign Secretary Sir Edward Grey hammered out an agreement to end the war on London's terms. If Germany would not accept an American offer to mediate a settlement, the United States "probably" would enter the war on the Allied side. The British cabinet rejected the deal. Wilson rewrote the House-Grey memorandum into a general statement that did not commit America to war. Henry Ford attempted to mediate, sending pacifists to Europe aboard a "peace ship." If he could manufacture cars, Ford said, he could make people stop killing each other.

★ EDWARD M. HOUSE: THE QUIET CAMPAIGNER ★

> My ambition has been so great that it has never
> seemed to me worthwhile to strive to satisfy it.
> —EDWARD M. HOUSE

A DIMINUTIVE, soft-spoken man who refused appointment to high office, Colonel Edward M. House (1858–1938) came to wield more authority than most of the highest officials in the United States. As Woodrow Wilson's chief adviser, especially in foreign policy, House preferred to work outside the channels of government as the president's representative.

Born in Houston, Texas, to the southern aristocracy and educated in elite schools, House held ambitions for political office but fragile health and a weak voice forced him to be content with the role of adviser. Aligned with the reform wing of the Democratic Party, he was awarded the title of "colonel" by the governor of Texas.

In 1912, House met Wilson as the New Jersey governor campaigned for president, and found a soul mate. "We found ourselves in such complete sympathy, in so many ways, that we soon learned to know what each was thinking without either having expressed himself," House wrote. After Wilson's election, House became a behind-the-scenes mover in the administration. An enigmatic figure with a fertile imagination, he penned a novel about a private citizen who imposed world peace in 1912. House's influence waxed during the Great War.

Distrusting the judgment of his secretary of state, William Jennings Bryan, Wilson increasingly relied on House's discretion. House's friendship with the British Foreign Secretary, Sir Edward Grey, facilitated negotiations with the British, who regarded him highly.

After the United States declared war on Germany in 1917, House served as the president's confidant in negotiations with the Allies. He helped Wilson draft the Fourteen Points and accompanied the president to the peace conference at Versailles in 1919, acting in Wilson's place when the president was ill. House disappointed his mentor by his willingness to compromise with the harsher terms demanded by Great Britain and France. Now Wilson came to distrust House, believing that his old friend betrayed their ideals. After Versailles, Wilson never spoke to House again. Once one of America's most powerful men, House returned from France with no political position or importance. He worked on Franklin D. Roosevelt's presidential campaign in 1932, but never exercised any influence over his administration.

Sources: For the relationship between House and Wilson, see Alexander L. George and Juliette L. George, *Woodrow Wilson and Colonel House* (1956). For House and Grey's negotiations, see Joyce Grigsby Williams, *Colonel House and Sir Edward Grey* (1984).

Wilson faced a formidable Republican challenger in the 1916 presidential campaign, Charles Evans Hughes, former progressive governor of New York and U.S. Supreme Court justice. The Democrats campaigned as the peace party. Wilson reluctantly accepted the slogan "He kept us out of war," although he feared war was imminent. International tensions overshadowed Wilson's accomplishments in domestic policy. The incumbent trailed most of the night until late wins in Ohio and California reelected him, one of the closest elections of the century. Wilson won 49 percent of the popular vote to 46 percent for Hughes. Wilson's margin in the Electoral College was 277 to 254. The congressional vote showed a decline in the progressive movement. Conservatives prepared to take up the reins of government and to limit Wilson's leadership. Outside government, debates over government's role in regulation waned, superseded by issues related to the war, business, consumerism, and cultural rebellion. Although these developments would be postponed by the necessities of war and temporary government involvement, their seeds were planted in the last election before American boys embarked for the battlefields of Europe.

"A Message of Death"

Late in 1916 Wilson sought once more to broker a peace. He described his proposals in a speech to the Senate on January 22, 1917. He wanted "peace without victory" and an international organization where nations would resolve differences. Proud idealism led him to think he could impose these provisions for the peace settlement without entering the war. His goal of peace could not be pursued while he defended neutral rights.

Early in 1917 German military leaders concluded that the British blockade would strangle their nation if they did not mount a massive offensive to win. A ground assault and resumption of submarine warfare, they realized, would draw the United States into the war, but they believed combat would end before America could make a difference. Germany gambled it could win by sinking all ships bound for Britain. On January 31, Berlin informed the United States that Germany would proclaim a war zone around Britain, France, and Italy, and that the *Sussex* pledge would no longer be observed. Wilson broke relations with Germany.

War grew imminent in February, when the British intercepted and decoded a telegram from German Foreign Secretary Arthur Zimmermann to the German Embassy in Mexico. Zimmermann instructed his envoy to negotiate an alliance with Mexico in the event of war with America. Mexico was to try to persuade Japan to switch sides and declare war on the United States. In return, Germany would give Mexico territory lost

★ JEANNETTE RANKIN: WARRIOR FOR PEACE ★

*This woman has more courage and packs a harder punch
than a regiment of regular-line politicians.*

—FIORELLO LA GUARDIA, WHO SERVED IN CONGRESS WITH RANKIN

FIRST WOMAN IN CONGRESS
Jeannette Rankin opposed the war.
(Library of Congress)

JEANNETTE RANKIN served just two terms in the House of Representatives, more than twenty years apart. But she made a lasting impact as a feminist, as the first woman ever elected to Congress—and as the only member of Congress to vote against American involvement in both world wars.

Elected from Montana in 1916, Rankin found herself tested by her first vote, cast on April 6, 1917. She felt intense pressure to vote for war; the majority of her supporters in the women's suffrage movement urged her to do so. Striving to keep an open mind, she listened to the debate and waited until the second roll call. When her name was finally called, the chamber grew silent and every eye fixed on her. Slowly Rankin half rose, clutching a chair, and whispered, "I want to stand by my country, but I cannot vote for war." The "no" vote that followed was nearly lost in the muttering of colleagues and a smattering of applause from the galleries. She had cast a stunning vote and defied tradition by commenting on a roll call.

For the rest of her term, Rankin supported the war effort and championed reforms affecting women and children. None of her work, however, quelled the clamor against her antiwar vote. She never regretted the vote, although she was warned that it would cost her reelection. "I'm not interested in that," she said. "All I'm interested in is what they'll say fifty years from now." Gerrymandered into a predominantly Democratic district, Rankin ran instead for a U.S. Senate seat, and lost.

In the 1920s and 1930s, Rankin worked as a lobbyist for peace groups. "You can no more win a war than win an earthquake," she said. In 1940, fearing the United States would be pulled into World War II, Rankin ran again for the House from Montana and won. After Japan attacked Pearl Harbor on December 7, 1941, she once more defied public opinion by opposing the declaration of war—the only vote in Congress against war on the Japanese. Once more, Rankin's subsequent support of the war effort did not deter the public backlash against her vote. She retired from

Congress when her term expired. Her colleagues praised her courage, yet considered her vote folly.

During the next quarter century, Rankin traveled around the world—including India, where she became a disciple of Mahatma Gandhi—but lived reclusively. Then in 1968 she lent her name to the Jeannette Rankin Brigade, an organization of women opposing the Vietnam War, and led several thousand women in a protest march to the national Capitol. "We have to get it into our heads once and for all that we cannot settle disputes by eliminating human beings," Rankin said. Later, one congressman called her "the original dove in Congress" and told her, "Look at the record now. We're voting your way, Jeannette." She spoke publicly for peace and government reform until a few months before her death in 1973 at the age of ninety-two.

In Rankin's long lifetime of activity, she remembered one act above the rest. "The most important accomplishment, I believe, was my voting against the First World War."

Sources: The most useful short treatment of Jeannette Rankin is Glen Jeansonne, "The Lone Dissenting Voice," *American History*, Vol. XXXIV (April 1999), pp. 46–54. Also see Kevin S. Giles, *Flight of the Dove: The Story of Jeannette Rankin* (1980).

in the Mexican-American War of 1846–1848, including Texas, Arizona, and New Mexico. Britain gave the telegram to the U.S. government, and reports of the document in the press increased the clamor for hostilities. Wilson still opposed war. Instead, he asked Congress to authorize the arming of merchant ships. The bill passed the House but was killed by a Senate filibuster by a handful of isolationists. "A little group of willful men, representing no opinion but their own, have rendered the great government of the United States helpless and contemptible," Wilson complained. Later, the president found legal grounds to justify arming the vessels by executive order.

Overseas, the Russian Revolution overthrew the czar and momentarily ushered in a democratic government under the liberal Alexander Kerensky, who pledged to continue the war. To Wilson, the mission of the Great War now seemed clear-cut: democracy must defeat autocracy. By joining the war, America could gain a voice at the peacemaking and ensure a permanent peace. On April 2, 1917, Wilson stood before a joint session of Congress to urge America to wage war.

Wilson addressed the lawmakers with majestic rhetoric but a sad heart. American entry, he knew, would postpone reform and inspire intolerance. Nevertheless, the world had to be made safe for democracy. "It is a fearful thing to lead this great peaceful people into war, the most terrible and disastrous of all wars, civilization itself seeming to be in the balance. But the right is more precious than the peace . . . the day has come when America is privileged to spend her blood and her might for the principles that gave her birth and happiness and the peace which she has treasured. God helping her, she can do no other."

At his conclusion, the lawmakers stood and applauded. "Think what it was they were applauding," Wilson told his secretary, Joseph Tumulty. "My message today was a message of death for our young men. How strange it seems to applaud that." In the next four days, both houses of Congress supported the commander in chief's call for war against Germany. The United States would devote its energies, its souls, its young men, to Europe's most awesome catastrophe since the Black Death killed one-third of the population in the 1340s.

CHAPTER SIX

From World War
to Lost Peace

THE PARADOXES of Woodrow Wilson's presidency closed the Era of Awakening. A renowned academic, successful governor, and reform president, he emerged in his second term as a great war president, an eloquent statesman for world peace, and, ultimately, a failed peacemaker. He is often considered a tragic figure, abandoned by all but history. Yet out of his one magnificent failure grew lessons and an appreciation of the enormity of the task he had undertaken. "Show me a hero and I will write you a tragedy," the novelist F. Scott Fitzgerald wrote.

Home Front Management

Even before running as the peace candidate in 1916, Woodrow Wilson prepared for war. The army had just one hundred thousand soldiers, the fewest of any major nation. The navy ranked third in battleships behind Britain and Germany and had an antiquated command structure and supply system. Wilson's preparedness program met with opposition from Secretary of State William Jenning Bryan's dovish followers in Congress. Wilson compromised, dropping its most controversial feature, a reserve force to be known as the Continental Army. War Secretary Lindley Garrison, the architect of the plan, resigned in protest, so it was up to his replacement, Newton D. Baker, to push the scaled-down proposal through Congress.

Two weeks after declaring war in April 1917, Congress gave Wilson authority to draft men between twenty-one and thirty-five into the Army. Around 10 million registered, 2.7 million were drafted, and 1.5 million volunteered. Some 520,000 volunteered for the Navy and Marines, neither of which held a draft. Many draftees were disqualified because of ill health. Some conscientious objectors on religious grounds were assigned

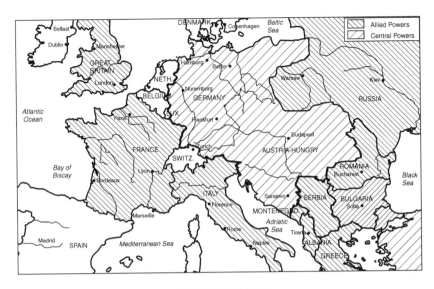

WWI IN EUROPE
Allied and Central Powers

to noncombatant military jobs in the United States. A few changed their minds and fought overseas, including the greatest Army hero, Sergeant Alvin C. York. A reluctant soldier owing to his religion (Christian Union), he had learned marksmanship by hunting in his mountainous Tennessee home, a talent he used to kill 25 Germans with 25 shots and capture 132 prisoners and 35 machine guns.

To finance the war, the Revenue Acts of 1917 and 1918 raised income taxes to their highest rates, peaking at 79 percent. Taxes, however, supplied only part of the money required. The rest came from large-denomination Treasury bonds and smaller Liberty Bonds. The return on Liberty Bonds was low, so the government made profits tax-exempt and urged their purchase as a patriotic contribution. Federal borrowing redirected capital from open markets, and government spending and economic expansion almost doubled the amount of money in circulation between 1916 and 1920. The size of the federal government doubled during the war, as the budget grew from $712,967,000 in 1916 to $18 billion in 1919. The national debt rose from $1 billion in 1916 to $24 billion in 1920.

Academics and businessmen advised economic planning, the latter receiving a dollar per year in pay from the government and the rest of their salaries from their companies. Business received waivers from antitrust prosecutions, government contracts, and permissions to merge. To spur production, the government guaranteed profits. Wall Street speculator Bernard

Baruch, head of the War Industries Board, applied coercion. When the automobile industry resisted converting to military production, he threatened to deny it steel. When railroads failed to provide efficient transportation, the government took them over. The government also fixed commodity prices and supervised the production of coal, oil, and food.

Herbert Hoover won accolades by furnishing food for Belgium, pinched between German occupation and a British blockade. After America entered the war, Hoover became Wilson's food administrator. Through a combination of conservation, small gardens, and scientific methods, he enabled farmers to provide enough food and fiber to supply the American armed forces, the civilian population, the Allies, and, after the war, much of Europe and the Soviet Union. Hoover relied on voluntarism, and appeals to patriotism, and limited regulation.

While Hoover fed bellies, George Creel, who headed the Committee on Public Information, the chief propaganda agency, sought to feed minds.

ALCOHOL DOWN THE DRAIN
Prohibition agents pouring liquor into the sewer, circa 1920.
(Library of Congress)

His army of writers, cartoonists, and speakers stuffed Americans with facts, figures, and patriotic speeches. Celebrities were recruited to deliver speeches, sometimes in theaters before films were shown. Historians wrote pamphlets justifying America's fight. Some of Creel's messages amounted to unnecessary hyperbole that incited hatred.

In wartime, alcohol consumption seemed wasteful. Prohibitionists finally achieved their goal, first in temporary legislation to conserve grain and prevent drinking near military bases in 1917. In December of that year, Congress passed the Eighteenth Amendment prohibiting the manufacture, transportation, and sale of alcohol. By January 1919 the amendment had been ratified. The Volstead Act, passed over Wilson's veto, defined an alcoholic beverage as one containing at least 0.5 percent alcohol by volume and allocated enforcement to the Bureau of Internal Revenue. The Prohibition Era had begun.

Women, too, achieved goals. One and a half million went to work, mainly in war industries, earning higher wages than previously. Though not all the work was permanent, it helped demonstrate the competence of women in a variety of occupations. The biggest gain, however, was suffrage, approved by Congress in 1919 and ratified by a sufficient number of states in August 1920. Women voted for the first time nationally three months later and joined men in the Warren G. Harding landslide.

"Over There"

Americans marched to war to the tune of George M. Cohan's "Over There" and vowed "We won't be back until it's over, over there." When the blare of the horns stilled, the doughboys (infantrymen) fought one of the most grisly wars in history. Their involvement was short, but violent and victorious. Their impact lay less in their victories than in their timing. With an endless caravan of fresh troops stretching across the Atlantic, Germany had to win quickly or lose. The American contribution was both small and potentially infinite; Europe was exhausted; America was rested and ready. The American commander, General John J. Pershing, a West Point graduate, had fought in Cuba, the Philippines, and Mexico. The American Expeditionary Force, which eventually reached 2 million, of whom 1.8 million engaged in combat, for the most part fought under an independent identity, at Pershing's insistence. He believed if Americans were integrated into Allied units their contribution would be less visible, and less impressive at the peace table.

The Rainbow Division, commanded by the army's youngest general, Douglas MacArthur, established a high standard for heroism and esprit de corps. Comprised of the star soldiers selected nationally from National

WINNING THE RIGHT TO VOTE
Women demonstrate for suffrage, 1917.
(Library of Congress)

Guard units, they emulated the dash of their commander. Americans had few military planes, yet built more than thirty thousand engines used by British planes. The United States contributed eleven thousand pilots, half assigned to France. The most famous was Captain Eddie Rickenbacker, who shot down twenty-six German planes.

The armed services treatment of its African American soldiers and sailors tarnished the nation's commitment to democracy. Blacks were barred from the Marines and could serve in the navy but only as cooks or in menial capacities. Tensions erupted occasionally. Taunted by white civilians, black soldiers rioted in Houston in August 1917, killing seventeen white people. After a summary trial, thirteen black soldiers were hanged for mutiny and murder and forty were sentenced to prison. Still, given the opportunity, African Americans served with distinction. The all-black 369th Infantry Regiment, integrated into the French Army because of emergency needs for replacements, was the first Allied unit to reach the Rhine. It served the longest of any American regiment attached to a foreign army; the 369th never lost territory or a man through capture. American Indians also felt the paradox of fighting for a democracy whose benefits they did not entirely share. Indians, unlike African Americans, did not fight in segregated units. Pershing used Apaches chiefly as scouts and, after two Choctaws used their native language, as a radio code.

Theodore Roosevelt yearned to duplicate his heroism in the Spanish-American War by leading a volunteer regiment. Wilson refused, stating

AFRICAN AMERICANS AT WAR
A segregated unit at attention.
(Library of Congress)

times had changed. The army needed professionals trained in the technology of modern warfare. To invite the aged, partially blind Rough Rider would politicalize the conflict, and perhaps cost Roosevelt his life. Sadly, TR's youngest son, Quentin, a pilot, was shot down behind German lines and killed in July 1918.

Roosevelt's romantic view of war denied reality. Technology killed more efficiently than medicine could cure. Lacking antibiotics, amputation was the chief method to prevent infection from spreading. Machine guns, barbed war, and primitive tanks made massed charges suicidal. Most heinous was poison gas, which could kill its users if the wind changed direction. It proved so ghastly it was outlawed for future wars. Soldiers fought in the stench and human waste of trenches, drenched by rain, baked by the sun, paralyzed by the cold. French troops mutinied, refused to charge, and were court-martialed. Perhaps only because America's involvement was short was it spared the massive casualties and some of the deadening mental pain that poisoned morale.

Germany was sinking beneath the onslaught of infinite numbers of enemy troops, diminishing supplies, and the threat of mutiny. In 1918 the generals decided to gamble on a spring offensive that would win the war on the Western Front or lose it. Then, like a bolt from Heaven, their eastern enemy, Russia, dropped out. A second revolution, following the overthrow of the czar, overthrew the Alexander Kerensky democratic government. The Bolshevik victors, facing a civil war at home, surrendered to Germany on draconian terms, giving up Latvia, Lithuania, Belorussia, Poland, and the Ukraine. The new communist government, by the Treaty of Brest-Litovsk, yielded 386,000 square miles of territory, 40 percent of Russia's iron and steel production, and 75 percent of its coal deposits. Some Americans romanticized the new regime under V. I. Lenin, believing the Bolshevik humanitarians would reform the nation oppressed by the czars. Wilson, on the other hand, refused to recognize the new regime.

Shortly before Russia withdrew, Wilson delivered a speech specifying Fourteen Points. He hoped to outflank the appeal of communism with his idealism and generous peace terms. The president's recommendations included freedom of the seas, free trade, restoration of Belgian independence and Russian territory, and adjustment of colonial claims with consideration for subjects. The program was embraced by the masses, but European heads of states were dubious. Russia, its people, and its new leaders, were exhausted and not inclined to trust the president's promise.

Japan, too, received Wilson's attention. An ally of the Entente, the Japanese seized German zones in China, extending its domination to the Shantung Peninsula. Wilson wanted to retain Japan as an ally, yet preserve China's territorial integrity. In the Lansing-Ishii agreement of November 2, 1917, the United States sanctioned Japanese economic domination of China, yet the Chinese interpreted it to imply military and political domination as well.

America sent troops to Russia, along with Japan, France, and Britain, to observe the civil war that followed the Bolshevik Revolution. London and Paris hoped to encourage the victory of the noncommunist White Army, and Tokyo aspired to seize concessions in the Far East. Although he favored the White Army, Wilson believed intervention unwise and impractical. There was no way to dictate the outcome without a massive investment of military resources that would be unacceptable to the American public. Wilson, however, wanted to remain on good terms with the Allies, protect American property, and counter Japanese influence. Wilson also hoped to enable anti-German Czech forces in Russia to reach the United States via Siberia and the Pacific, then cross the Atlantic to fight Germany. By the time this unrealistic plan materialized, the war was over. The only tangible result of the Western occupation, which lasted until 1920, was to foster communist resentment.

On the Western Front in March 1918, the Allies faced a German offensive strengthened by the release of thousands of troops from the East after the Russian surrender. But inexperienced American soldiers helped repel Germany at Cantigny in May and at Chateau-Thierry and Belleau Wood in June. The initiative shifted to the Allies after their victory in the Battle of the Marne in July. Having exhausted themselves in the offensive, the Germans fell back, now confronting an adversary with virtually unlimited manpower. In a war of attrition, they could not win.

The Allied commander, French General Ferdinand Foch, gave the Americans a central role in the counteroffensive of September 1918. They were, first, to reduce the German salient behind the village of St. Mihiel, and, second, to attack the main German lines to the northwest of Verdun through fortified terrain bounded by the Meuse River on the west and the Argonne Forest on the east. The main objective was to sever the railroad connection at Sedan. Some 550,000 American troops were committed to St. Mihiel and 1.2 million to the Meuse-Argonne offensive. Although the St. Mihiel campaign caught the Germans evacuating and drove them out easily, the Meuse-Argonne offensive found a deeply entrenched foe difficult to dislodge. Still, the progress of the Americans, who could replace casualties as Germany could not, was inexorable, and they won their objective.

Foch planned to use almost 2 million American troops for an offensive in early 1919 that would cross the Rhine and take the war to German soil. This action proved unnecessary because Germany's army and civilians were spent; to continue the war, their military leaders felt, would mean humiliation. Desiring to salvage their armed forces, officials asked Wilson to arrange an armistice based on the Fourteen Points. A new government headed by Prince Max of Baden conveyed the request through the Swiss in early October. Wilson declined to deal with the Kaiser, who abdicated and escaped Germany on November 9 after a naval mutiny at Kiel and the outbreak of a revolution in Bavaria. By this time Austria had surrendered. France and Britain, however, did not favor the Fourteen Points as a basis for negotiations.

Wilson turned the final negotiations over to Foch. Germany agreed to evacuate the Western Front immediately, release prisoners of war, and accept the British blockade until a treaty was signed. A republican government under socialist Friedrich Ebert, signed a truce on November 11, 1918. The United States won a seat at the peace negotiations without suffering the staggering casualties of the other warriors. America lost 53,000 killed and 204,000 wounded in battle; another 63,000 died from disease, most in the 1918–1919 influenza epidemic. Germany lost the most to bat- tle, 1.8 million, followed by Russia, 1.7 million, France, 1.4 million (one- third of its combat-age men) and Britain, 900,000. In proportion to population, the French suffered the most deaths and maimings.

The "war to end all wars," as Wilson called it, proved a misnomer. Yet, the Era of Awakening ended as it had begun, with victory in a military con- flict, this time a major one. Arguably the greatest economic power at the turn of the century, the United States was now the most potent military power, certainly the one with the most potential. Yet if the war provided an explosion of America's military might, the aftermath produced a dud. A short period of intolerance was capped by a generation of withdrawal.

Intolerance and the Red Scare

While America fought for liberty abroad, the government cracked down on civil liberties. The degree should not be exaggerated and must be placed in the context of the time. All wars limit freedoms until victory is in sight, and in comparison with the other democracies, the United States was not the worst. Still, America was, and should be held to high standards. The nation's prestige was tarnished by its excesses, and hatred is never justified, not even in wartime.

To stifle dissent, the government enacted the Espionage Act, which prohibited sabotage and criticism of the war effort. A second law, the Trading with the Enemy Act, barred trade with enemy nations and autho- rized censorship of foreign language publications. In 1918 two additional laws were passed. The Alien Act permitted the deportation of noncitizens considered a threat; the Sedition Act outlawed criticism of the Allied cause. Leftists were stigmatized. Anarchists Emma Goldman and Alexander Berkman were convicted of inciting draft resistance, fined, sentenced to jail, and deported. Socialist Roger Baldwin defied the draft and was sent to prison. Victor Berger, a Wisconsin socialist who had won a congressional election, was sentenced to jail for publishing antiwar articles. However, Berger's conviction was overturned by the Supreme Court. Eugene V. Debs was sentenced to ten years for disputing Wilson's claim that the war was waged to uphold democracy. Some 160 members of the Industrial Workers of the World, including William Haywood and Elizabeth Gurley Flynn, were sentenced to long terms for violating the Sedition Act.

The Supreme Court reluctantly upheld most convictions, although it overturned some. In *Schenck v. United States* Justice Oliver Wendell Holmes wrote, in upholding the conviction of Debs, that the right of free speech was not absolute. Context was a key. Falsely shouting "Fire!" in a theater, for example, was unacceptable. Holmes helped establish the precedent that talk constituting a "clear-and-present danger" was illegal.

The public was intolerant of Germany. German food was taken off restaurant menus and German books were removed from library shelves. At a time when the military needed translators, some schools ceased teaching German. The fear and prejudice culminated in the Red Scare of 1919. The catalysts were a large number of high-profile strikes in 1919, the Bolshevik Revolution of 1917, and militant speech and some violent action by homegrown radicals. Most concern was directed at the American Communist Party, the Communist Labor Party, and the Socialist Party. More action-oriented, a few anarchists mailed bombs to federal officials in New York, Pittsburgh, Boston, and Washington. Postal officials defused most, yet a bomb exploded on the front porch of Attorney General A. Mitchell Palmer, who became the Red Scare leader. Uninjured, Palmer ordered raids to round up and deport aliens suspected of radicalism. In November 1919, 250 aliens were netted in a twelve-city sweep, followed by 249 rounded up in December. Among those sent to the Soviet Union were Goldman and her lover, Berkman. The raids peaked on January 2, 1920, when 4,000 radicals were arrested and 550 deported.

The Red Scare was based on fear, not a realistic threat. To some degree, it expanded beyond fear of the overthrow of the government to fear of those who were different. Some of the fear was generated by the idea that determined minorities had power beyond their numbers. The Bolsheviks, for example, had been a tiny minority when they overthrew the Russian government. Of course, America was not Russia, although some Americans advocated tactics similar to the Russian regime. Some states banned Communist flags. The New York State Legislature expelled five duly elected Socialists. Palmer predicted a communist takeover attempt on May 1, 1920, a coup that did not transpire. In a last burst of terrorist activity, anarchists detonated a bomb on Wall Street on September 16, killing thirty-eight and injuring two hundred.

Fear of radicalism ebbed after Palmer's false prediction, and the country turned to other matters. On the uplift of war the economy soared, particularly infant industries such as radio and aviation. A key economic indicator, the gross national product (GNP), the value of all goods and services produced in the country, swelled from $48.3 billion in 1916 to $84.0 billion in 1919. The largest debtor in the world, the United States became the largest creditor, and the dollar replaced the British pound as the foundation for international trade. Still, reconversion to a peacetime economy on a massive scale had no precedent. Wilson's task was vexing. When he removed curbs on wages and prices, inflation climbed, increasing the cost of living and motivating labor to demand higher wages. The wartime experiments in government economic planning, called "wartime socialism," were terminated. Although many believed the railroads had been better operated in government hands than in private ones, they were returned to their owners under the Esch-Cummings Transportation Act of 1920.

The difficulty of reconversion was only one of a host of problems the United States confronted near the end of the Era of Awakening. In the last years of the decade the anxieties included not only the Red Scare and the labor unrest and extremist agitation that precipitated it, but also racial unrest; Wilson's illness; and a global influenza epidemic that claimed some 686,000 American lives in 1918 and 1919, far exceeding the U.S. toll from the war.

The Peace Conference

If the war seemed comparable to the Battle of Armageddon, the peace conference that convened in Paris represented the Day of Judgment. To this day came Wilson, deciding to attend the conclave because he trusted only himself to shape its outcome. The world's most respected statesman in 1919, he was showered by the European masses with cheers, flowers, and honors. He headed an American delegation that included Robert Lansing; Colonel Edward M. House; Tasker Bliss, the general who had represented America on the Allies' Supreme War Council; Henry White, a diplomat and the only registered Republican in the delegation; and a group of thirteen hundred experts called the Inquiry. Wilson, however, consulted just a few men he trusted.

The major decisions were made by the Council of Four: Wilson, British Prime Minister David Lloyd George, French President Georges Clemenceau, and Italian Prime Minister Vittorio Orlando (Japan was represented in some sessions). Each had different priorities. Wilson wanted lasting peace policed by a League of Nations. Clemenceau wanted to disarm and weaken Germany. Lloyd George wanted to maintain Britain's supremacy at sea and preserve its empire. Italy coveted territory the Allies promised it in the secret 1915 Treaty of London. Japan desired to expand its domination of China and to include language recognizing racial equality. The cynical nationalist Clemenceau complained that the idealistic Wilson "thought himself another Jesus Christ come upon the Earth to reform men." Wilson's self-righteousness, Clemenceau predicted, would wear thin. "God has given man Ten Commandments. He broke every one. Wilson has his Fourteen Points. We shall see."

Battling Clemenceau and others tried Wilson's patience, and strained his frail health. At the end of March he suffered from what might have been a viral infection or a series of minor strokes. Still Wilson persisted, and the conference worked out the treaty that Germany signed in the Palace of Versailles on June 28, 1919. The reconfiguration of Europe marked the greatest changes since the Congress of Vienna ended the Napoleonic era. Poland reappeared on the map, with a route to the sea carved from German territory. Yugoslavia and Czechoslovakia were created to provide ethnic self-determination—Wilson's principle that political units should reflect the will of the ethnic groups within them. France received a demilitarized buffer zone between itself and the Germans taken from the Rhineland, in addition to a temporary right to occupy the Saar Basin coal region in Germany.

Italy's boundary was moved north to annex the Brenner Pass, but Wilson refused to concede the port city of Fiume because it was not populated by Italians and because Yugoslavia needed a port. Nor did the Japanese receive everything they sought, for the conference did not adopt a statement promising racial equality. Wilson, whose pledge for self-determination did not include nonwhite races, realized that the British and the French, each possessing colonies, would not tolerate such a statement, which would embarrass Americans as well. Yet the conference offered the Japanese something they wanted more: control over the Shandong Peninsula.

Although the terms were less harsh than those that a victorious Germany might have imposed, the Germans were furious. They were judged guilty of causing the war, shorn of their colonies, disarmed, and ordered to pay $56 billion in reparations to the Allies. Their country lost 6.5 million people and one-eighth of its territory. Any German government that signed such a document was certain to be vilified by its people. The Germans haggled over the terms for six weeks before representatives of a new republic created at Weimar signed the treaty.

In an absolute sense, the treaty was unduly punitive toward Germany. In a relative sense, it was fairer than most treaties of such magnitude. Much of the world had assumed that Wilson, despite being only one player at the peace table, held the cards and could deal the hand he chose. It was unrealistic to assume the Americans, who intervened late and shed less blood than the British and the French, could unilaterally dictate the terms. Wilson, nonetheless, had substantial influence. Without his contributions, the pact would have been worse. What was surprising was that he incorporated as many of the Fourteen Points as he did, not that he was thwarted on many issues, British statesman Winston Churchill observed. The recognition of independence for Poland and Baltic states, the formation of Czechoslovakia and Yugoslavia, the system providing for Allied trusteeship of the former German and Turkish colonies as a theoretical prelude to self-government—all these reflected Wilson's beliefs in democracy and self-determination. And, of course, the treaty included the League of Nations.

"Dare We Reject It?"

The narrow straits of European diplomacy, churned by centuries of ethnic, religious, and national turmoil, were less perilous than the treacherous currents of politics in the United States. Wilson had an opportunity to name Republicans to the American delegation at Paris, but included only White. Then, during the 1918 election campaign in the closing weeks of the war, he urged voters to return a Democratic majority to Congress to support his plans. This partisanship misfired. Republicans gained control of both houses. Returning home in February 1919, the president received a petition from Massachusetts Republican Henry Cabot Lodge, chair of the Senate Foreign Relations Committee, stating that thirty-nine GOP senators or senators-elect—enough to prevent ratification—opposed the League Covenant. Upon his return to Paris, Wilson had to negotiate changes. He satisfied the Republicans by having the covenant amended to exclude tariff and immigration issues and regional security arrangements, such as the Monroe Doctrine.

When Wilson brought home the completed treaty in July 1919, he believed the Senate would ratify it quickly. "Dare we reject it and break the heart of the world?" he asked. Probably a majority of the Senate, and a majority of the people, favored ratification, although there was no consensus on the nature of treaty they wanted. In the Senate a two-thirds majority was required. Moreover, Lodge, the Senate majority leader and the president's political and intellectual foil, hated Wilson and was dubious of the League. He delayed consideration by reading the entire treaty into the *Congressional Record*, which took two weeks. Then he held six weeks of hearings and drafted a series of amendments, or reservations. Of the reservations, the most important mandated congressional approval before the United States could dispatch armed forces under the League's peacekeeping obligations.

To build support, Wilson embarked upon a speaking tour in which he covered eight thousand miles in three weeks and delivered thirty-six speeches. He ridiculed the argument of some that the League would order soldiers from the United States to distant lands to keep the peace, insisting that Americans would be involved only near their borders, where their interests were at stake. "If you want to put out a fire in Utah, you do not send to Oklahoma for a fire engine. If you want to put out a fire in the Balkans

. . . you do not send to the United States for troops." Wilson's speeches stirred the masses, yet did not gain votes in the Senate. After an address at Pueblo, Colorado, on September 26, 1919, he collapsed and was rushed to Washington. On October 2 the president suffered a stroke that paralyzed his left side, slurred his speech, and disturbed his emotional stability.

For a few days Wilson lingered between life and death; for the next six weeks he did little work. With no chief, Edith Wilson and her husband's doctors concealed his infirmity from the public, limited his contacts, and protected him from stress. Some of his strength returned, yet Wilson remained in bed or in a wheelchair. Prone to outbursts, he fired Lansing, accusing him of disloyalty. The president refused to compromise to win Senate approval.

Wilson believed Lodge's reservations would "cut the heart" from the treaty. Accordingly, he ordered pro-League Democrats to vote against the treaty with reservations. On November 19, 1919, they obliged, joining the "Irreconcilables," senators who would not support any form of

BLOCKING THE TREATY
Henry Cabot Lodge defeats
Wilson's plan for world peace.
(Library of Congress)

League, to defeat the treaty with the reservations, 39 votes in favor and 55 opposed. The treaty also failed without the reservations, 38 to 53.

Shocked by the rejections, moderates pleaded for compromise. Instead, Wilson insisted that the issue be placed before Americans as a "solemn referendum" in the 1920 presidential election, in which he would be the Democratic candidate. Practically, this scheme was impossible because of the two-term tradition and his poor health. Lodge agreed to hold another vote, on March 19, 1920, and it was closer, as 21 Democrats ignored their president to support the treaty with reservations. It passed, 49 to 35—seven votes short of a two-thirds majority. The League would have to keep peace without the United States.

Wilson ended his public career a tragic figure, much like Roosevelt who had died on January 6, 1919. For a time Wilson was blamed for arrogance and pride that led to the defeat of the Treaty. Yet after World War II his reputation rose, his idealism and inspiration were revived again, and some speculated that a League, such as Wilson envisioned, might have stifled Nazism. A retrospective look, however, does not comfort the observer with the thought that the League might have contained Adolf Hitler and other aggressors. It offered a way to do so, but not the will, which was not strong enough in the world between the wars. Not until after World War II would Wilsonian ideas of an international peacekeeping body and collective security have their day.

Having dreams of greatness for humanity, Wilson would have been foolish not to pursue them. Yet, if there is nothing so powerful as an idea whose time has come, there is nothing so futile as an idea that is premature. Wilson appreciated this in the twilight of his life, when he said to his eldest daughter: "I think it was best after all that the United States did not join the League of Nations. Now when the American people join the League, it will be because they are convinced it is the right thing to do, and then will be the *only right* time for them to do it." He smiled and added, "Perhaps God knew better than I did after all."

Bibliographic Essay

BECAUSE OF space constraints, the compilations of supplementary readings in this book emphasize general and more recent studies (although older, seminal works receive their due).

The 1890s

On the populists, see John D. Hicks, *The Populist Revolt* (1931), dated but essential; Lawrence Goodwyn, *The Populist Moment: A Short History of the Agrarian Rebels in America* (1978); O. Michael Kazin, *The Populist Persuasion: An American History* (1995); and Robert C. McMath, *American Populism: A Social History, 1877–1898* (1993). Other works on politics include three books by Richard Hofstadter, *The Age of Reform: From Bryan to F.D.R.* (1955), *The American Political Tradition and the Men Who Made It* (1948), and *The Paranoid Style in American Politics and Other Essays* (1964); C. Vann Woodward; *The Strange Career of Jim Crow* (1974), another seminal work; Michael E. McGerr, *The Decline of Popular Politics: The American North, 1865–1928* (1986); Joel Williamson, *A Rage for Order: Black–White Relations in the American South since Emancipation* (1986); and Nancy Cohen, *The Reconstruction of American Liberalism, 1865–1914* (2002). For foreign policy, see Ernest R. May, *Imperial Democracy: The Emergence of America as a Great Power* (1961); Walter LaFeber, *The New Empire: An Interpretation of American Expansion, 1860–1898* (1963); David F. Healy, *U.S. Expansionism: The Imperialist Urge in the 1890s* (1970); Robert L. Beisner, *Twelve against Empire: The Anti-Imperialists, 1898–1900* (1985); and *From the Old Diplomacy to the New, 1865–1900* (1986), both excellent; and the revisionist William Appleman Williams, *The Tragedy of American Diplomacy* (rev. ed., 1989).

Useful business, labor, and technology studies include Melvin Dubofsky, *Industrialism and the American Worker, 1865–1920* (1975); James Tobin,

To Conquer the Air: The Wright Brothers and the Great Race for Flight (2003); Leon Fink, *Workingmen's Democracy: The Knights of Labor and American Politics* (1983); and Paul Krause, *The Battle for Homestead, 1880–1892: Politics, Culture, and Steel* (1992).

1900–1920

Valuable works include H. Wiebe, *The Search for Order: 1877–1920* (1967); a study of social modernization; Eric F. Goldman, *Rendezvous with Destiny* (1952); Otis L. Graham, *The Great Campaigns: Reforms and War in America, 1900–1928* (1978); James MacGregor Burns, *The Workshop of Democracy* (1985), beautifully written; Lewis L. Gould, *Reform and Regulation: American Politics from Roosevelt to Wilson* (2nd ed., 1986); Nell Irvin Painter, *Standing at Armageddon: The United States, 1877–1919* (1987), strong on women, African Americans, and labor; and John M. Cooper Jr., *Pivotal Decades: The United States, 1900–1920* (1990).

The worst natural disaster of the century's first decade is described in Philip L. Fradkin, *The Great Earthquake and Firestorms of 1906: How San Francisco Nearly Destroyed Itself* (2005).

Progressivism

On progressivism, start with Eldon J. Eisenbach, *The Lost Promise of Progressivism* (1983); William L. O'Neill, *The Progressive Years: America Comes of Age* (1975); John Whiteclay Chambers II, *The Tyranny of Change: America in the Progressive Era, 1900–1917* (2000); Steven J. Diner, *A Very Different Age: Americans of the Progressive Era* (1998); Louis L. Gould, *America in the Progressive Era* (2000); Michael E. McGerr, *A Fierce Discontent: The Rise and Fall of the Progressive Movement in America, 1870–1920* (2003); and Alan Dawley, *Changing the World: American Progressivism in War and Revolution* (2003). For unconventional interpretations, see Gabriel Kolko, *The Triumph of Conservatism* (1963) and *Railroads and Regulation, 1877–1916* (1965); and James Weinstein, *The Corporate Ideal in the Liberal State* (1968). Among the best regional studies of Progressivism are C. Vann Woodward, *Origins of the New South, 1877–1913* (1951); Russell B. Nye, *Midwestern Progressive Politics* (1951); George B. Tindall, *The Emergence of the New South* (1967); Jack Temple Kirby, *Darkness at the Dawning: Race and Reform in the Progressive South* (1972); Monroe Lee Billington, *The Political South in the Twentieth Century* (1975); David P. Thelen, *The New Citizenship: Origins of*

Progressivism in Wisconsin, 1885–1900 (1972); Herbert F. Margulies, *The Decline of Progressivism in Wisconsin* (1968); Spencer W. Olin Jr., *California's Prodigal Sons: Hiram Johnson and the Progressives* (1968); James Wright, *The Progressive Yankees: Republican Reformers in New Hampshire, 1900–1916* (1987); Dewey W. Grantham Jr., *Southern Progressivism: The Reconciliation of Progress and Tradition* (1983); and Lewis L. Gould, *Progressives and Prohibitionists: Texas Democrats in the Wilson Era* (1973).

Major Political Leaders

The literature on the major political leaders of the era is rich. On Theodore Roosevelt, Edmund Morris, *The Rise of Theodore Roosevelt* (1979), and David McCullough, *Mornings on Horseback* (1981) are important for his early life. Edmund Morris, *Theodore Rex* (2001), describes Roosevelt's life during the presidential years. Perhaps the best complete biographies are H. W. Brands, *T.R.: The Last Romantic* (1997), and William H. Harbaugh, *The Life and Times of Theodore Roosevelt* (rev. ed., 1975). Also good are Lewis L. Gould, *The Presidency of Theodore Roosevelt* (1991), an administrative history. George E. Mowry, *Theodore Roosevelt and the Progressive Movement* (1946) and *The Era of Theodore Roosevelt and the Birth of Modern America* (1958), and John Morton Blum, *The Republican Roosevelt* (1954), are important studies of his political career. Roosevelt's foreign policy is described in Raymond A. Esthus, *Theodore Roosevelt and the International Rivalries* (1970), and Frederick W. Marks III, *Velvet on Iron: The Diplomacy of Theodore Roosevelt* (1979). On the Panama Canal see David McCullough, *The Path between the Seas* (1977).

The essential works on William Howard Taft include Henry F. Pringle, *The Life and Times of William Howard Taft* (2 vols., 1939), and James R. Anderson, *William Howard Taft: A Conservative's Conception of the Presidency* (1973). Taft's foreign policies are the subject of Walter Scholes and Marie Scholes, *The Foreign Policies of the Taft Administration* (1970).

Woodrow Wilson has inspired numerous studies. The most comprehensive biography is Arthur S. Link, *Wilson* (5 vols., 1947–1965). Kendrick A. Clements, *Woodrow Wilson* (1987), is a reliable portrait. John Cooper, *The Warrior and the Priest: Woodrow Wilson and Theodore Roosevelt* (1983), is an outstanding dual biography. Also important are Arthur S. Link, *Woodrow Wilson and the Progressive Era, 1910–1917* (1954); John Morton Blum, *Woodrow Wilson and the Politics of Morality* (1956); and Edwin A. Weinstein, *Woodrow Wilson: A Medical and Psychological Biography* (1981).

Other Political Figures

Works on other politicians include Horace S. Merrill and Marian C. Merrill, *The Republican Command, 1897–1913* (1971); David Sarasohn, *The Party of Reform: The Democrats in the Progressive Era* (1989); Paolo E. Coletta, *William Jennings Bryan* (3 vols., 1964–1969); Lawrence W. Levine, *Defender of the Faith: Bryan, the Last Decade, 1915–1925* (1965); Kendrick A. Clements, *William Jennings Bryan, Missionary Isolationist* (1983); Le Roy Ashby, *William Jennings Bryan* (1987); Robert W. Cherny, *A Righteous Cause: The Life of William Jennings Bryan* (1994); David P. Thelen, *Robert M. La Follette and the Insurgent Spirit* (1976); Nancy C. Unger, *Fighting Bob La Follette: The Righteous Reformer* (2000); and Stephen Kantrowitz, *Ben Tillman and the Reconstruction of White Supremacy* (2000).

Racial Issues, Sound Reform, Business, and Labor

Aspects of racial issues, social reform, business, and labor are treated in Robert M. Crunden, *Ministers of Reform: The Progressives' Achievement in American Civilization, 1889–1920* (1982); Robert H. Wiebe, *Businessmen and Reform* (1962); Nick Salvatore, *Eugene Victor Debs, Citizen and Socialist* (1982); James Weinstein, *The Decline of Socialism in America, 1912–1925* (1967); Philip Taft, *The A.F.L. in the Time of Gompers* (1957); Melvin Dubofsky, *We Shall Be All: A History of the Industrial Workers of the World* (1969); W. Elliott Brownlee, *The Dynamics of Ascent* (1974), which traces the rise of business and the economy, as does Alfred D. Chandler, *Strategy and Structure* (1982), and *The Visible Hand: The Managerial Revolution in American Business* (1977). Paul S. Boyer, *Urban Masses and Moral Order in America, 1820–1920* (1978); George Chauncey, *Gay New York: Gender, Urban Culture, and the Making of the Gay Male World, 1890–1940* (1994); and John D'Emilio and Estelle Freedman, *Intimate Matters: A History of Sexuality in America* (1988), describe aspects of the sexual revolution.

Some excellent works on African Americans include Mary Frances Berry and John W. Blassingame, *Long Memory: The Black Experience in America* (1982); Herbert G. Gutman, *The Black Family in Struggle and Freedom, 1750–1925* (1976); August Meier, *Negro Thought in America: Racial Ideologies in the Age of Booker T. Washington, 1880–1915* (1963); Louis R. Harlan, *Booker T. Washington* (2 vols., 1972–1983); Manning Marable, *W.E.B. Du Bois* (1986); and David Levering Lewis, *W.E.B. Du Bois* (2 vols., 1994, 2000).

On women, see Aileen Kraditor, *The Ideas of the Woman Suffrage Movement, 1890–1920* (1965); William L. O'Neill, *Everyone Was Brave: The Rise and Fall of Feminism in America* (1969); Mari Jo Buhle, *Women and American Socialism, 1870–1920* (1981); Nancy Woloch, *Women and the American Experience* (1984); Carl Degler, *At Odds: Women and the Family from the Revolution to the Present* (1980); Nancy F. Cott, *The Grounding of Modern Feminism* (1987); and Eric Rauchway, *The Refuge of Affections: Family and American Reform Politics, 1900–1920* (2001).

Immigration history is covered in Oscar Handlin, *The Uprooted* (rev. ed. 1973); John Higham, *Strangers in the Land: Patterns of American Nativism, 1865–1925* (1955); John Bodnar, *The Transplanted: A History of Immigrants in Urban America* (1985); Thomas Archdeacon, *Becoming American* (1983); Alan M. Kraut, *The Huddled Masses: The Immigrant in American Society, 1880–1921* (1982); Victor Greene, *The Slavic Community on Strike: Immigrant Labor in Pennsylvania Anthracite* (1968); James S. Olson, *Catholic Immigrants in America* (1987); Irving Howe and Kenneth Libo, *World of Our Fathers: The Journey of East European Jews to America and the Life They Found and Made* (1976); and H. L. Kitano and Roger Daniels, *Asian Americans: Emerging Minorities* (2nd ed., 1988).

On intellectual and cultural history, consult Richard Hofstadter, *Anti-Intellectualism in American Life* (1962); Christopher Lasch, *The New Radicalism in America* (1965); Lawrence N. Levine, *Highbrow/Lowbrow: The Emergence of a Cultural Hierarchy in America* (1988); Daniel J. Singal, *Modernist Culture in America* (1991), extremely useful; Henry F. May, *The End of American Innocence: A Study of the First Years of Our Own Time, 1912–1917* (1959); and Christine Stansell, *American Moderns: Bohemian New York and the Creation of a New Century* (2000).

Diplomacy and War

The best overview of the era's foreign policy is Warren Zimmerman, *First Great Triumph: How Five Americans Made Their Country a World Power* (2002), which examines Theodore Roosevelt, Alfred Thayer Mahan, Henry Cabot Lodge, John Hay, and Elihu Root. Also see Walter LaFeber, *The American Search for Opportunity, 1865–1913* (1993); Akira Iriye, *The Globalizing of America, 1913–1945* (1993); George F. Kennan, *American Diplomacy, 1900–1950* (1951); and Robert E. Osgood, *Ideals and Self-Interest in America's Foreign Relations* (1953). On prewar diplomacy and World War I, begin with John Cooper, ed., *The Causes and Consequences of World War I* (1971). On Wilson's foreign policy see Arthur S. Link, *Woodrow Wilson: Revolution, War, and Peace* (1979); and Link, ed., *Woodrow*

Wilson and a Revolutionary World, 1913–1921 (1982); N. Gordon Levin Jr., *Woodrow Wilson and World Politics: America's Response to War and Revolution* (1967); Patrick Devlin, *Too Proud to Fight: Woodrow Wilson's Neutrality* (1975); Gnonel Kolko, *Century of War: Politics, Conflict and Society Since 1914* (1994); Lloyd C. Gardner, *Safe for Democracy: The Anglo-American Response to Revolution, 1913–1923* (1984); Robert H. Ferrell, *Woodrow Wilson and World War I, 1917–1921* (1985); Thomas J. Knock, *To End All Wars: Woodrow Wilson and the Quest for a New World Order* (1992); and David Steigerwald, *Wilsonian Idealism in America* (1994).

On the military history of the war, Edward M. Coffman, *The War to End All Wars: The American Military Experience in World War* (1968), is the best work, but see also John S. D. Eisenhower, *Yanks* (2001); and Jennifer D. Keene, *Doughboys, the Great War, and the Remaking of America* (2001). For other topics, consult William J. Breen, *Uncle Sam at Home Civilian Mobilization, Wartime Federalism and the Committee for National Defense* (1984), and Stephen L. Vaughn, *Holding Fast the Inner Lines: Democracy, Nationalism, and the Committee on Public Information* (1980). On the peace negotiations, the best work is Margaret MacMillan, *Paris 1919* (2002). Also see Arthur Walworth, *Woodrow Wilson and His Peacemakers* (1983). On Wilson's efforts for the League of Nations, see John Cooper, *Breaking the Heart of the World: Woodrow Wilson and the Fight for the League of Nations* (2001); and Lloyd G. Ambrosius, *Woodrow Wilson and the American Diplomatic Tradition: The Treaty Fight in Perspective* (1988).

For the effects of the war on the United States, see John Cooper, *The Vanity of Power: American Isolationism and the First World War* (1969); David Kennedy, *Over Here: The First World War and American Society* (1980); Maureen W. Greenwald, *Women, War, and Work: The Impact of World War I on Women Workers in the United States* (1980); Robert K. Murray, *Red Scare: A Study in American Hysteria*; Norman H. Clark, *Deliver Us from Evil: An Interpretation of American Prohibition* (1976); Paul Murphy, *World War I and the Origins of Civil Liberties in the United States* (1979); Gina Kolata, *Flu: The Story of the Great Influenza Pandemic of 1918 and the Search for the Virus That Caused It* (1999); John M. Barry, *The Great Influenza: The Epic Story of the Deadliest Plague in History* (2005); Stuart D. Rochester, *American Liberal Disillusionment in the Wake of World War I* (1977); and David Burner, *The Politics of Provincialism: The Democratic Party in Transition* (1986).

PART

★ II ★

An Era of
Trial and Triumph,
1920–1945

Prologue

A DECADE of prosperity, political conservatism, and cultural bohemi-
anism, the 1920s were followed by a mirror image, a decade of depression, political change, and cultural retrenchment, and then by World War
II, the greatest transforming event of the century. The Era of Trial and
Triumph ushered in more change than many periods twice or three times
as long. Mature Americans in 1900, who might have been comfortable in
1921, would have found themselves in a different world by 1945. The generation that came of age during this era, literary historian Malcolm Cowley
wrote, "belonged to a period of transition from values already fixed to values that had to be created. Its members were seceding from the old and yet
could adhere to nothing new; they groped their way toward another scheme
of life, as yet undefined; in the midst of their doubts and uneasy gestures of
defiance they felt homesick for the certainties of their childhood."

Hopes and dreams were realized, crushed, reborn. It seemed that the
nation repeatedly was poised on a precipice above a canyon of despair, made
a leap of faith, and landed on the other side. No roller-coaster ride could
have been more dizzying. Still, one takes only a small risk in riding a roller-
coaster. People who bet on the stock market, moved from Mississippi to
Massachusetts, or landed at Normandy took risks that defined, or ended,
their lives. Anyone who lived through the era should have emerged
exhausted. Instead, most people were grateful, subdued, and optimistic.
These years constituted neither a steady march toward greater democracy
nor a story of inexorable oppression. "Never did bitterer disappointment
follow high hopes," historian James Harvey Robinson wrote. Whatever the
chagrin, though, the age was ultimately one of affirmation; far more people
subscribed to capitalism and democracy than rejected them. Answering
grave challenges to these systems when many considered their country in
decline, Americans made their nation wiser and richer.

Throughout the era, change, whether cultural or political, was met with resistance and consequently occurred in spurts, with lapses and regressions. A society in dynamic tension between change and resistance characterized the period (such tension is present to some degree in all periods but its impact in this era is unrivaled). The former happened despite the latter, although the resistance partly shaped the nature and pace of change. Not all of the change was positive; to win both an economic war and a military war, the United States had to pay dearly in dollars and lives, and the victories were not guaranteed to last. Perhaps more environmental pollution occurred during the war than over the next thirty years, yet this facet of the war is rarely mentioned. Moreover, the end of World War II unveiled new perils, making the planet more dangerous than at the opening of the era in 1921.

The most important change was an explosive increase in knowledge, precipitating modernization, the adaptation of institutions to knowledge. Previously such increases had occurred incrementally over hundreds, even thousands, of years. Yet World War II, requiring reorganization of politics, centralization of government, and rationalization of industry and transportation, accelerated the pace of modernization. The greatest pushes were the rapid advance of scientific knowledge and the speed with which scientific discoveries made an impact upon jobs, lifestyles, and beliefs. Race and gender issues gathered momentum, accompanied by rising expectations. The federal government grew enormously, first during the depression, then during the war. After Republican political domination during the 1920s, the Democrats seized control with the election of Franklin D. Roosevelt, who became one of the most powerful presidents in history.

As knowledge grew, the basis of belief in traditional verities was shaken. Changing more swiftly than religion or politics, science introduced ideas and standards by which to judge old verities; truth became relative or contextual, not eternal or absolute. Institutions were judged by utility, not by abstract criteria. Those who sided with only custom or science were apt to be ostracized or ridiculed by the other side. Those who tried to adhere to both were pulled in different directions: they could no longer believe things they wanted to believe, and they began to believe some things that shattered their serenity. It was widely debated whether science was a tyrant or a liberator, whether the future was radiant with promise or dark with foreboding.

Modernization was related to, but differed from, a movement in the arts known as modernism. Modernism arose partly in reaction to modernization. Modernists applauded scientific knowledge but criticized the dehumanizing aspects of the machine civilization and government bureaucracy. Modernists argued that the prevailing Victorian culture and the conventional in the fine and literary arts stifled self-expression by suppressing the emotional side of human nature. With modernism, the aim was integration of the emotional and the rational. In the short run it rejuvenated the emotional aspects of humankind, expressed through abstract art, Freudian psychiatry, rejection of materialism, and sexual experimentation. To traditionalists, modernism was a fad; to modernists, traditionalists were archaic. Their struggle, waged in literary journals, art galleries, and intellectual discussions, raged over the period, the modernists appealing to the avant garde, the traditionalists to the masses.

Sexuality, which aggravated generational and religious conflicts, opened one rift between traditionalists and modernists. Habits such as smoking and drinking were linked to sexuality. Conservatives deplored women who were openly sexual, used cosmetics, bobbed their hair, and shortened their skirts. Birth control, more technologically feasible than before, led to moral and social dilemmas. Yet the age was not so libertine as the movies and magazines might have us believe. There were clear boundaries, and the predominant practice among singles was sexuality without intercourse, except among engaged couples.

Cultural sterility and materialism were attacked before the Great Depression by writers who insisted that a prosperous society meant neither cultural sophistication nor economic equality. H. L. Mencken satirized materialism, and Sinclair Lewis depicted the hypocrisy and banality of small town life. Ironically, the people they ridiculed bought and read their books.

In no sphere were hypocrisy, inequality, and neglect more poignant than in race relations. The prosperity of the 1920s largely eluded minorities, particularly African Americans, most of whom lived in the rural South, mired in poverty and lacking in educational opportunities. They would later make economic progress during the era, but not political progress, and despite their accomplishments, many failed to share the nation's bounty. So did the millions of other Americans who lived in poverty and crowded into city tenements or farm shacks without running water or electricity. Millions more, many of them children, toiled in unhealthy factories for subsistence wages; women were underpaid and confined to gender-segregated jobs; and ethnic and religious groups felt the sting of discrimination.

In foreign relations, there were tensions between crusades for peace and the stark reality of a violent world. The public was nationalistic and cautious throughout much of the period. Isolationists and internationalists clashed in the late 1930s until a world in turmoil overwhelmed them all.

Nevertheless, during the 1920s social stresses and weaknesses were an undercurrent, not the mainstream. Republican Presidents Warren Harding and Calvin Coolidge presided over an economy of abundance with limited intervention. Business was ascendant. Literature and art flourished. Henry Ford put the nation on wheels. New forms of entertainment, including radio and the movies, helped change the morals of a newly urban nation. Puritanism was in retreat. Bootleg liquor was abundant.

Then a way of life crashed with the stock market in 1929, and easy money vanished. After living in a fool's paradise, the United States, led by the once-vaunted progressive Republican Herbert Hoover, grimly tried to cope with privation. Hoover, a transitional figure, was more inventive than previous chief executives. He struggled valiantly and rationally to combat conditions largely beyond his control, failing because he lacked precedents to learn from. There had never been such a severe, long-lasting depression in our history. Hoover's successor, Franklin Roosevelt, would be bolder, yet he would not end the Depression either. World War II would.

Roosevelt evinced initial reluctance to change, but reacted to circumstances, aided by overwhelming Democratic majorities in Congress. Winning four elections, he fundamentally altered the presidency, the government, politics, and the economy. Under his New Deal, a domestic revolution, government provided the spark that restarted the economic engine and restored hope, if not prosperity. Labor realized significant gains, and the government acted as an employer of last resort. With the United States' entrance into World War II, the government focused on winning the war and the New Deal retreated into the background. Roosevelt proved a great war leader as well as an innovative domestic president. Although the war ended the Depression, the New Deal brought long-overdue reforms, swelling the size and power of the government, which grew further during the war. The conflict ended in a flash over Hiroshima that brought a new weapon of unlimited destruction into the arsenal of warfare. Eventually human beings would rush to build bombs that could destroy one another many times over. One could hardly imagine an era more tense than the Era of Trial and Triumph. Yet in the decades that followed, the Era of Uncertainty, an arms race and domestic divisions would make stress unrelenting. We had leaped out of the fire of war and into the cauldron of a potential atomic apocalypse that made life more uncertain than ever.

Time Line

An Era of Trial and Triumph, 1920–1945

August 26, 1920 Nineteenth Amendment, women's suffrage, ratified.

November 2, 1920 Warren G. Harding elected president.

November 2, 1920 KDKA, Pittsburgh, first radio station, broadcast presidential returns.

April 7, 1922 Lease granted for Teapot Dome oil field.

August 2, 1923 President Warren G. Harding dies; Vice President Calvin Coolidge succeeds him.

July 10, 1925 Scopes "Monkey trial" opens in Tennessee; concerns teaching of evolution.

May 20 and 21, 1927 Charles A. Lindbergh becomes first person to make solo, non-stop flight across Atlantic.

October 6, 1927 "The Jazz Singer," first "talkie" motion picture, is released.

October 29, 1929 Stock market crashes.

November 8, 1932 Franklin D. Roosevelt elected president.

January 23, 1933 Twentieth Amendment which moves presidential inauguration to January 20 from March 4 ratified.

December 5, 1933 Twenty-First Amendment repealing Prohibition ratified.

July 5, 1935 National Labor Relations Act passed.

August 14, 1935 Social Security Act passed.

December 7, 1941 Japan bombs Pearl Harbor.

June 6, 1944 Allies launch D-Day invasion of France.

April 12, 1945 Roosevelt dies and Vice President Harry S Truman succeeds him.

May 7, 1945 Germany surrenders.

August 6 and 9, 1945 United States drops atomic bombs on Hiroshima and Nagasaki, Japan.

September 2, 1945 Japan surrenders.

October 25–26, 1945 United Nations established.

CHAPTER SEVEN

The 1920s: Decade of Fear, Decade of Excess

A PERIOD OF hedonism and materialism, the 1920s elicited from songwriter Hoagy Carmichael the observation that "The postwar world came in with a bang of bad booze, flappers with bare legs, jangled morals and wild weekends." The time was dubbed the Jazz Age, although the Elastic Age might have been more appropriate, for in the tug-of-war between permissiveness and restraint, the country's institutions and patience were stretched nearly to the breaking point. Some people clung to the past and lashed out against new people and new ideas, a loss of tolerance felt in many nations after the Great War. Both the forces of the change and the forces of reaction were strong in this decade, with the paradox of progress amidst intolerance reflected in the era's trials and triumphs.

Intolerance and Discrimination

Of the forces of reaction, the strongest was the Ku Klux Klan. The Klan practiced intimidation and violence against minorities; allied with fundamentalist Protestant churches, it was a potent reactionary influence. The Klan of this decade represented a powerful social current. The growth of its membership, from five thousand in 1920 to five million in 1924, and its virtual demise just a few years later, epitomize the ascendancy and defeat of ultraconservatism.

Created to promote white supremacy in the Reconstruction South, the original Klan became discredited because of its violence against former slaves and faded by the mid-1870s. In 1915 a former minister, William J. Simmons, revived the organization, inspired by the popularity of fraternal groups, not only white supremacy. He devised an elaborate ritual and costume based partly on those of the Reconstruction Klan. He added the

CROSSES BURNING IN THE NIGHT
Ku Klux Klan spreads terror in Swainsboro, Georgia.
(Library of Congress)

burning cross, an emblem the first Klan had not used, borrowed from the movie *Birth of a Nation*. Under Simmons the Klan was a small organization until 1920, when he hired public relations experts Edward Y. Clarke and Elizabeth Tyler to increase membership. Hiram Evans replaced Simmons as Klan "Imperial Wizard" in 1922, but the changes set in motion through Clarke and Tyler persisted. Their techniques included advertising, the use of recruiters who received commissions for selling memberships, and an appeal based on self-righteous morality. Clarke and Tyler created possibilities for growth outside the South by expanding Klan enemies to include Catholics, Jews, Bolsheviks, and foreigners. Animosity toward these groups soon eclipsed hostility toward African Americans. At its peak, the Klan had more members in New Jersey than in Alabama, more in Oregon than in Louisiana, and more than 40 percent of the membership was in the midwestern states of Illinois, Indiana, and Ohio.

Paradoxically, the Klan had a positive program as well as a negative mission: Klansmen were expected to attend a Protestant church, abstain from alcohol, support their families, and practice patriotism. When Klansmen felt their values threatened, they became bigoted, reckless, and criminal, particularly when opposing Catholics. The typical Catholic was loyal to the pope rather than the United States, the Klan argued. As church-required celibacy of priests and nuns was unnatural, said the Klan, they must be engaging in illicit sex; if children resulted from these liaisons, they must have been aborted or buried alive. Catholic schools should be abolished because they trained children to undermine American democracy and prepare the country for a takeover by the pope, who would invade by tunneling under the Atlantic Ocean. Jews, too, were seen as a danger. The Jew personified vices Klansmen identified with modernity, among them chain stores, large banks, motion pictures, and sensuous music. Jews supposedly refused to assimilate, planned wars to slaughter gentiles, lured young girls into prostitution, and spearheaded communism and racial equality for black people.

Women joined Klan auxiliaries, the Kamelias, the Queens of the Golden Mask, and the Women of the Ku Klux Klan, the last becoming the largest, with about five hundred thousand members. Some women considered the Klan a protector from abusive husbands. Klansmen tried to shield the virtue of Nordic women by driving prostitutes out of town, searching country roads for teen couples in parked cars, and thwarting interracial marriages.

The Klan's fall was partly a product of its gratuitous violence, a divisive battle over the leadership of the organization, and the moral lapses of its Indiana "Grand Dragon," David C. Stephenson. Stephenson kidnapped a young woman and raped her; an overdose of sleeping pills took her life. When he was sent to prison, he exposed the illegal deeds of his political cronies. The Klan evaporated in his state, losing 335,000 members within a year, but part of the Klan's demise was due to its successes. Accomplishing its objectives of restricting immigration and muffling radicalism in a time of political conservatism, the organization was shorn of its purpose. The Klan worked to defeat the presidential candidacy of Catholic Al Smith in 1928, then lingered until 1944, when it became bankrupt.

Minorities continued their struggle for respect and fairness. The administration of Warren G. Harding proved less biased against African Americans than had the administration of Woodrow Wilson, and Harding appointed some black people to minor positions in the federal bureaucracy and diplomatic corps. In October 1921 he became the first chief executive since the Civil War to deliver a speech in a southern city, Birmingham, Alabama, urging amicable race relations. Belying his words, though, he would not denounce the Klan and was woefully ignorant about black culture and achievements; he had never heard of Booker T. Washington, for example.

Harding's successor, Calvin Coolidge, urged Congress to make lynching a federal crime, yet he was not much interested in race relations. Democratic nominating primaries barred blacks from voting in a region where Republicans were too weak to meaningfully contest elections. The labor movement also resisted black participation, but A. Philip Randolph persisted in seeking a voice for his constituents. The only African American leader of his generation to fuse the economic uplift message of Washington and the civil rights emphasis of W.E.B. Du Bois, he became head of the first major black union, the Brotherhood of Sleeping Car Porters. His unionization of the porters set a precedent for organizing black workers when many AFL unions discouraged them from joining. After Randolph won a decade-long fight for AFL recognition, he became a major force for African Americans in the labor movement.

Like African Americans, Hispanics knew poverty and discrimination. The promise of prosperity brought millions of Hispanics, mostly Mexicans, to the United States, many of them migrant workers on Western farms and ranches. About 728,203 Mexicans crossed the border between 1901 and 1930, and demand for Mexican labor rose as European immigration ebbed. Hispanic workers were unorganized, and their living conditions were primitive—shacks without running water or an indoor toilet. Wages were meager. Entire families had to work in the fields, meaning that children seldom received an education. Most Mexicans settled in California and Texas, and some started businesses that lifted them from poverty. The flow reversed during the 1930s. Mexicans returned to their native land because the Great Depression ended the Western labor shortage. Some were forcibly repatriated under Hoover administration policy. Native Americans were made citizens by virtue of federal policy, but continued to endure the most hardships of any minority.

Protests of injustice were at the heart of the Sacco-Vanzetti case. Two Italian anarchists, Nicola Sacco and Bartolomeo Vanzetti, were tried and sentenced to death for robbing a shoe company payroll and murdering a paymaster and his guard in 1920 in South Braintree, Massachusetts. They were armed when arrested, and ballistics tests suggested the gun found on Sacco had been taken from the guard and used to slay him; it also had a nick in the handle, matching a witness's description of the guard's firearm. Several witnesses identified Sacco and Vanzetti as the culprits. Such eminent intellectuals as H. L. Mencken and John Dewey argued that the two were found guilty because of their atheistic and anticapitalist views. Communists seized on the case as proof that capitalism was immoral. However, thorough reviews of the court record failed to reveal any procedural errors, the only basis for appeal.

Several men convicted of other crimes confessed to the robbery and murders, yet their versions of the crime did not equate with the known facts, and appeals were denied. After the Massachusetts Supreme Court affirmed the conviction and the U.S. Supreme Court decided it had no jurisdiction, Governor Alvan T. Fuller appointed a commission to review the case. The commission concluded that the two were guilty, and they were executed on August 22, 1927, martyrs to radicals. Novels, a play, and poems were written to denounce the legal system. Belief in the innocence of Sacco and Vanzetti became a dogma vindicated sixty years afterward when Governor Michael Dukakis expunged their guilt from the record.

Ballistics tests conducted in 1961, employing more precise scientific instruments than were available in the 1920s, indicated that the gun found on Sacco was the murder weapon. The significance of the case, though, does not lie in the guilt or innocence of Sacco and Vanzetti. Its importance is twofold: it was exploited to become a trial of America, of traditional values and unconventional ideas; and despite the duo's probable guilt, the controversy demonstrated the persistence of the paradox that in the land of equality, some were more equal than others.

Prosperity and Poverty

The 1920s are known as prosperous, but two sectors of the economy, labor and agriculture, floundered. Government and the media favored industry; bankers and business titans were the idols of the time. The stock market was portrayed as the way to make a fortune in a hurry. Workers and farmers were hurt by decline in demand for the products they supplied; wartime demand for labor and food was temporary, and export markets contracted. Technology, paradoxically, was both boon and bane. It increased productivity and wages, but it stole jobs, and wages failed to keep pace with profits. Greater productivity was especially ruinous for farmers, who overproduced. In retrospect, the decade was less stable than it appeared. Beneath the glitter of Wall Street was an undercurrent of anguish by those who were excluded from the carnival of wealth.

One of the most heated fights of the decade pitted unions in an unequal contest against employers for a greater share of profits and control of the workplace. During the 1920s the proportion of nonagricultural workers holding union cards plunged from 19.4 percent to 10.2 percent. AFL membership reached a high of 4.079 million in 1920, only to fall to 2.926 million in only three years. Organized labor was concentrated in a handful of industries—coal, construction, railroads, garment, manufacturing, longshoremen—and had no presence among clerical workers, unskilled and semiskilled

LONG HOURS, DANGEROUS CONDITIONS
A child laborer in a South Carolina textile mill photographed by Lewis Hine, 1908.
(National Archives)

factory workers, white-collar workers, and domestic servants. Several factors were responsible for the limited reach of unions. Productivity was high because of new technology; yearly wages increased 10.8 percent between 1923 and 1928. Credit buying raised the purchasing power of workers higher than their incomes; more married women workers enhanced family incomes; and the variety of inexpensive items for sale left laborers relatively content. The migration of African Americans northward between 1915 and 1928 provided cheap competition to white union workers. Labor leaders, such as William Green, Gompers's successor as AFL president in 1924 were less aggressive than Gompers. Green's reticence earned him a reputation as the "Calvin Coolidge of the labor movement."

The Republicans in the White House in the 1920s were no friends of labor, although Harding, encouraged by Hoover, helped negotiate a voluntary eight-hour day to replace the twelve-hour day in the steel industry and tried to stay neutral in labor disputes. His attorney general, Harry Daugherty, had no qualms about breaking strikes, however. When railroad workers struck in 1922 after two wage cuts, he obtained the most sweeping injunction in labor history to crush the strike. Unrest among railroad laborers led to the creation in 1926 of a presidentially appointed mediation board that sought to persuade parties to submit to arbitration. (Not until the Railway Labor Act of 1934 and the elimination of company unions during the New Deal did genuine progress occur in negotiating railroad labor peace.) John L. Lewis's United Mine Workers (UMW), likewise made little headway. Its national strike over wage reductions in 1922 became violent, resurrecting the Red Scare; public opinion turned against the strikers, who settled for preserving wage levels. UMW membership, largest in the nation among unions in 1920, declined steadily because of overproduction and the availability of cheap, nonunion southern miners.

Industrialists sought to forestall worker radicalism by allowing profit sharing, retirement plans, health insurance, and labor-management committees, all under the aegis of company unions, which helped make workplaces safer but lacked bargaining power. Commerce Secretary Herbert Hoover spearheaded the effort to make labor and capital partners, a philosophy that appealed to capitalist chieftains because they held the upper hand. Another supporter, the Supreme Court, favored business and voided more prolabor laws than it had in decades. The justices limited picketing outside factories, ruled boycotts illegal under most conditions, and nullified laws prohibiting injunctions against unions and setting minimum wages for women. It interpreted the Clayton Antitrust Act in a way that allowed labor few rights. Further, the tribunal and other federal courts upheld employers' use of "yellow-dog" contracts requiring that workers agree not to join a union.

Violent strikes ignited in 1929, precursors of the labor unrest of the 1930s. These were concentrated in the largely unorganized southern textile industry, which faced excess capacity and competition from synthetic fabrics. The mills paid workers, many of them women and children, lower wages and required longer hours than any factories. Strikes left demonstrators and police dead and caused extensive property damage. A strike in Gastonia, North Carolina, won notoriety because of the role of communists in trying to organize the mills and because seven strikers convicted of killing a police officer jumped bail and escaped to the Soviet Union.

Business was poised to dominate the decade because the world war that had ravaged Europe left the United States untouched—except to stimulate industry, consolidate banking, and hasten scientific discoveries. American industry became the most efficient on the planet, owing to mass production, technical wizardry, higher productivity per worker, and use of the movable assembly line that Henry Ford adapted to the automobile industry. New products appeared—the automobile, radios, rayon, cosmetics, telephones, and electric appliances—many sold in chain stores such as

Sears, Roebuck and Company, and J. C. Penney, and through catalogues. Mass advertising, making up 80 percent of all mail and 60 percent of newspaper space, stimulated demand for the goods and services and fed the economic boom. Ads beckoned buyers with themes of sex, eternal youth, and envy. One told of a man whose "faulty elimination" blocked him from climbing the ladder of executive success until he began eating Post Bran Flakes. Charles Atlas advocated "dynamic tension," or isometric exercise, which transformed him from a "ninety-eight-pound weakling" into "the world's most perfectly developed man."

Incomes rose consistently, even though richer Americans reaped the most and many did not share in the plenty. Because wage increases lagged behind business profits, eventually purchasing power would be limited and business would decline. Even during the boom, the coal, textile, shipbuilding, shoes, leather, and farm sectors languished. Understandably, none of this troubled middle-class Americans while they prospered and admired the wealthy. Business leaders were believed to have judgment superior to that of artists or intellectuals and experience that was valuable in government. Hoover, who had made unprofitable mines lucrative, had the chance to reorganize on a larger scale once he became secretary of commerce, prompting a contemporary to say, "He is engineering our material civilization as a whole." The pursuit of fortune was deemed character-building. One's worth was determined by one's wealth.

The acquisitive ethos was derived not from Mammon, the god of lucre, but from the Christian God who ordained the capitalist system and bestowed favor upon businessmen in the form of riches. Metaphors linking riches with holiness proliferated. A wildcatter who struck oil nearly every time he drilled linked his results to tithing. "I couldn't miss because I was in partnership with the Big Fellow and He made geology," he observed. Salesmen could follow the example of Moses, portrayed in an insurance company tract as the first successful realtor. Jesus "spent more time in marketplaces than in synagogues," one writer pointed out. The Last Supper was interpreted as the first Rotary Club luncheon, and a minister called Christ "the first president of Lions International. I quote you from the Bible: He was "Lion of the tribe of Judah." God's son, in fact, was the greatest businessman of all time, according to Bruce Barton, an advertising executive and politician whose biography of Jesus, *The Man Nobody Knows* (1924), was the number one best seller two successive years. The "proof" that he was a businessman was his reply to the doctors in the temple, "Wist ye not that I must be about my father's business?"

Business captains could take credit for substantial accomplishments, yet in their zeal, irresponsible elements among them grew greedy, sought too much, and, in the ultimate irony, wrecked themselves with rampant stock speculation. A force for modernization at the start of the decade, business hardened into defense of the status quo at the end of the 1920s, a paradoxical switch from progress to reaction.

Lindbergh and Ford: Heroes in the Air, on the Road

Although businessmen were heroes in the 1920s, no hero soared as high or as far as Charles A. Lindbergh, the first person to make a solo flight across the Atlantic Ocean. His flight from New York to Paris in May 1927 set off a celebration greater than the one that greeted the armistice ending World War I. Americans hungered for heroes and were anxious to replenish their idealism in the wake of the Great War and failed peace. Conqueror of one of the last frontiers, Lindbergh filled these needs, his flight commanding more newspaper space than any event in the decade.

A stunt flier and airmail pilot, Lindbergh was intrigued when Frenchman Raymond Orteig offered $25,000 to anyone who would fly nonstop from New York to Paris. With financing from businessmen in his base of St. Louis, Lindbergh designed and built a single-engine monoplane, *The Spirit of St. Louis*, with abundant fuel reserves. Because each pound he saved meant an extra quart of gasoline, he eliminated all excess weight, flying without a navigator or radio operator, eschewing a radio, carrying no parachute, and even tearing extra pages from his notebook. Unable to sleep the night before, Lindbergh faced more than thirty hours in the air with no sleep, confronting hazardous weather. But on the morning of May 20 he took off in the rain, barely clearing the runway in his gasoline-laden plane. Lindbergh remained on course despite crude navigation devices. Then he was over Ireland, over England, over the French coast. Thirty-three hours and twenty-nine minutes after takeoff, Lindbergh landed in Paris, where one hundred thousand people welcomed him. The journey for the man who had "flown like a poem into the heart of America," as the *New York Post* stated, was just beginning.

Lindbergh met the kings of Belgium and England. President Coolidge sent a cruiser to bring him to Washington, where the elite of the political and social worlds waited. Lawmakers pinned medal after medal on him. He was offered millions to star in movies and endorse products, yet modestly refused. Lindbergh did write a book, *We*, about himself and his plane, for which he received $200,000. Initially enjoying the publicity, he soon resented his loss of privacy and the public's expectations intimidated him. When one is on top of the world at twenty-five, there is no where to go but down.

In 1929 Lindbergh married Anne Morrow, who became his copilot and navigator and wrote books about their flights to Latin America, Africa, and China. In 1930 she gave birth to a son, Charles, at their country estate in New Jersey. Nineteen months later the infant was kidnapped from his bedroom and murdered despite a ransom. Evidence incriminated a German American, Bruno Richard Hauptmann, who was tried, convicted, and executed for the crime, although there were doubts about his guilt. Before the execution the Lindberghs fled to England to escape the press and to build a home for their growing family. America did not forget them, however, and Charles Lindbergh returned in 1939, urging Americans to avoid war with Germany, a war he said the United States could not win because of the might of the Luftwaffe.

Yet another hero of the 1920s was Ford, whose autos freed Americans from barriers of time and geography. Cars had been on the scene since early in the century, although it was not until this decade that Americans started their love-hate relationship with the automobile. Auto registration jumped from eight thousand in 1900 to 8 million in 1920 and close to 23 million in 1930. By 1925, there were 20 percent more cars than telephones, and 60 percent of farm families had a car, whereas just 12 percent had running water. A farm wife explained her family's decision to own a car but not a bathtub, saying, "You can't go to town in a bathtub." But technology that offers to liberate individuals from restraints also inspires the state to regulate. Thus, the noisy contraptions that clanked along dusty roads and frightened horses prompted requests to lawmakers to curb their use. Tennessee adopted a law requiring a motorist to advertise his plan to drive one week in advance. In Illinois, a proposed statute stated that when approaching a corner that allowed no view of the road ahead, "the automobilist must stop not less than one hundred yards from the turn, toot his horn, fire a revolver, halloo, and send up three bombs at intervals of five minutes."

Some uses of the automobile especially concerned ministers and parents. A juvenile court judge called the vehicle a "house of prostitution on wheels" because one-third of the girls appearing before him on sex charges had committed their offenses in cars. Technology once more battled tradition and facilitated sexuality. The automobile made dates chaperon-free and encouraged the advent of motels, which were "little more than camouflaged brothels," Federal Bureau of Investigation (FBI) Director J. Edgar Hoover said. Sociologists found that three-quarters of the patrons of Dallas tourist camps were local couples, not tourists, and that one cabin had been rented sixteen times in a single night.

Serious crime—bank robbery, bootlegging, kidnapping, insurance fraud, car theft, and drunken driving—also became easier because of the car. On the other hand, automobiles aided law enforcement by allowing police to cover more territory, particularly when dispatched by radio, and ambulances could speed the ill or injured to hospitals.

Both city and farm were transformed. Previously compact cities could sprawl, encouraging the growth of suburbs, branch offices of businesses, and shopping centers. School buses helped eliminate the one-room school in favor of consolidated schools. Wasteland became prime real estate when a major highway traversed it. Rural life was reinvigorated as automobiles eased isolation and loneliness, and gasoline-powered threshers, tractors, and reapers made arduous hand labor unnecessary. Millions began to vacation via automobile. Tourists traveled to once isolated destinations such as Florida and California. Already fluid, the pace of society quickened.

The automotive industry paid some of the highest wages in the United States and stimulated the economy. By 1928 it was the nation's largest industry, and by 1929 it employed one of every ten workers. It consumed 85 percent of the rubber imported, 19 percent of the iron and steel manufactured, 67 percent of the plate glass, 27 percent of the lead—and practically all the gasoline. Ford, the high priest of the industry, was the first to conceive of his car as a product for the masses rather than the elite and, by the early 1920s, had captured 60 percent of the market. He made just one model in one color, black, but it was dependable and cheap, because Ford cut the price yearly to outsell competitors: in 1924 the Model T sold for a mere $290, down from $450 ten years before. Forward-looking in technology but backward-looking in politics, Ford was voted the third-greatest figure in world history in a poll of college students (Jesus was first and Napoleon second). Nevertheless, he fell behind the times, so much that by 1927 General Motors Chevrolet was outselling the Model T. Ford's answer was to halt production while he designed the Model A, in part to satisfy women's demands that cars be stylish and comfortable. When it appeared on December 2, 1927, he overtook General Motors and regained his luster. Ford even received a fan letter from bank robber Clyde Barrow, who was proud to write that he drove Fords exclusively whenever he could get away with one.

New Manners and Morals

Victorian morality, a code stressing restraint, silence about sex, prim and proper women, and starkly delineated gender roles, yielded to a morality that was less disciplined and more tolerant, an environment that considered love erotic and sex enjoyable. Young people were in the forefront of this revolution, which emerged from the temporary couplings of World

War I, the exposure of troops and nurses to looser European lifestyles, and a live-for-the-moment mentality. Rebellion began among an elite, college students on urban campuses, and spread to rural areas and high schoolers, although it was less apparent on farms and in small villages. By the end of the decade, however, the rebels, their free spirits disseminated by the mass media, had won the cultural battle. The sexual revolution that surfaced most prominently in the 1920s (and again in the 1960s) was, arguably, the most significant revolution of the twentieth century.

A woman who flaunted her sexuality, the flapper, personified the young insurgent. The word "flapper" came from the fad of college women wearing open galoshes that flapped when they walked. Ignoring petticoats, corsets, and girdles, the flapper wore short skirts and short-sleeved dresses, bobbed her hair, and applied cosmetics. She accentuated her sexuality by appearing provocative and naughty.

Sexual rebels had a supporter in Sigmund Freud, whose writings spread to the United States in popularized form after the war and were embraced by Americans. His emphasis on sex and his thesis that sexual repression was unhealthy and caused mental illness fascinated and titillated. From Freud, sexual experimentation attained the imprimatur of science, and people spoke more frankly about sex, except for homosexual relationships, for the mainstream rejected them.

Contributing to the new sexuality in a different way, Margaret Sanger crusaded for birth control. She devoted a magazine and several books to her cause, established the American Birth Control League, forerunner of the Planned Parenthood Federation of America, and started three hundred clinics. Fought by traditionalists, Sanger was incarcerated for "maintaining a public menace," but by 1930, allied with physicians, she was gaining support. Meanwhile, with condoms, spermicides, and diaphragms available, increasing numbers of couples practiced birth control.

The new practice of dating abetted the sexual revolution. In Victorian times, ladies invited men to their homes, where they would spend an evening in the parlor or on the front porch with chaperons. Dating shifted the initiative to men, who invited women to a restaurant or a movie or for a drive. It was assumed the man worked and the woman did not, hence he paid. Dates became acts of consumption in which a woman sold her company; the higher the price she commanded and the more dates she had, the more popular she was considered. There was an element of competition—of women getting invited on numerous dates and of men striving to be seen with attractive females. Couples were expected to neck and pet. In the slang of the time, necking involved caresses above the neck and petting involved caresses below the neck, including genital stimulation short of intercourse. Men expected to pet in exchange for spending money on a date.

Movies and magazines encouraged sexual libertines. Watching stars such as the voluptuous Greta Garbo taught women how to kiss and to hold a cigarette and a drink. Mass magazines were accused of inciting lust. *True Story* had three hundred thousand readers by 1923, four years after it started, and almost 2 million by 1926. It published articles titled "Indolent Kisses" and "What I Told My Daughter the Night before Her Marriage." Promiscuity, nonetheless, was not so widespread as the magazines might suggest. A survey in the early 1930s found that around one-fourth of the women and one-half of the men had sex before marrying, and that three-fourths of the women limited it to sex with their fiancés. Attitudes about sexuality changed more than practices. Virginity was no longer an ideal.

Grace Coolidge became the first president's wife to light a cigarette in the White House. From 1911 to 1928 yearly cigarette sales doubled, largely because of women. Advertisements showed pretty women asking men to blow smoke their way. The American Tobacco Company, aiming at women determined to win gender equality, labeled cigarettes "torches of freedom" and staged a march of women smokers at the 1928 New York Easter parade. Smoking became an emblem of sexuality, as was drinking, which women began doing more often in the company of men. Nice girls, who would not have sipped gin before, liked to get drunk. Hip flasks were evident at school dances and football games, and women carried dainty versions in their purses. "In order to be collegiate, one must drink," the University of Chicago handbook announced. Drinking was illegal under Prohibition, of course, yet this only made it a more powerful weapon in the arsenal of youthful rebellion.

Many watched the relaxing of standards with dismay. The rate of divorces to marriages climbed from about 1 in 10 to 1 in 6 during the 1920s. Women initiated two-thirds of the divorces. Divorce, attributed in part to promiscuity, lost some of its stigma, and people were unwilling to endure unhappy unions, even for the sake of children. Traditionalists tried to clamp down on sexuality with legislation. A Utah lawmaker wanted to imprison women caught wearing skirts higher than three inches above the ankle; Virginia thought of banning dresses that exposed more than three inches of a woman's throat; and Ohio considered a bill to outlaw "any garment which unduly displays or accentuates the lines of the female figure." Colleges banned women from smoking or confined it to off-campus areas, penalizing violators by withholding their degrees or expelling them. Universities imposed curfews or forbade students from owning cars and women from riding in them, rules designed to make sex logistically difficult.

Women, paradoxically, held a central place in the culture wars on both sides, as advocates of transformation and as disciples of tradition: they grew less passive in all aspects of life. They were liberated not only from sexual taboos but also from laborious housework because of advances in food preparation, electrical appliances, and smaller houses. They worked more outside the home. By the close of the decade, 10.6 million women did such work, up from 8.3 million ten years previously. Some 11 percent of white married women and 31 percent of African American married women were employed as domestics, clerical workers, and factory laborers. Some fields opened for women, yet most jobs remained segregated by gender. In the professions women fared poorly, losing ground numerically or proportionally among physicians, architects, chemists, lawyers, college students, and holders of doctorates.

Women's incentive for taking jobs was usually financial exigency instead of personal fulfillment. For single women, work was believed to be a stopgap, something to do until they married and raised families. The main goal of the flapper, for all her rebelliousness, was to get a man, wed him, and raise children. Hard-pressed to meet the demands on their time, women were expected to keep themselves attractive if they were to hold on to their husbands and to bring up their youngsters properly, despite the confusing advice that child-rearing experts dispensed. Mothers were told that too much attention would hinder a child's development but that too little was also harmful. John B. Watson, the most famous child psychologist, counseled women to prepare to send children into the world as independent persons as soon as the age of two. "Never hug and kiss them, never let them sit in your lap," he wrote.

Religion: Beacon of Hope; Ally of Prejudice

After 1900 most immigrants to the United States were Catholics, and by the 1920s, 23 million lived in the country, making Catholicism the largest denomination in the nation. No other large religious group inspired such a wave of nativism and ethnocentricity. As with Protestants and Jews, disputes between traditionalists and modernists divided Catholics. Many American priests and bishops were more liberal on theological and social issues than their European counterparts. In the 1920s most American Catholics practiced birth control (although opposing it in theory), and there was an increase in divorce among them. Joining Catholics as a persecuted minority, Jews faced prejudice common among wealthy Americans such as Ford, who lent the prestige of his industrial empire to the publication of anti-Semitic articles in his newspaper, the *Dearborn Independent*.

Most Jewish immigrants were impoverished, but Jews prospered faster than any minority group and became prominent philanthropists, intellectuals, and civil libertarians.

Protestants, polarized between liberal and conservative factions, debated issues such as the literal truth of the Bible, tithing, prayer, and church attendance. The majority of churchgoers showed up only on Sundays, and churches devised gimmicks to fill pews. A midwestern minister held an "auto Sunday" at which he awarded a prize to the person who could squeeze the most people in a car and bring them to church. The next Sunday he promised a prize to the church member with the biggest feet (the minister himself won). One New York congregation, tying itself to the prestige of business, gave an engraved certificate of stock in the kingdom of God to anyone who donated $100 to the church building fund.

One of the most puzzling religious phenomena of the decade, as far as liberals were concerned, was the persistence of fundamentalism. "Heave an egg out of a Pullman and you will hit a fundamentalist almost everywhere in the United States," said Mencken, who, like other secular commentators,

RELIGION FOR THE MASSES
Aimee Semple McPherson, circa 1931.
(Used by permission of the Heritage Department of the
International Church of the Foursquare Gospel)

did not respect or understand fundamentalists. In fact, it was quite easy to learn where fundamentalists stood: belief in the literal truth of the Bible, in the virgin birth and deity of Jesus, in his literal resurrection and atonement for the world's sins, and in his second coming in bodily form. The leading fundamentalist of the period was Billy Sunday, one of the first evangelists to apply modern business and organizational techniques to his crusades. Renowned more for emotional enthusiasm than for theological sophistication—"I don't know any more about theology than a jack-rabbit knows about Ping Pong," he said, "but I'm on my way to glory"—he converted listeners by the hundreds.

The flamboyant Aimee Semple McPherson settled in Los Angeles, where she preached to huge crowds, held faith-healing sessions, and constructed a five-thousand-seat, $1.5 million temple. In May 1926 she vanished while swimming in the Pacific Ocean and was believed to have drowned, stunning the world thirty-two days later by emerging in a Mexican village and claiming she had been abducted. The "disappearance," one of the major news stories of the decade, was exposed as a hoax when neither the kidnappers nor the cabin where they allegedly held her was found. Actually, McPherson was having an affair with the married man who operated her radio station, and they fled Los Angeles together. Returning to her temple, she continued to draw larger crowds with dramatic sermons. McPherson created mission churches and planned to establish a "Salvation Navy." Although membership in her denomination, the Four-Square Gospel, increased, the Salvation Navy never sailed. Her personal life grew more unstable, and McPherson died in 1944 of a barbiturate overdose, possibly a suicide.

McPherson, Sunday, and their fellow believers were alarmed because they lived in a time of transition in which their views became minority ones. They became counterrevolutionaries, buffers against modernization. "This is not a battle, it is a war from which there is no discharge," said W. B. Riley, a leading fundamentalist minister. The clash culminated in a debate over whether Charles Darwin's theory of evolution should be taught in schools. Fundamentalists argued that the theory undercut belief in the biblical story of creation and, by implication, the credibility of the Bible. Modernists retorted that academic freedom protected teachers from censorship. Further, they considered the Bible an unreliable source for science. By 1925 Oklahoma and Tennessee passed laws banning the teaching of evolution in public schools, and almost half the states were considering such measures. Looking for courts to declare the laws unconstitutional, the American Civil Liberties Union offered to finance the defense of any teacher who would violate an antievolution statute. High school teacher John T. Scopes volunteered after business leaders in his farm community of Dayton, Tennessee, asked him to raise the issue so the town could attract tourists.

More than one hundred newspapers sent reporters, including Mencken, to cover the trial, the first broadcast on radio. Revivalists flocked to Dayton to preach on street corners, bookstores marketed volumes on theology, and hot dog vendors set up stands. Obviously it was naive to presume that the issue of biblical vs. scientific truth would be resolved in a brief trial in a small Tennessee town before a county judge; the real battle was for public opinion. To compete for that opinion, the prosecution welcomed William Jennings Bryan, the famous orator, secretary of state, and three-time presidential nominee. The defense boasted Clarence Darrow, one of the most brilliant trial lawyers in America. With each unwilling to concede that the other might be acting on good faith or had a right to his beliefs, their debate was irreconcilable.

Frustrated when Judge John T. Raulston would not allow scientific experts to testify for the defense in the presence of jurors, Darrow asked to put Bryan on the stand as a biblical authority. Accepting, Bryan testified that the world was created in 4004 B.C., that Eve was literally created from Adam's rib, that the world's languages originated at the Tower of Babel— responses that offended modernists, who believed the Bible should be interpreted metaphorically. For the judge and jury, however, the case did not concern the validity of the Bible, only whether Scopes flouted the law. He was convicted, and Raulston fined him $100. Inadvertently, Raulston violated the law, which specified that juries, not judges, should set the fine, an error that the Tennessee Supreme Court cited a year later to nullify the sentence and avoid the issue of the statute's constitutionality. There the case ended, for the ruling meant that opponents of the law could not appeal it to federal courts.

Mencken and other journalists decided that fundamentalism had been exposed as a fraud because of Bryan's testimony. Bryan, who did not regret his role in Dayton, died in his sleep five days after the trial ended, his reputation in decline. Some believed that Darrow's renown, too, was wounded, as the attorney had showed a mean-spirited, vindictive streak. In fact, neither made many converts, and for all the ridicule heaped on it, fundamentalism never disappeared. By the end of the century, it remained a vital force in the United States, its churches adding members more rapidly than mainstream Protestant denominations. The Tennessee law remained in force until 1967, yet was not enforced to avoid another test.

Prohibition in Triumph and Trial

Prohibition has become one of the best-remembered symbols of the 1920s. The authors of the Eighteenth Amendment did not expect to stop all drinking, but they hoped people would respect the Constitution. Aiming to punish only makers and sellers of booze, not ordinary people, they did not criminalize possession. Initially their ideas appeared plausible, for consumption declined, yet by the late 1920s the sale of alcohol had become a profitable paradox, and enforcement became impractical. There were simply too many ways that someone determined to drink could get an alcoholic beverage. Alcohol could be smuggled across 18,700 miles of borders and coastline, overwhelming security. Underpaid enforcement officials accepted bribes, and local judges and juries set bootleggers free with small fines.

If one could not afford costly smuggled liquor, alcohol could be obtained with a doctor's prescription or it could be made. All the equipment needed to construct a still was sold in hardware stores, and the U.S. Agriculture Department helpfully published a pamphlet on how to manufacture home brew. Near-beer with little or no alcohol was available, and many people bought wort, a mixture that could be converted to beer by adding yeast. Also, speakeasies served drinks almost openly in big cities. A Treasury agent found one just thirty-five seconds after arriving in New Orleans. Bootleggers sold dangerous concoctions such as Jamaica Jake, 90 percent alcohol, that paralyzed people, and Jackass Brandy, which caused internal bleeding. Alcoholics resorted to antifreeze, wood alcohol, hair tonic, and patent medicines containing alcohol. Midwestern farmhands drank fluids from the bottoms of silos, where silage had rotted and fermented. Moonshiners were so busy making money they rarely stopped to wash their tubs and vats, where agents discovered cats, mice, rats, and cockroaches that were attracted by the odor, fell in, and drowned.

Prohibition became a bonanza for organized crime. By intimidating or murdering competitors, a gang could secure a monopoly on the alcohol trade and a share of the $2 billion yearly that bootleggers earned in the United States, at a time when the federal budget was $3 billion to $6 billion. Al Capone, the most notorious bootlegger, dominated Chicago and suburban Cicero, grossing $60 million from beer and distilled liquor, as well as his take from gambling, prostitution, and the "protection" racket. Paradoxically, he thrived because he served a need, albeit illegal. To embellish his image, he gave away food and coal to the poor, donated money to charity, and invested in legitimate businesses (he shunned stocks, though, claiming that Wall Street was crooked). Yet few could admire Capone or dismiss him after St. Valentine's Day in 1929, when his men massacred six members of a rival gang. In 1931 he was imprisoned for federal income tax evasion.

Herbert Hoover was the only president to exert a sincere effort to enforce Prohibition, increasing penalties, transferring jurisdiction from the Treasury Department to the Justice Department, and placing enforcement agents under civil service rules for salaries and professional advancement. In addition, he appointed a commission led by former Attorney General George Wickersham to study federal law enforcement, particularly the alcohol ban. The commission reported that Prohibition violators were straining the federal prison system. As early as 1924 half of all federal prisoners were incarcerated because of Prohibition offenses, even though they represented just a fraction of those who disobeyed the law. Eventually most reformers concluded that the ban was unenforceable. The clinching argument, during the Great Depression, was that the return of the legitimate industry would create jobs, furnish revenue for the government, and aid recovery.

By 1932 the Republican and Democratic platforms called for repeal or alteration of the Eighteenth Amendment. After Democrat Franklin D. Roosevelt unseated Hoover that year, the lame-duck Congress that met before his inauguration enacted the Twenty-First Amendment, repealing the Eighteenth. Ratified in December 1933, it closed the Prohibition Era. Still, eight states and several counties remained dry, and Prohibition was not universally branded a failure. Defenders reminded people that alcohol consumption, auto accidents, and diseases such as cirrhosis of the liver declined under the alcohol ban; nor could illicit drinking be held responsible by itself for organized crime, when urbanization, the auto, the availability of guns, and greater criminal sophistication contributed. Alcoholism exacted a heavy toll on individuals, persuading Prohibition supporters to help found Alcoholics Anonymous in 1935. Repeal did not solve problems any more than did Prohibition. Compulsive drinkers resorted to the bottle to escape anxiety, and in no decade did they seek escape so desperately, and so unsuccessfully, as in "the Roaring Twenties."

CHAPTER EIGHT

Republicanism from Prosperity to the Great Depression

THE 1920S WERE paradoxical in that they resembled a second Gilded Age (1877–1900), an era that appeared golden on the surface, yet in fact was only gilded. The glitter of society was fascinating, yet the reality beneath lacked substance. The Republican presidents were popular in their time and have some significant accomplishments to their credit, yet their reputations, and the economy, floated on thin ice.

The 1920 Election

Its luster fading with Woodrow Wilson, the Democratic Party's star was in decline by 1919, and the Republicans' was ascendant. There had been just two Democratic chief executives since the Civil War. The second, Wilson, won in 1912 only because of a GOP split, and he barely defeated his Republican foe in 1916. By 1920 Wilson was infirm and unpopular, his party discredited, because he could not secure approval of the Versailles Treaty, and because he neglected to plan adequately for conversion to a peacetime economy. Registered Republicans outnumbered Democrats.

The chief problem for the Republicans in 1920 was to find a suitable candidate after Theodore Roosevelt's death on January 6, 1919. General Leonard Wood, who had commanded the Rough Riders and considered himself Roosevelt's heir, Illinois Governor Frank Lowden and U.S. Senator Hiram Johnson of California led the field. Both parties made overtures to Herbert Hoover, a fabulously successful mining engineer and humanitarian, yet Hoover would not campaign for the job.

IN A PLAYFUL MOOD
Warren G. Harding with his dog at the White House.
(Library of Congress)

Ohio Senator Warren G. Harding, who had announced his candidacy in 1919, ran a low-key campaign. Harding had nominated William Howard Taft for president in 1912 and had delivered his party's keynote address in 1916, in his first term in the U.S. Senate. In 1918 and 1919 Harding delivered speeches nationwide, positioning himself as a potential nominee. His campaign strategist, Harry Daugherty, devised the tactic of collecting pledges to Harding as a second choice should the leading candidates deadlock. A newspaper publisher, Harding was a friendly unifier who understood intuitively the mood of the nation. Shaken by a victorious war followed by a lost peace and a declining economy, America wanted what Harding termed "normalcy." Not a profound orator by present standards, Harding's patriotic, alliterative speeches were effective because of their delivery, though lacking in intellectual content. A Democratic opponent labeled them "an army of pompous phrases moving over the landscape in search of an idea."

As the convention approached, Harding's campaign gained momentum. Wood was injured by an investigation into his campaign finances; as was Johnson, when it was learned he had helped inspire the investigation to discredit Wood. The leading candidates were destroying one another. This fratricide made Harding's superficial calm attractive. Florence Harding, the candidate's wife, played a major role. Initially, she did not want him to run. She knew, as the public did not, that Harding had entered a Michigan hospital on several occasions for treatment of stress. Yet once Harding entered, she would not let him quit. After her husband was trounced in the Indiana primary, she insisted he remain a candidate. But Florence had premonitions. She had a reading with a Washington psychic, Madame Marcia, who predicted that a deadlock would develop at Chicago leading to Harding's nomination and election. However, he would die before his term ended.

The deadlock predicted by the psychic and hoped for by Daugherty materialized. Wood led the first ballot but could not expand beyond his core of delegates. Neither could Lowden or Johnson. They disliked each other, and neither would release their delegates to another front runner. Yet this animosity did not extend to Harding.

When the convention adjourned temporarily to sort out the mess, Daugherty's second-choice pledges began to cash in their chips. Many believed Harding could win the election. Although not a party leader, neither was he a novice. He had served in the Ohio senate, as lieutenant governor of Ohio, and as a U.S. senator. He was likeable and a reliable party regular. He came from an elector-rich, closely contested state.

Harding was nominated after the leading candidates released their delegates. The nominee grasped Lowden's hand and said, "I am not sure that I would be happier, Frank, if I were congratulating you." Daugherty, once exiled to a cameo role by the political heavyweights, was now grudgingly respected as Machiavelli reborn. Harding left the selection of a vice presidential running mate to the convention, which chose the diminutive governor of Massachusetts, Calvin Coolidge. Coolidge had become a symbol for law and order when he dispatched a blunt telegram to labor leader Samuel Gompers during the Boston police strike of 1919: "There is no right to strike against the public safety by anybody, anywhere, any time."

Not everyone considered Harding a model leader. *The Nation* wrote: "In truth he is a dummy, an animated automaton, a marionette that moves when the strings are pulled." And Florence Harding, having witnessed the fulfillment of the first installment of Madame Marcia's prophecy, now feared fulfillment of the latter, telling reporters, "I can see but one word written over the head of my husband if he is elected and that word is 'tragedy'."

Two weeks after Harding's nomination, the Democratic convention in San Francisco also bogged down. Wilson wanted a third term to make the election a referendum on his treaty, but his physical condition prevented it. The leading candidates were William G. McAdoo, Wilson's treasury secretary, and A. Mitchell Palmer, the attorney general and Red Scare leader. It took eight days and forty-four ballots before the party nominated a compromise choice, Ohio Governor James M. Cox. The vice presidential nominee was another surprise: Franklin D. Roosevelt, selected because delegates thought his name might appeal to Republican voters who remembered his distant cousin, Theodore. He was well liked in both parties, but many leading politicians did not consider him a serious person.

Harding paced his campaign deliberately. Initially he remained home, speaking to delegations who hiked to his front yard. The press appreciated his candor and affability. Neither party found the public responsive to the League of Nations issue. A racist professor wrote a book and compiled a fake genealogy purporting that Harding was part black. Cox and Roosevelt refused to exploit it. In early August, Harding took to the campaign trail delivering 112 speeches before November 2. Coolidge did little campaigning. The Democratic ticket campaigned energetically, yet could not escape the clouds of Wilson's turbulent presidency.

Florence Harding voted for her husband, thanks to the Twentieth Amendment, one of a tidal wave of voters who swept Harding into the White House. The Republican won 404 electoral votes, the greatest total up to that time, and 16.2 million popular votes, or 60.4 percent, one of the highest percentages in American history. Cox carried just eleven states, 127 electoral votes, and 9.1 million popular votes. The GOP controlled both houses of Congress. The main protest candidate, Eugene V. Debs of the American Socialist Party, was serving a federal prison sentence for subversion, having delivered a speech against the war. Debs, whose campaign literature featured his prison number, received almost 920,000 votes, the most ever for a Socialist candidate.

Harding's Presidency

Always modest, some said with good reason, Harding asserted: "I should not be fit to hold the high office of President if I did not frankly say that it is a task which I have no intention of undertaking alone." He planned to tap "the best minds in the United States" as cabinet members, and with a few exceptions succeeded. Most of Harding's cabinet members were generalists rather than specialists. The most important were Herbert Hoover, young, assertive, and imaginative, as secretary of commerce; and Andrew Mellon, the second-richest man in the world, who, financial journals predicted, would become the greatest secretary of the treasury since Alexander Hamilton. Harding nominated Charles Evans Hughes, a man with a brilliant legal mind, as secretary of state. Albert Fall, who sat next to Harding in the Senate, became his secretary of the interior. The most controversial nominee was Harding's friend Daugherty for attorney general. The *New York Times* wrote of rumors of Daugherty's appointment: "It would be universally regarded as the payment of a political debt. But it would be worse than that. It would be the naming of a man not believed to be competent to do the important work to be placed in his hands." The cabinet, for the most part, had good minds, indeed. But the advice it gave him was hydra-headed rather than uniform or consistent. Harding despaired of his own indecisiveness.

At the time Harding entered office, the nation had been drifting under the declining health of President Wilson, unable to provide a rudder for the Ship of State. The presidency was listing, foreign policy was in chaos, domestic policy was unattended. The postwar economy was a shambles. Nonfarm unemployment grew from 2.3 percent in 1919 to 4.0 percent in 1920 to 11.9 percent in 1921. Harding made uprighting the economy and restoring domestic calm his primary objectives.

Excelling at public relations, and gregarious, Harding kept the White House gate open and the curtain drawn, and every day during the lunch hour he greeted anyone who wished to meet him, shaking hands with a quarter of a million people in three years. His generosity was expressed through pardons of Debs and other political prisoners shortly before Christmas 1921. Wanting to be successful, Harding worked hard, arriving at the Oval Office by 7:00 A.M. and often remaining until midnight.

Harding's first message to Congress stated his priorities: negotiate a separate peace with Germany, Austria, and Hungary; cut government expenditures by creating a Bureau of the Budget; enact an emergency tariff followed by a permanent tariff and aid farmers. He wanted Congress to limit immigration; regulate new technology such as aviation, radio, and automobiles; create a department of public welfare; and enact antilynching legislation. This was not a reactionary agenda, and some of it was progressive. Harding was responding to public demands in some areas; in others, such as the Bureau of the Budget, a department of public welfare, and antilynching legislation, he was moving ahead of public opinion, demonstrating a degree of leadership.

Congress quickly passed and Harding signed the Emergency Immigration Act of 1921. Workers feared loss of jobs to immigrants, and racial and ethnic bias determined the apportionment. The act, which Harding signed on May 19, 1921, reduced immigration quotas to 3 percent of a country's nationals residing in the United States in 1910. Not until after Harding's death, in 1924, did Congress pass a more permanent, more restrictive statute. About a week after authorizing the measure, Harding signed his second major measure, an emergency tariff law. Expected to help protect farmers from foreign competition, it did little to relieve their plight. Farmers overproduced for American markets and retaliatory tariffs shut down foreign sales. They would have to produce less or sell on world markets. A second, more lasting act, the Fordney-McCumber Tariff, signed in 1922, raised tariffs and provided favors to special interest groups.

The administration's greatest domestic accomplishment was the Budget and Accounting Act of June 10, 1921. The Bureau of the Budget organized and balanced expenditures with income, helped cut taxes, and eliminated waste and duplication. Charles G. Dawes, a Chicago banker, became the first director. Harding asked Dawes to slice $1 billion from the federal budget; Dawes did better.

Veterans began agitating for a bonus for their service in World War I during Harding's tenure, and he vetoed the first measure to pass Congress in 1922. As farmers continued to languish and tariffs did not prove their salvation, the administration enacted ameliorative measures. These included the Capper-Volstead Act (1922) to exempt farm cooperatives from antitrust prosecution (sometimes called agriculture's "Magna Carta"), appointment of a farm representative to the Federal Reserve Board, the Grain Futures Acts of 1921 and 1922, restricting speculation, and the Packers and Stockyard Act (1921) to regulate prices charged by livestock processors.

Harding found it difficult to work with the lawmakers, because he rarely provided the leadership needed to overcome opposition. Only when there was broad agreement did he publicly campaign for bills. With the nation in a recession in 1921, both parties favored a tax cut to stimulate the economy. Mellon believed that tax cuts for the wealthy would make capital available for investment, and progressives preferred broader reductions. Ultimately Harding endorsed Mellon's proposal, yet the law that emerged was a compromise. General tax rates were unchanged, exemptions were raised, and the excess profits levy was abolished. The maximum surtax on incomes greater than $1 million was dropped from 65 to 50 percent, the corporate tax was raised from 10 to 12 percent, and the first-ever capital gains tax, 12.5 percent, was imposed. This was hardly a "soak-the-poor" law; under it most working-class Americans paid nothing. For the other half of his financial formula, Mellon, with the aid of Harding and Dawes reduced spending and helped retire the federal debt, which fell from $23.1 billion in 1921, to $21.8 billion in 1923, and to $16.5 billion in 1929. Hoover organized a national conference on unemployment, collected and distributed economic statistics, helped manufacturers eliminate waste and duplication, and encouraged industry to cooperate through trade associations.

Harding's Supreme Court appointments were one of his most endur-ing accomplishments. His first appointee, former President William Howard Taft, had a fine legal mind and led a strict constructionist court. In addition, Harding appointed George Sutherland (1922), Pierce Butler (1923), and Edward T. Sanford (1923), the latter three upon the recom-mendation of Taft.

Scandal and History's Verdict

On December 8, 1922, Harding delivered his second State of the Union address. The economy had pulled out of its slump and was growing. Harding moved in a progressive direction, calling for internal improve-ments, conservation, federal development of waterpower and electricity, and an end to child labor.

Yet Harding's health waned even as his oratory waxed. He appeared calm and in command, but the stress of the presidency was straining his already damaged heart. Harding enjoyed the ceremonial and interpersonal aspects of the presidency, although he was a poor administrator, meticu-lous to a fault. Not until late in his short term did he learn to delegate or set priorities. Although it has been written that Harding was lazy, just the opposite was true. He was a perfectionist in human relations because he did not like to hurt people. Harding's chief problem was that he could not relax amid undone work. "I never find myself done," he said. "I never find myself with my work complete. I don't believe there is a human being who can do all the work there is to be done in the President's office." His var-ious attempts at recreation—golf, poker, and heavy drinking—were in part efforts to escape tension and depression. Like other men who sought the presidency, the power ceased to become an honor and grew into a burden. The White House became a prison he had to pretend he liked. Like presi-dents before and after him, the public image was at odds with reality.

Harding kept working despite a severe case of influenza contracted in early 1923. Some doctors believe the flu was accompanied by an undiag-nosed heart attack. The president's morale began to sag when he learned of rumors of scandals in his administration. Inklings came that Charles R. Forbes was looting Veterans Administration hospitals. Forbes took kickbacks for giving lucrative government contracts to friends and selling hospital sup-plies below cost, while buying expensive new supplies. Forbes traveled to Europe, where he resigned, but was belatedly brought to justice after Harding's death. His confederate, Charles F. Cramer, committed suicide during a Senate investigation. A friend of Attorney General Daugherty, Jesse Smith, accused of selling pardons and alien property seized during the war, committed suicide when his crimes were uncovered. Meanwhile, Secretary of Interior Fall, the culprit in the most famous scandal, resigned from the cabinet on January 2, 1923, to become effective on March 4.

Of the brewing scandals, Harding knew most about Forbes. He probably suspected others. The president planned a cross-country railroad tour to lift his spirits and revive his health. Before departing, he altered his will and sold the *Marion Star*. The vacation only aggravated his angst. He played bridge compulsively. He asked Hoover, aboard for the trip, what he would do if he learned of a scandal in the administration. After Hoover advised him to reveal it, Harding refused to elaborate. Harding ended the journey in Alaska, Washington, Oregon, and California. After a series of strokes he succumbed to pneumonia in California.

Harding's death on August 2, 1923, had the impact of a comet crashing into earth. His body was borne on a train back to Washington as tens of thousands lined the tracks and sang his favorite hymn, "Nearer My God to Thee." To them, he was a man with an average mind but a generous nature, calm, patient, patriotic, whose kind voice was silenced.

History has not treated Harding as generously as his contemporaries. Journalists, congressional committees, and enemies began to drive silver stakes through his reputation. Within months of the president's death a pall of scandal that has not lifted to this day had enveloped Harding's administration. The best known, probably because of its catchy name, was the Teapot Dome scandal, so named because of a teapot-shaped rock formation that dominated the landscape at a government oil reserve in Wyoming. Another oilfield at Elk Hills, California, was equally involved but is less remembered.

Believing World War I's ultimate weapon, the battleship, would need fuel to patrol the seas, the government bought oil lands and placed them under the Department of the Navy. Navy transferred them to Interior at the request of Secretary of the Interior Fall. Fall, in turn, leased them to two oilmen, Harry Sinclair and Edward Doheny, without competitive bids. The oilmen promised to build pipelines and storage tanks to deliver the oil to the fleet, including a base at Pearl Harbor. The arrangement made logistical sense and might have been acceptable had not Fall accepted bribes for the leases. Fall, eventually convicted of bribery, became the first member or former member of the cabinet to serve time, though only nine months. Tried by separate juries, Sinclair and Doheny were acquitted of bribing Fall, though Sinclair was convicted of contempt. The cases, handled by a special prosecutor, dragged on into the Coolidge administration.

Harding's reputation slid rapidly downward after Nan Britton, who claimed to be his mistress, published her memoirs in 1927. She described trysts in the Oval Office and the birth of a baby girl fathered by Harding.

Later, it was learned that Harding had a second affair, this one with Carrie Phillips, the wife of his best friend in Marion. Their romance cooled after Harding refused to leave his wife to marry her. Neither affair was known to the public during the president's lifetime. The sexual revolution had reached the White House.

What the public of the 1920s knew of Harding's administration, we now know, was the tip of the iceberg. The scandals repeated in history books through generations made Harding seem one of the most corrupt presidents in history. Yet it is more accurate to say that the Harding administration was corrupt than to label Harding himself financially corrupt. He was responsible for the deeds of those he appointed, of course, and if he did not know of their misdeeds, he should have. Still, Harding's greatest failure was neither personal corruption nor lack of intelligence. A unifier, a man who made friends easily, who won a huge popular victory in 1920, he failed as a politician. His loose-reined approach could not harness the wild horses he unloosed upon the national treasury.

"Silent Cal"

When Harding died, most politicians issued respectful condolences. However, Henry Cabot Lodge's first reaction was "My God, that means Coolidge is president!" Asked later what his first thought was, the new chief executive said, "I thought I could swing it." Lacking a dynamic personality and leadership qualities, Calvin Coolidge might not have been considered presidential timber, yet he possessed assets that politicians covet. Shrewd, cautious, lucky, and opportunistic, he gauged voters' attitudes as perceptively as any politician of his era. Nor was Coolidge lazy; his long afternoon naps were due to poor health, particularly stomach disorders, not lassitude. Known as "Silent Cal," he was reticent because of depression. The fear of death haunted his family. His mother died when he was twelve, his sister when he was fifteen; his stepmother died in 1920; and he lost his father and younger son while president. Coolidge was not as silent as some observers portrayed him, but he was shy and laconic. Unlike his immediate predecessor, it was impossible to suspect him of dishonesty; he was so frugal he quibbled about nickels.

An archetypical New Englander, Coolidge never truly felt that he left the green hills and stony soil of his native Vermont. Born in 1872 in the hamlet of Plymouth Notch, Coolidge worked on his father's farm and, after outgrowing the local school, went to a Ludlow boarding school and then Amherst College in Massachusetts, where he earned a Phi Beta Kappa key. He had few close friends and rarely participated in extracurricular activities. When Coolidge filled out a questionnaire asking seniors what they expected to do after graduation, he wrote, "Nothing, I reckon." Instead he settled in nearby Northampton and studied law. In the early 1890s he entered politics at the local level and became adept at winning elections, with an approach that included few promises. In 1905 he married the gregarious and witty Grace Goodhue, an unlikely pairing, as Grace was as spontaneous as her husband was reserved.

The public confidence he inspired enabled Coolidge to serve as mayor of Northampton, a member of the Massachusetts legislature, and lieutenant governor before becoming governor. As vice president, though, Coolidge became known as a quaint nonentity who spent much of his time attending banquets and delivering speeches. Asked why he attended so many dinners when he clearly did not enjoy socializing, he answered, "Got to eat somewhere." Grace Coolidge enjoyed telling stories about her spouse's reputation for silence, which the press reported in an effort to make him interesting. A reporter who sat with the Coolidges through a baseball game said that Coolidge spoke only once during nine innings, when he asked Grace, "What time is it?"

When Coolidge rose to the presidency, his surface calm charmed the country and reassured business. He rarely intervened in congressional affairs unless a crisis arose, and during his presidency there were few crises. So relatively tranquil was his tenure that near its end, when a woman asked Coolidge what had worried him most, he said, "The White House hams," explaining that he never found out what happened to the leftovers. Typically he followed a dictum he had laid down as governor: "A great many times if you let a situation alone, it takes care of itself." His program, was of limited governmental activity, in consonance with the times. Coolidge's liabilities, nevertheless, were substantial. He lacked vision, procrastinated, and ignored advice. Confronted with problems, he diverted conversations to irrelevancies. The chief executive did not understand the complexities of government, economics, or human relations, and he read superficially. He did not fathom the modern world and was largely ignorant of the vast, pluralistic nation over which he presided.

Philosophically, Coolidge was more conservative than Harding. To Coolidge, economy in government was a sacred principle; to Harding, it was expedient. In his first message to Congress after Harding died, Coolidge called for more cuts in taxes and spending, better race relations, aid for African American education, a constitutional amendment to restrict child labor, and a minimum wage for women. Like Harding, Coolidge did not lobby Congress to pass legislation, so only the tax and budget cuts were enacted. His first budget was just $3.3 billion, the lowest since World War I.

The Revenue Act of 1924 reduced income taxes to 2 percent on the first $4,000, from 4 percent; to 4 percent on the next $4,000, from 8 percent; and to 6 percent on the rest, from 8 percent. The maximum surtax was sliced from 50 to 40 percent and applied only to incomes greater than $500,000, up from $200,000. Despite the tax reductions, federal revenue increased, and Mellon continued retiring the national debt.

In his standpat posture and his disposal of the Harding scandals, Coolidge became a formidable candidate for a full term. No one mounted a serious challenge for the 1924 GOP nomination, and the president was selected on the first ballot. Coolidge did not choose a running mate, so delegates nominated Lowden, who declined, then chose Dawes, who accepted. In sharp contrast with the Republican conclave, the raucous Democratic convention, fittingly, took place in New York's Madison Square Garden, the site of many prizefights. The party was split between an urban, liberal wing that opposed Prohibition and a rural, conservative faction that favored it. Another polarizing issue was the Ku Klux Klan; a motion to condemn it in the platform failed narrowly. On the choice of a presidential nominee, the convention could not decide between New York Governor Al Smith and McAdoo, somewhat tainted because he was Doheny's attorney in the Teapot Dome scandal. Needing a two-thirds majority to nominate a candidate, the Democrats exhausted themselves by balloting endlessly. "This thing has got to come to an end," humorist Will Rogers wrote in his newspaper column. "New York invited you people here as guests, not to live." McAdoo offered to release his delegates to support his friend from Indiana, Senator Samuel Ralston, who declined because of poor health. Finally, on the 103rd ballot, the party nominated a compromise candidate, John W. Davis, a corporate lawyer from West Virginia who had served as a congressman and ambassador to Britain. His running mate was Nebraska Governor Charles W. Bryan, the younger brother of William Jennings Bryan.

Finding little reason to back Davis or Coolidge, some liberals supported Senator Robert M. La Follette, the Progressive Party candidate, who called for federal ownership of railroads and hydroelectric power and a constitutional amendment permitting Congress to override Supreme Court decisions. Most of La Follette's support came at Davis's expense; without his candidacy the Democrats would have posed a stronger threat to Coolidge. The Republicans' chief strengths were prosperity and that theirs was the majority party. Henry Ford expressed the views of many voters when he said: "The country is perfectly safe with Coolidge. Why change?"

Polls showed Coolidge leading throughout the campaign, helped by Republican spending that topped Democrats' almost 5 to 2. The result: the Coolidge-Dawes ticket won 382 electoral votes and 15.7 million popular votes, to 136 and 8.4 million for the Democrats, who carried only the South, and to 13 electoral votes for the Progressives. Further, the GOP won safe majorities in Congress.

The Economy According to Coolidge

Coolidge and Mellon continued to cut taxes and spending. The Revenue Act of 1926 reduced maximum inheritance and surtax rates to 20 percent (from 40 percent), repealed the gift tax, and raised personal exemptions. The income tax was lowered to 1.5 percent on the first $4,000 (from 4 percent) and to 5 percent on the rest (from 6 percent). The corporate income tax rose to 12.5 percent in 1926, up 0.5 of a percent, and to 13.5 percent the next year. The tax reductions were hailed, although farmers, who continued to languish, resented Coolidge for twice vetoing bills that would have provided agricultural price supports. Known as the McNary-Haugen plan, the legislation had been under consideration since the Harding administration. It would have set a high domestic price for agricultural products; the federal government would have bought surpluses and sold them abroad at a loss, to be compensated with a tax on food processing. Coolidge, however, was correct in pointing out that the plan would encourage farmers to produce more when overproduction was the reason prices were low. Production limits might have helped, but neither the government nor farmers were willing to require them. Farm unrest persisted, one reason the Republicans lost seats in the 1926 congressional elections.

Coolidge signed a bill providing $165 million to construct federal buildings despite curtailing most spending. He even pared a flood control appropriation to $500 million, from the $1.4 billion that Congress wanted, after a flood in the Ohio and Mississippi valley left two hundred people dead and 1.5 million homeless and caused millions of dollars in damages. Business expanded, with new products such as automobiles and electrical appliances flowing off assembly lines, prompting investment in stocks that seemed destined to rise. The paradox of such plenty was that the economy was overheating.

Almost all groups that benefited from Coolidge prosperity voted Republican in the 1920s. Women, who voted nationally for the first time in 1920, seem to have voted for Harding and Coolidge in about the same percentages as men. They voted much less than did men in the decade—about 74 percent of eligible males cast ballots, compared with only about 46 percent of eligible women—but steadily increased their political involvement as delegates to national party conventions. In 1920, ninety-six women were Democratic delegates (9 percent of the delegate total) and twenty-six were Republican delegates (2 percent); in 1928 the numbers had risen to 156 Democrats (14 percent) and seventy Republicans (6 percent), and the national committees of each party included women, including a vice chair. Women's officeholding for the decade peaked in 1928, when there were seven women in Congress, 131 in state legislatures, two heading state treasuries, and one woman serving as a state Supreme Court justice. Two women succeeded their husbands as governors.

Women were active in political clubs and pressure groups, including the League of Women Voters, the General Federation of Women's Clubs, the Women's Trade Union League, and the mostly female National Consumer's League. The smallest and most militant, the National Woman's Party led by Alice Paul, had eight thousand members. The party made its sole objective enactment of an Equal Rights Amendment to the Constitution, that would eliminate all discrimination against women as well as nullify laws giving them special protection. Many women's groups opposed the amendment, believing they would lose more from the abolition of protective laws than they would gain from an end to discrimination. Introduced in each session from 1923 through 1970, the amendment was never adopted. An amendment outlawing child labor, which the Women's Joint Congressional Committee and the National Child Labor Committee promoted, passed Congress, only to win ratification in just four states.

It was assumed that women would join men in reelecting Coolidge in 1928. The president, though, had grown ill in the White House, with an ailing stomach and heart, and his spirits waned after Calvin Jr.'s death from an infection in 1924. "When he went, the power and the glory of the presidency went with him," Coolidge said. The office had become a painful paradox for him, much as it had been for Harding. On vacation in August 1927, Coolidge issued a statement that was enigmatic in its brevity: "I do not choose to run for President in 1928," he said, without elaboration. Enjoying inscrutability, he had consulted no one about his decision, not even his wife, who learned of it from a senator.

Coolidge has been maligned for inaction while the economy hurtled toward the stock market crash in 1929. Many of what appeared his virtues in the 1920s were viewed as vices in the 1930s, yet it must be remembered that in the 1920s there was no demand for a New Deal—and that after 1929 there was no demand for a lackadaisical president. Coolidge was fortunate to have retired from presidential politics when he did, for if he had won in 1928, he, and not his successor, Hoover, would have been blamed for the Great Depression.

Coolidge retired to Northampton, never again to participate actively in politics. His health failing, he sometimes sat on his front porch and watched motorists drive by to look at a former president in his rocking chair. Asked if he was pleased to see so many cars, he answered: "Not as many as yesterday. Yesterday there were 163 of them."

Hoover from Triumph to Tragedy

With Coolidge's withdrawal, Hoover became the leading Republican candidate and won the 1928 nomination on the first ballot; delegates chose Kansas Senator Charles Curtis as his running mate. Using words that would be ironic in depression America, Hoover said in his acceptance speech: "We in America today are nearer to the final triumph over poverty than ever before in the history of the land. The poorhouse is vanishing from among us. We shall soon with the help of God be in sight of the day when poverty is banished from this nation." Of course, at the time, such optimism was widely shared. The GOP claimed credit for prosperity, and Hoover's background inspired faith that the nominee would preside over good times.

A native of West Branch, Iowa, Hoover was the first president from west of the Mississippi River. Only Abraham Lincoln's birthplace was more humble than his. Orphaned in childhood and raised by relatives in Oregon, Hoover did not regularly attend high school, but enrolled in the first class of Stanford University. There, he was an outstanding student because of his ability to organize, raise money, and serve others. Graduating with a degree in geological engineering in 1895, he eventually joined an English mining firm that sent him to Australia, then to China. With a reputation for good judgment and dealing effectively with difficult people, Hoover managed international mining operations for thirteen years, becoming a millionaire by forty.

Hoover's wife, Lou Henry, was Stanford's first female graduate in geological engineering. After marriage, Lou devoted herself to her husband, two sons, volunteer work, outdoor activities, and writing. Never a political activist, she did not work outside the home, except for volunteer activities such as the Girl Scouts of America.

When World War I broke out, Hoover, in London, aided Americans stranded in Europe, helping some pay passage to the United States with his own money. In one of the great humanitarian endeavors in history, he fed Belgium, trapped between German occupation and the British blockade. Once the United States entered the war, Hoover, as food administrator under Wilson, fed America and Europe. Following the armistice, he spent eight years as commerce secretary, among the most creative cabinet tenures in memory. Hoover distinguished himself in alleviating the great Mississippi flood of 1927, supervising rescue work, refugee care, and rehabilitation, and helping enact the Mississippi Flood Control Act of 1928.

HOOVER AND
HOLLYWOOD
Actress Mary Pickford
gives President Hoover
a ticket for a film industry
benefit for the unem-
ployed, 1931.
(Herbert Hoover
Presidential Library)

Hoover's Democratic foe in 1928, Al Smith, was another rags-to-riches story. Smith was born in the shadow of the Brooklyn Bridge, as quintessentially urban as Hoover was rural—so provincially eastern that he thought Wisconsin was east of Lake Michigan and asked, while traveling through the prairies, "What do people do out here?" His East Side accent and his nervous fidgeting made him ineffective on radio, although he was witty in person. Unlike Hoover, Smith was a seasoned politician who rose through the ranks of Tammany Hall as state assemblyman, sheriff of New York, and president of the Board of Aldermen. He championed equal pay for women teachers, better health care for the disabled, and adequate appropriations for public education; he reorganized and consolidated state government and revamped welfare. Paradoxically, Smith later opposed programs on the national level similar to his innovations on the state level, and his closest ally in the 1928 campaign, Franklin D. Roosevelt, became his most bitter rival. As paradoxical a figure as Hoover, Smith reflected the complexities of changing times.

The first major party Catholic presidential nominee, Smith found religious prejudice an obstacle. "If this man Smith is elected, the pope is going to come over here with all his wives and concubines and live in the White

House and run the country," a Delaware man said. What hindered Smith most, however, was Republican prosperity. Almost any GOP candidate would have defeated Smith. Hoover polled 21.4 million popular votes and 444 electoral votes to Smith's 15 million and 87; Republicans also increased their majorities in the House by 30 seats, to a margin of 100, and in the Senate by 7, to a margin of 17.

The new chief executive planned to provide stronger leadership than Coolidge, yet he cautioned admirers that he was no magician. In terms that ring ironic, Hoover said, "If some unprecedented calamity should come upon the nation I would be sacrificed to the unreasoning disappointment of a people who expected too much." Hoover did expect much of himself, working seven days a week without diversion, becoming the first president to have a telephone on his desk, mothballing the White House yacht, and closing the White House stables.

On the activist side of his ledger, Hoover supported civil rights, entertained an African American in the White House, addressed Congress on lynching, appointed more African Americans to middle-level jobs than did Harding and Coolidge combined, launched a program to reduce black illiteracy, and devised a plan to give sharecroppers money to purchase land. Also, he undertook prison reform, designed plans for child care and protection, upgraded the condition of Indians, and restricted oil drilling on public lands. A conservationist who spent much of his early life in the outdoors, the president increased the National Park Service budget 46 percent in two years and added 2 million acres to national forests. He planned inland waterways and the St. Lawrence Seaway. His appointments to the Supreme Court were distinguished—Charles Evans Hughes, Benjamin Cardozo, and Owen Roberts. On the debit side, Hoover failed to publicize his achievements. He was not adept at getting bills enacted, and achieved his most significant accomplishments through executive order instead of legislation. A better administrator than a politician, he expected lawmakers to accept his proposals because they were logical, not politically expedient. The president misfired with one of his high court nominees, John J. Parker, whom the Senate rejected after unions and African Americans opposed him. In ordinary times he might have been an above average chief executive, but after the first six months of his term, times were no longer ordinary.

The Stock Market Crash and
Onset of the Great Depression

A speculative land boom in Florida in 1925 and 1926 preceded the bull market that gave way to the 1929 stock market crash. Land values soared far above the worth of the properties, only to collapse after the market grew saturated. From the episode, investors learned little. During the decade too much money was borrowed for stock speculation, and share prices were pushed artificially high. Imprudently, bankers entered the market, speculating with depositors' money; corporations lent money to brokers, discovering that lending was more profitable than investment in productivity. Brokers, the agents for stock buyers and sellers, lent money to people to purchase shares, a practice that worked well only when stocks went up, facilitating repayment. Nationwide there were probably not even 1 million speculators, although they wielded a consequence beyond their numbers, soaking up capital, dominating the news and culture, and feeding the notion of easy riches for grab.

Booms, obviously, always end, whether from a deliberate decline at an early point or from a cataclysmic crash later. Hoover said he considered values inflated and speculation risky, disposed of some of his stocks, and asked newspapers and magazines to tone down statements that encouraged market players. But no one in authority appreciated the dimensions of the danger, signaled in a stock market that trickled, then gushed downhill in September. Next month came the deluge. On the morning of "Black Thursday," October 24, prices staggered on the New York Stock Exchange, a slide halted only when bankers tried to soothe investors' nerves and bought millions in major stocks. The plunge could not be arrested for long, and on "Black Tuesday," October 29, an unprecedented 16.4 million shares were traded at shockingly low prices, summarized the next day in a *Variety* headline, "WALL STREET LAYS AN EGG." In a few weeks the market lost $30 billion, equal to the U.S. expenditures in World War I and almost twice the national debt. By the end of November the market saw $100 billion vanish.

The crash would not have led inexorably to a depression if consumers had been able to keep buying the products pouring forth from factories and farms. Yet given an overproducing economy, depression would have arrived sometime, even without the crash. Backlogs of merchandise accumulated, and as orders slowed manufacturers cut production and laid off workers. International trade could not alleviate the surplus, for when the 1930 Hawley-Smoot Tariff raised rates, foreign nations erected walls against American imports. The conditions that led to the depression evolved from World War I, which undermined European economies, saddled them with huge debt, and created a large temporary demand for American goods. In Europe, democracy shuddered. The German dictator Adolf Hitler spellbound his nation behind programs of nationalism, racism, and militarism, like Benito Mussolini in Italy. Paradox carved a canyon through the Era of Trial and Triumph: world war helped trigger a depression that led to another world war that ultimately ended the depression.

Back home, merchants desperately cut prices, accelerating deflation, which was problematic for those who owed money, particularly farmers, because they had to repay debts in dollars more valuable than those they had borrowed. Businesses and banks toppled. That people could not consume all that industry and agriculture produced was in part a result of an inequitable distribution of wealth. Almost everyone enjoyed a rising standard of living in the 1920's, but the rich had grown richer faster than the poor had become less poor. During the decade real wages increased 13 percent, whereas returns to industry grew 70 percent; in 1926, 1 percent of the people owned 60 percent of the wealth; and one year later, two hundred of the largest corporations controlled more than 44 percent of all business assets. Companies gobbled up others with impunity, creating monopolies, fixing prices, and cowing labor. Trade associations contributed to vast oligopolies, stifling competition and fixing prices. Banks incorporated investment affiliates that made irresponsible investments with depositors' money. Trusts and holding companies were created to exploit investors. Such concentrated wealth diminished consuming power, made the economy dependent upon the sale of luxuries, and encouraged speculation. Money that might have gone into wages and salaries was invested in stocks and bonds, bloating the market. Employee productivity, spurred by technological advances, outpaced the rate of pay increases, so producing power exceeded consuming power. The wage scale was lowered further, and unemployment was swelled, when farmers who had failed at agriculture, sought industrial jobs. Credit purchases mitigated some of the disparity, yet loans had to be repaid, requiring saving that necessitated a decline in consumption. High taxes on imports provoked retaliation against American imports, hobbling international trade.

As the economy spiraled downward, so did Americans' faith in capitalism, in democracy, in themselves. Unprecedented because of the magnitude of the depression, the panic ushered in an atmosphere in which industrialists were afraid to invest and consumers were afraid to buy. Money was hoarded and demand kept plunging. The federal government, whose policies had done much to bring on the economic peril and, hence, low morale, might have helped prevent depression via stricter business regulation, higher taxes on the wealthy, and encouragement of labor organization. It would have taken remarkable political will and vision to adopt the necessary actions, however, and no presidential aspirant or Congress was likely to advocate them. Production controls and price supports that might have assisted farmers, for example, had been proposed, and not enacted, because farmers opposed them.

Misery was pervasive. Unemployment, the most conspicuous sign of the depression, rose from about 2 million in 1929 to a range of 13 to 14 million in 1932; from 1930 to 1940, the average jobless rate only once dipped

★ SAMUEL INSULL: NAPOLEON ABDICATES ★

With him—to the top and then to the bottom—went hundreds of thousands
of stockholders who shared his faith in his own invulnerability.
—FORREST MCDONALD, INSULL'S BIOGRAPHER

EMPIRE OF ELECTRICITY
Utility magnate Samuel Insull.
(Library of Congress)

AT HIS PINNACLE in 1929, Samuel Insull reigned over
a $2.5 billion Midwest-based utility empire that
encompassed six thousand power plants in thirty-nine
states. The magnate's companies furnished nearly one-
eighth of the electric power in the country and had 1 million investors; his securities, people swore, were safer
than government bonds. His personal fortune was $150
million, and he lived in a mansion that had gold-plated
bathroom fixtures. His estate had the nation's only post
office on private property. The most powerful man in his
home area of Chicago, he was once told that he was practically as powerful as Napoleon. Insull sneered, "Napoleon
was only a soldier." Insull's wife had a different view:
"Sam, you should learn about that man and what happened to him. If you don't, that's what's going to happen
to you." Her warning was prescient, for her husband, like
the French emperor, brought about his downfall because he extended his empire
beyond his resources to control it.

Insull came to the United States from England at twenty-one to become private
secretary to Thomas Edison. An organizational wizard, he took over the Chicago
Edison Company, then absorbed competitors and created holding companies to build
five corporate systems with more than 150 subsidiaries. The financing defied comprehension—ultimately perhaps even Insull's. Acquiring properties for inflated prices,
he issued overvalued stocks against them and siphoned profits from operating companies into holding companies.

Unfortunately, after the 1929 stock market crash, the profits dried up, and Insull,
like a juggler juggling too many balls, could not control his vast corporate structure.
In a dramatic illustration of depression tragedy, his companies collapsed—the largest
business failure in history. His investors lost $750 million. Insull retreated, quit every
one of his corporate offices, and became "too broke to be bankrupt." Later, he
recouped enough to live on. A conquering hero during the apogee of business in the
1920s, he became a villain, a betrayer, because his stockholders went down with him.

Vilified by politicians who held him up as an archetype of business corruption,
pursued by creditors and the law, Insull fled to Europe in 1932, prepared to remain

abroad until the American mood mellowed enough to allow him a fair trial. "Why am I not more popular in the United States?" he wondered. "What have I done that every banker and business magnate has not done in the course of business?" Proposing to answer him, the government extradited Insull from Turkey in 1934 to face charges of fraud and embezzlement. Three times he stood trial in Chicago; three times he won acquittal. But the American public never forgave Insull, and he spent most of his remaining life in Paris. He did leave America a legacy, however, by provoking an outcry that resulted in New Deal financial reforms, the Tennessee Valley Authority, and the Rural Electrification Association.

Insull was found on a Paris subway platform on July 16, 1938, killed by a heart attack at age seventy-nine, with only eighty-five cents. Like others of the Era of Trial and Triumph, Insull found that money purchased notoriety and power, yet the long-term price was stress and humiliation. The Great Depression did not play favorites.

Sources: Samuel Insull's biography is Forrest McDonald, *Insull* (1962). Edward Robb Ellis, *A Nation in Torment* (1970), contains a useful, shorter treatment of his career. Arthur M. Schlesinger Jr., *The Age of Roosevelt*, vol. 1, *The Crisis of the Old Order, 1919–1933* (1957), is also helpful.

below 8 million, in 1937. At times, 25 percent of the workforce was without employment. Labor income declined from $50 billion in 1929 to $29 billion in 1933, gross farm income from $12 billion in 1929 to 5.3 billion in 1932, corporate income from an $8.7 billion profit in 1929 to a $5.6 billion deficit in 1932, and national income from $81.1 billion to $40 billion. Farm income dived 20 percent in 1930 and 30 percent the next year. People wandered among breadlines and soup kitchens. Men lived in sewer pipes in Oakland, California, in shacks in Central Park in New York, and in squalid shantytowns called "Hoovervilles." The president's name was seized for other grim symbols: "Hoover hogs" were rabbits that farmers shot for food; "Hoover flags" were empty pockets turned inside out. Weddings were postponed, husbands deserted families, and evictions multiplied. The home of a Chicago municipal worker was auctioned off because he was $34 in arrears in city taxes; meanwhile, the city owed him $850 in unpaid salary. Schoolchildren were undernourished and fatigued, in no condition to learn.

With surpluses on their hands, northwestern farmers gave apples on credit to unemployed men, who tried to sell them for a nickel apiece with the slogan, "Buy an apple a day and eat the depression away"; in 1930, there were six thousand apple peddlers on New York streets. "Apple sellers crouched at the street corners like half-remembered sins sitting upon the conscience of the town," a Manhattan reporter wrote. While millions hungered in cities or wore ragged clothes, crops that could not be sold rotted in the countryside. Compounding the despair, in 1930 the worst drought in history parched the Missouri Valley. As animals died from the lack of fodder, Hoover provided feed, provoking the caustic criticism that he fed cattle, not people. The rich, too, felt the depression—the Rockefeller fortune shrank to one-fifth its precrash size—but some of the privileged did not comprehend the anguish of the poor. One of the Du Ponts, asked to advertise his products on Sunday afternoon radio, objected, "At three o'clock on Sunday afternoons everybody is playing polo."

Marshaling the financial and moral resources of the nation, Hoover displayed unprecedented activism. Unlike previous chief executives, he was unwilling to trust the economic cycle alone to bring recovery. He tried to persuade those who could afford it to open their pocketbooks. He obtained pledges from industrialists not to cut wages or dismiss workers and promises from union leaders not to strike. Hoover hoped that private charity, supplemented by local action, could provide effective, decentralized relief, but he believed that states and the federal government should intervene if necessary. "I insisted that the first obligation of direct relief rested on local communities, and that they should not call upon the state and federal governments until the load overtaxed their capacities." Hoover urged the Red Cross to feed the hungry, yet the charity rejected federal aid, as did forty-seven governors, including Franklin D. Roosevelt of New York. As the depression deepened, Hoover, government, and charities began to change their minds about government involvement. But after privation appeared intractable, politicians and the public turned on Hoover for clinging to views they had shared earlier.

As the depression deepened, Hoover moved more slowly than the public desired, yet he was far from inactive. At the president's request, Congress appropriated $800 million and reduced taxes by $160 million to stimulate spending and investment. Hoover also created a pool of money contributed by bankers to provide loans to businesses, yet the $500 million fund was insufficient. Then he submitted a bill, enacted, creating the Reconstruction Finance Corporation (RFC) to aid exports, stimulate employment, and lend money to agricultural cooperatives, banks, railroads, and manufacturers. The RFC became a mainstay of the New Deal under Hoover's successor, Roosevelt. Hoover and Congress additionally established Home Loan Discount Banks to enable banks to borrow from the federal government, using mortgages they held as collateral. With such resources available, banks could avoid foreclosures. As for farmers, the Agriculture Marketing Act of 1929, enacted before the stock market crash, provided for the Federal Farm Board, which promoted voluntary acreage controls and lent money to

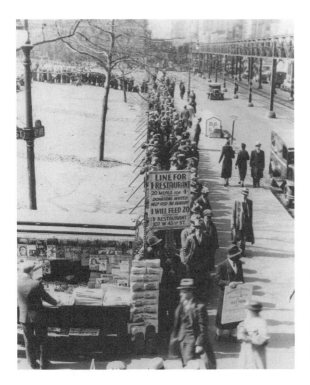

WAITING FOR
THE DEPRESSION
TO END
A breadline in New
York City, 1932.
(Franklin D. Roosevelt
Presidential Library)

cooperatives. Stabilization corporations were set up to buy grain, cotton, and other commodities to sustain prices. Failing to generate farm prosperity, the board at least preserved price levels until 1931, and without it the prices of 1932 would have been lower.

To boost business morale, Hoover believed he must protect the gold standard. Gold was flowing abroad because creditors redeemed securities for gold, considering gold safer than paper money. It appeared that the Treasury might exhaust its gold supply, creating more panic. Yet certain kinds of "eligible" paper, besides gold, backed dollars, and by increasing the eligible paper, the gold drain might be stemmed and the gold standard preserved. Legislation containing such provisions was enacted as the Glass-Steagall Act of 1932. The act liberalized Federal Reserve requirements for collateral, making more member banks eligible for loans and, thus, making more credit available to business. Seeking to boost the economy, Hoover also planned more public works than any of his predecessors. By the end of his term, 360 public structures had been completed and 460 were under construction. His administration began or completed buildings for the city of Washington: the Supreme Court; the Commerce, Labor, and Justice departments; the Post Office; the Interstate Commerce Commission; and the National Archives, as well as additions to the House and Senate buildings. Hoover's program was plausible, and his opponents offered no feasible alternative. Raymond Moley and Rexford Tugwell, advisers to FDR, wrote in their memoirs that many of the New Deal programs were borrowed from Hoover's ideas. Under Hoover, the United States weathered the early years of the depression more successfully than much of the Western world, and the nation's institutions remained intact.

Hoover's greatest failure lay in public relations. He could not inspire, lacked communication skills, and could be stubborn and self-righteous. He was accustomed to getting his way. Persuasive before small groups, Hoover was less effective with the masses and with Congress. His approach seemed inflexible and uncaring. Hoover reinforced this image by refusing to show his empathy, which was real, deep, and intellectually honest. The opposition caricatured him as stubborn and hard-hearted, and Hoover, the "fighting Quaker," did not strike back. Hoover was imaginative and a skilled administrator, yet what he needed was the magic of an alchemist. A tragedy for millions, the Great Depression was a personal humiliation for Hoover. Sandwiched between Coolidge prosperity and the frenetic pace of the New Deal, the Hoover administration is sometimes dismissed as a time when nothing happened, or when only bad things happened. Such was not the case.

"I Pledge . . . A New Deal"

Believing that the economy was improving in 1932, Hoover felt he had to run to vindicate his administration. The Republicans, who had reaped the harvest of prosperity, now were trapped in the whirlwind that swept it away. Regardless, the Hoover-Curtis team was renominated because the GOP was not prepared to repudiate incumbents. Democratic hopefuls knew Hoover was vulnerable, and competition for their presidential nomination was avid. The candidates included Al Smith and House Speaker John Nance Garner, yet the front-runner was New York Governor Franklin D. Roosevelt. Garner helped break a log jam, giving Roosevelt the nomination, and was named his running mate. Breaking tradition by flying to the Chicago convention to accept the nomination, FDR said, "I pledge you, I pledge myself, to a new deal for the American people." A cartoonist highlighted the phrase "new deal" the next day, establishing the term for Roosevelt's program.

Like Hoover, Roosevelt was a millionaire, a protégé of Woodrow Wilson's, an opponent of federal relief, and an advocate of a balanced budget. In temperament the candidates were a striking contrast, for FDR was more gregarious, eloquent, and optimistic. If Roosevelt appeared too eager to please, indecisive, and superficial, "all clay and no granite," as Felix Frankfurter said, he had courage that at least matched Hoover's and had overcome polio as the Republican had overcome poverty. People had overestimated Hoover's potential for the presidency in 1928, and they underestimated Roosevelt's four years afterward.

In the deepest irony, neither presidential nominee made the Depression the chief issue of the campaign. Rather, they talked more about peripheral issues, such as Prohibition, with Roosevelt considered somewhat stronger for repeal. Still, there was a drama that enlivened the campaign, outraged the public, and damaged the Republican. In the summer of 1932, some twenty-two thousand impoverished World War I veterans, dubbed the "Bonus Expeditionary Force" or the "Bonus Army," descended on Washington to seek payment of a bonus for their service. The veterans were paid $1 a day during the war, while shipyard workers' earned $90 per week, an inequity that Congress redressed by enacting over Coolidge's veto in 1925 a bill to credit each veteran with additional money, cashable in twenty years. Thirteen years ahead of the payoff, the veterans assembled to lobby for a measure that would provide it immediately.

Showing some care for the Bonus Army, Hoover supplied the Washington police chief, Pelham Glassford, with food, eating utensils, and tents for the veterans, many of whom camped in Anacostia Flats, on the outskirts of the District of Columbia. Many Washingtonians, though, were alarmed over the veterans' presence, and Hoover refused to meet with the protest leaders, fearing that such a course would encourage disorder. Confounding his apprehensions for the moment, the men assembled peaceably to learn that the repayment bill failed in the Senate, sang "God Bless America," then returned to their camps. But Glassford was ordered to evict veterans who had occupied abandoned federal buildings scheduled for demolition. Ironically, new public buildings, designed to stimulate employment, were to be built on the site. Glassford warned there might be violence during the eviction, and there was. Two veterans died.

Fearing a combustible situation, Hoover ordered the army to drive the veterans out of town while leaving their camps intact and persuaded Congress to appropriate $100,000 to pay for train fare home. General Douglas MacArthur directed troops in dispersing the veterans over the objections of a junior officer, Dwight D. Eisenhower; in the resulting tumult, a brick struck another of MacArthur's subordinates, George S. Patton. Preceded by tanks and tear gas, soldiers with fixed bayonets evicted the Bonus Army from the city. MacArthur then directed his charges to defy Hoover's orders and cross the Anacostia Bridge to destroy the veterans'

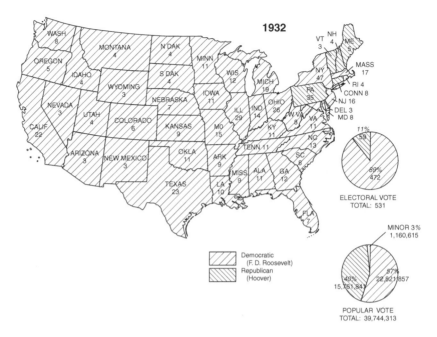

Election of 1932

Camp Anacostia, which was burned; a few veterans resisted, most fled. Hoover worsened the situation by not reprimanding MacArthur.

The electorate chose Roosevelt, even though it did not know exactly what to expect from the Democrat, who polled 22.8 million popular votes and 472 electoral votes to 15.8 million and 59 for Hoover. Socialist Norman Thomas led the minor candidates with more than 872,000 popular votes. Uncertainty grew between the election and the inauguration in March 1933. The depression reached its nadir as banks failed and businesses closed, declines that Hoover blamed on Roosevelt, reasoning that the country had more to fear from an incoming president than an outgoing one. Already some people detested Roosevelt. On February 15 in Miami, Giuseppe Zangara, who hated the privileged and who had tried to assassinate the Italian king, fired a pistol at FDR. Zangara's aim was deflected, but he killed Chicago Mayor Anton Cermak, who was accompanying Roosevelt.

It was left to Roosevelt to do what Hoover could not. If he succeeded, a friend told him, he would go down in history as the greatest American president, and if he failed, he would be known as the worst. Roosevelt turned grim. "If I fail," he said, "I shall be the last one."

CHAPTER NINE

Franklin D. Roosevelt and the New Deal

F RANKLIN D. ROOSEVELT seemed as much a paradox as the New Deal he inspired. Born wealthy, he became a champion of the underdog. Handicapped by polio, he became the greatest politician of the twentieth century. He dominated the last half of the Era of Trial and Triumph as few Americans have dominated an epoch, before or since. In Roosevelt's era, it was the government, not rebellious, bootleg-guzzling flappers, that made the noise.

A Presidential Temperament

Descended from the old Dutch aristocracy of New York State, Franklin Delano Roosevelt was the only child of James Roosevelt, a railroad executive and businessman, and Sara Delano, also of an aristocratic family. Young Franklin met some of the nation's most famous people, including President Grover Cleveland, who made a wish for him: that the boy would never suffer the ordeal of becoming president. Roosevelt's first presidential vote, in 1904, was for his distant cousin, Theodore Roosevelt. Theodore's niece, Eleanor Roosevelt, was Franklin's fifth cousin and fiancée. Uncle Theodore gave away the bride when the couple wed in 1905.

After compiling mediocre academic records at Groton prep school and Harvard, Roosevelt enrolled at the Columbia University law school, but failed two courses and did not graduate. He learned enough to pass the New York State bar exam and through family influence was hired for a position with a Wall Street firm. His political allegiance wavered until a Democratic delegation, intending to take advantage of his name, asked him to run for the state legislature. The novice politician won an upset victory

THE FIRST LADY SPEAKS OUT
Eleanor Roosevelt at a WPA site in Des Moines, Iowa, in 1936.
(Franklin D. Roosevelt Presidential Library)

in a Republican district in 1910. In the assembly, Roosevelt achieved a reputation as a reformer. He soon moved from Albany to Washington. Roosevelt supported Woodrow Wilson for the 1912 Democratic presidential nomination and then became his assistant navy secretary. Franklin's career survived his affair with Lucy Page Mercer, Eleanor's social secretary. The Roosevelts did not divorce, but their marriage became one of respect without physical intimacy. Politically, Eleanor was more interested in racial justice and feminism than was her husband.

In 1920, FDR lost as Democratic vice presidential nominee to the Harding ticket. Soon afterward, Roosevelt caught polio, was paralyzed from the waist down, and never walked unaided again. Physical adversity strengthened him, teaching him patience, perseverance, and empathy. Retiring from political candidacy while striving to regain use of his legs, Roosevelt nominated his mentor, Al Smith, for president in 1924. Four years later Smith won the Democratic nomination, yet lost the election to a world-famous figure, Herbert Hoover. Roosevelt was elected governor of New York. After the stock market crashed in 1929, FDR practiced retrenchment and rejected federal aid. As the economy spiraled downward, however, Roosevelt developed a program that made New York one of the first states to provide public relief.

Following his election to the presidency in 1932, Roosevelt visited former Supreme Court Justice Oliver Wendell Holmes to celebrate the famed jurist's ninety-second birthday. "A second-class intellect. But a first-class temperament," Holmes declared of FDR. The assessment hit the mark. Roosevelt was not a deep thinker, although he had an above average mind, good judgment, and common sense. Although he had attended elite schools, he never immersed himself in government theory, preferring as president to surround himself with intellectuals and borrow ideas from them. Neither religious nor inquisitive about theological or philosophical questions, he possessed a sense of command that enabled him to deal on even terms with the world's best minds and most powerful leaders. He was confident, tough, and inspirational, eloquent in person and via radio. Roosevelt assembled a gallery of gifted speechwriters. The new president perceived the depression as a problem of morale, politics, and economics.

FDR had faced adversity before. "If you had spent two years in bed trying to wiggle your big toe, after that anything else would seem easy." His optimism inspired Winston Churchill to remark, "Meeting him is like opening a bottle of champagne." Roosevelt was an innovator and a pragmatist who relied on trial-and-error. He could boldly gamble, lose, and raise the stakes for the next hand. A man who had risen above a crippling disease was not easily intimidated; he only half-joked that if he was a pure guesser he would be right half the time. And the president was a man of action who enjoyed political battles and had huge Democratic majorities in Congress to work with.

Although he was born to an elitist family, had never experienced poverty and had no poor friends, Roosevelt connected with the indigent. In the Denver freight yards, a hobo scrawled in chalk, "Roosevelt is my friend." From his own class, the social stratum that produced plutocrats, Roosevelt elicited a different reaction, in which he was considered a dictator who was browbeating the country to ruin. He was no dictator, but a resourceful politician. His cabinet reflected all political views and regions and Roosevelt dominated it. Labor Secretary Frances Perkins became the first woman cabinet member. Outside the cabinet, FDR relied upon a group of intellectuals called the "Brains Trust."

THE SECRET
LIFE OF FDR
A rare photo of
Franklin D. Roosevelt
in a wheelchair.
(Franklin D. Roosevelt
Presidential Library)

The Hundred Days and the First New Deal

In his inaugural speech, FDR echoed Hoover's belief that the chief problem was psychological, predicting, "The only thing we have to fear is fear itself." He said he would not hesitate to use executive power to fight poverty—as if it were a military enemy. That evening, the new administration, with the aid of officials from Hoover's cabinet, worked late to address the banking crisis. Across the nation banks were shutting down while depositors lost their money. Hoover had sought from Roosevelt a joint resolution closing the banks but the incoming chief executive had declined. Now he had no choice. Twenty-two states had closed their banks. FDR declared a temporary banking holiday, during which Americans resorted to barter and credit. Instead of panic, there was relief.

To pass banking legislation, FDR summoned a special session of Congress. Roosevelt cracked the whip and Congress snapped to attention. Bills roared forth. The Emergency Banking Act passed the first day. Many of those who voted for it did not have the time to read it. The bill allowed for a federal audit of banks, classified them according to their stability, and permitted them to reopen on a phased-in basis; 75 percent were cleared to open on the first day. No one knew whether there would be a run on the banks when they reopened, yet before the reopening, Roosevelt delivered his first radio address, termed an informal "fireside chat," to persuade depositors the banks were safe. When the banks opened, $10 million more was deposited than withdrawn.

Roosevelt's next proposal, the Economy Bill, intended to help balance the federal budget by cutting government salaries by $100 million and veterans' pensions by $400 million, was unpopular. Later the president would be pushed, reluctantly, into deficit spending, which he considered a tool to be used only during economic decline. During his first term, however, he wanted to save money. Despite the opposition of most Democrats, who criticized the plan as deflationary, it passed because House Republicans favored it. Roosevelt also introduced a popular bill permitting the sale of beer and wine. Adopted swiftly, the Beer and Wine Revenue Act was an interim measure to legalize light alcohol while the states were ratifying the Twenty-First Amendment, approved by the previous Congress, to repeal the Eighteenth.

Roosevelt decided to use the momentum from his successes to keep legislators in Washington to deal with the depression. Lawmakers remained three months, a span known as the Hundred Days, the most productive New Deal session. With no program ready, FDR improvised. Asked to define his plans, he compared himself to a quarterback in a football game: the quarterback knows what the next play will be, yet beyond that, he cannot plan too rigidly because future plays will depend on how the next one works.

The New Deal orchestra sounded like a cacophony of contradictions. Indeed, it evolved without a grand design, precipitated by political necessity. Some programs were undermined by others. The ideological jumble did not bother Roosevelt. Congress complied, giving extraordinary authority on the chief executive and shifting the balance of power from the states to the federal government. Democratic majorities, coupled with divided Republicans who had no alternatives to FDR's bills, eased passage of the measures. Nevertheless, Congress shaped the president's program. Most bills did not emerge exactly as the administration drafted them, and some ideas originated in Congress.

One of the first bills Congress enacted addressed unemployment, the Civilian Conservation Corps (CCC), created to employ young men in semimilitary camps located in national forests and parks to plant trees, control erosion, and construct recreational facilities. By 1936 the CCC had employed some 1.6 million men. They planted more trees than had been planted in the entire previous history of the United States. Embraced by the public, the corps lasted until World War II. Also aimed at unemployment, the Federal Emergency Relief Administration (FERA) distributed money to cities and states to provide work.

Harry Hopkins, the FERA leader, helped persuade Roosevelt to implement a more ambitious policy to help the destitute through the harsh winter of 1933–1934. The New Deal created the Civil Works Administration (CWA), the first all-federal program focusing on job relief. Hopkins spent nearly $1 billion to employ 4 million workers before the CWA was terminated in the spring of 1934. The jobs included building and repairing roads, developing parks, digging sewers, and refurbishing neighborhoods. Given Hopkins's emphases on putting people to work and pumping spending power into the economy, some of the jobs amounted to no more than raking leaves, yet they provided income to those who performed them.

Whereas Hopkins's efforts were aimed at furnishing wages, the Home Owners Loan Act was intended to save homes from foreclosures. Commercial banks were allowed to use mortgages as collateral for government loans, effectively making the government the holder of the mortgages. The government had superior resources to individual banks and less urgency to foreclose. Banks and other businesses benefited from a revitalized Reconstruction Finance Corporation that distributed as much money as all of the work-relief programs.

Addressing the meager income of farmers—a primary cause of the depression, the Agricultural Adjustment Act (AAA) tried to adjust production to consumption. The AAA paid farmers to limit production in order to eliminate their surplus. Induced scarcity would raise prices. Money to pay farmers came from a tax on food processing. Because the agency was not organized until May 1933, after spring planting, about one-fourth of the cotton crop was plowed under and 6 million pigs were slaughtered before reaching maturity. A limited success, the AAA helped reduce deflation, yet it did not eliminate overproduction. Gross farm income rose from $4 billion in 1932 to $6 billion in 1936, but not until 1941 did income reach the 1929 level. Also, more cotton was produced in 1933 than in 1932, despite destruction of part of the crop; and higher domestic prices for cotton and wheat diminished the export market. Surpluses would have been greater if not for a severe drought in the South and West from 1932 to 1936, which dried out fields. The "Dust Bowl" destroyed crops and animals from Texas to the Dakotas. Thousands of farmers abandoned their land to seek work elsewhere, many in California. "Noon was like night," a train conductor said of the Dust Bowl. "There was no sun, and at times, it was impossible to see a yard." Dust blew as far east as the White House.

The AAA, which the Supreme Court declared unconstitutional in 1936, hurt sharecroppers and tenants because they saw nothing of the government checks that went to farmers who owned the land. Higher prices for crops pinched consumers, particularly those on fixed incomes. Because most farmers were in debt and had to borrow money to live until the next harvest, some hoped inflated dollars might relieve their hardship. Oklahoma Senator Elmer Thomas introduced an amendment to the AAA giving the president authority to provide inflation by coining silver, issuing paper currency, and devaluing the dollar. Roosevelt supported the amendment to avert more radical inflationary schemes, then used his authority to take the country off the gold standard.

The New Deal also helped rural people by creation of the Tennessee Valley Authority (TVA), an experiment to develop the Tennessee River basin in Tennessee, Alabama, Kentucky, and other states. Federal agencies implemented programs of flood control, soil conservation, tree planting, production of fertilizer and explosives, development of recreational facilities, and generation of electric power. The agency encountered opposition from businessmen, because the TVA competed with private utilities and used its cost of generating electricity as a yardstick to determine whether independent companies charged fair rates.

A plan to invigorate industry under the National Industrial Recovery Act (NIRA), the most complex legislation ever submitted, involved a government-business partnership. Again FDR embraced the scheme to avert a more radical remedy. Alabama Senator Hugo Black, for example, wanted to revive the economy by limiting the workweek to thirty hours without decreasing wages.

Based on the idea that ruthless competition was destructive, the law established a National Recovery Administration (NRA). Each industry drafted codes of fair competition, including maximum hours and minimum wages, elimination of duplication, and, in some cases, price fixing (the president could exempt industries from antitrust prosecution). Section 7(a) of the law ensured unions the right of collective bargaining but made no distinction between company unions and independent unions. Because the law provided no means of enforcing codes, the NRA director, General Hugh S. Johnson, resorted to social pressure, employing parades and mass rallies, publicizing the motto "We do our part" and featuring a blue eagle emblem for cooperating businesses. Patriotic consumers were supposed to patronize only businesses displaying the blue eagle. The reliance on voluntary compliance for the major New Deal program for business regulation was ironic, because Democrats (and, later, historians) criticized Hoover for relying on voluntarism.

The NRA had serious flaws. Small businesses had little voice in drafting codes, consumers had virtually no influence in determining prices, and micromanagement in the form of central planning was cumbersome. The NRA was a disappointment: production and employment increased at first, then declined, and national income for 1934 was down $10 billion from the previous year. The NRA was outlawed by the Supreme Court in 1936. Still, the NRA contributed to reform. It banned child labor, required collective bargaining, and established maximum hours and minimum wages.

The National Industrial Recovery Act created the Public Works Administration (PWA). With an initial appropriation of $3.3 billion, it was placed under the direction of Interior Secretary Harold Ickes, who was determined to prevent waste. Ickes's program employed skilled workers hired by private contractors and erected durable and colossal projects, including the Triborough Bridge in New York and the Grand Coulee Dam in Colorado. From 1933 to 1939 the PWA built 70 percent of the public schools, 65 percent of the courthouses and city halls, 35 percent of the hospitals, and two aircraft carriers. Fraud was absent.

Fearing public works did not infuse money into the economy rapidly enough, some of Roosevelt's advisers felt that manipulating the currency might achieve immediate results. By inflating the currency to produce cheaper dollars, they argued, the government could raise domestic prices and ease debts, and a weaker dollar would make American goods competitive abroad. One way to inject dollars into circulation was to pay more for gold than the market price. Thus, the government increased what it paid for gold daily, raising the price by random amounts to confuse speculators. Gold buying yielded neither recovery nor ruin, and in January 1934, Roosevelt ended it. Some New Dealers advocated the remonetization of silver over-valued to stimulate inflation. Farmers, miners, and other inflationists rallied behind silver, and the administration agreed to test the idea. In December 1933, the government agreed to buy the entire domestic production of silver at 21 cents per ounce above the market value. In the next fifteen years the government spent $1.5 billion on silver, more than it spent to support farm prices. The program was lucrative for the silver industry, which employed fewer than five thousand people, yet silver inflation proved no panacea for the economy.

Recognizing the Great Depression as an international problem, businessmen looked to London's world economic conference in June and July 1933 for solutions. Roosevelt sent a delegation divided along ideological lines. Brains Truster Raymond Moley arranged a compromise on international currency stabilization, but FDR rejected the compromise. After wavering between the advice of nationalists and internationalists, Roosevelt sided with the nationalists. He feared international currency stabilization might jeopardize his efforts to raise domestic prices. Unwisely, he rejected a global approach to the worldwide depression.

In another search for answers, the Senate Banking and Currency Committee investigated abuses in banking and businesses that led to the crash. The inquiry led to reforms in banking and the sale of stocks and securities, including a second Glass-Steagall Banking Act in 1933. Separating investment from commercial banking to prevent bankers from speculating with depositors' money, the law also created the Federal Deposit Insurance Corporation (FDIC) to guarantee deposits of less than $5,000. Under the measure, fewer banks failed than in any year of the prosperous 1920s. Securities were the focus of a 1933 law, the Truth in Securities Act, requiring publication of data relevant to the sale of stocks and securities, and a 1934 measure, the Securities Exchange Act. The latter established the Securities and Exchange Commission to license stock exchanges and brokers.

Pressure for inflation resumed in 1934. In March, Congress restored the salary and pension cuts made in the Economy Act, overriding Roosevelt's veto. Three months later, lawmakers passed the Silver Purchase Act, ordering the Treasury to increase the silver supply until it reached one-third the value of the gold it held and to issue certificates redeemable in silver.

Despite its inconsistencies Americans approved of the New Deal in the 1934 congressional elections. For only the second time in history, the president's party increased its congressional majority in an off-year vote. More demoralizing to conservative Republicans, GOP members who backed the New Deal fared better than Republicans who opposed it. Still, the acceptance of the early New Deal owed more to Roosevelt's leadership than to its success in easing privation. The program realized its most critical short-term approval by energizing politics and raising morale. In the long term, the New Deal suggested new possibilities that touched every citizen.

The Second New Deal

By late 1934 it was apparent that neither the NRA nor the AAA had produced recovery, and that Roosevelt's program had lost momentum. Concluding that he had to reevaluate his approach, FDR reacted with a shift to the left that preempted radical critics. The importance of the bills passed in the spring and summer of 1935 led some historians to label the period "the Second New Deal." Resembling the First New Deal, it was based less on ideology than expediency. However, it veered from the centralizing aspects of the NRA to a more fragmented economy in which smaller businesses competed. Roosevelt declared war on monopoly and earmarked aid to organized labor and farmers. Additionally, New Dealers recognized that unemployment was a long-range problem. The government should create additional jobs. Putting money into the hands of consumers was the most effective means of stimulating recovery. Unemployment insurance, retirement benefits, and support for collective bargaining, they argued, might mitigate the hardships of capitalism. Slum dwellers should be given the opportunity to reside in open spaces with clean air; farms should receive electricity.

In January 1935, Roosevelt asked Congress for $4 billion for work relief, the largest peacetime appropriation. With part of the money he created the Works Progress Administration (WPA), the centerpiece of job creation. Employment became a federal responsibility. Under Hopkins's direction, the WPA became the longest-lived New Deal agency. It lasted more than eight years; employed 8.5 million, chiefly unskilled workers—one-fifth of the workforce—paying wages higher than relief and lower than private wages. The WPA constructed 500,000 miles of highways, 100,000 public buildings, 8,000 parks, and thousands of irrigation ditches. It subsidized art, planted trees, strung rural electric lines, and prevented floods and erosion. Only a partial success despite these achievements, the WPA fell short of FDR's goal to provide every able-bodied unemployed person with a job. Still, it helped the economy grow and lifted gloom. Because the WPA did not use men and women under twenty-four, Eleanor Roosevelt advocated a program to keep young people in school and to teach them skills. Following her lead, Congress established the National Youth Administration (NYA), which hired 4.7 million part-time employees, increasing college enrollment, and keeping youths from competing with adults for jobs.

The WPA broke precedent by employing artists and humanists. Congress appropriated $27 million in 1935 to finance jobs in writing, music, the theater, and the visual arts. The Federal Writers Project employed about 6,500 at its peak in 1936 and aided promising novelists such as Conrad Aiken, Richard Wright, John Cheever, and Ralph Ellison. Fiction was too subjective and too controversial to subsidize, so the project used writers for tasks such as preparing guidebooks, taping oral histories, indexing newspapers, compiling inventories of historical records, and interviewing former slaves. This work bored creative writers, yet supported them while they wrote novels, poems, and plays during their free hours.

More than fifty thousand musicians were jobless. The Federal Music Project employed about fifteen thousand of them to perform and teach; they played in orchestras and bands and sang in choral groups in parks and schools, free of charge. By the time the project expired in 1939, 150 million Americans had heard 225,000 performances and 500,000 children had received free music lessons.

The most controversial venture was the Federal Theatre Project (FTP), under the direction of Hallie Flanagan, a Marxist playwright. Some performances were experimental; the Living Newspaper dramatized news stories, and Orson Welles produced *Macbeth* with an African American cast. The most ambitious production was a production of Sinclair Lewis's *It Can't Happen Here*, a story of fascism arising in America. Not all plays were ideological; the project staged *Cinderella*, Mark Twain stories, puppet shows, and Gilbert and Sullivan comic operas. Future stars such as Orson Welles, Burt Lancaster, and Arlene Francis appeared in FTP shows, aimed primarily at blue-collar audiences, staged in schools, public buildings, and CCC camps. By 1935, 12.5 million people had seen 924 government-sponsored plays, cheaply or free.

Some painters and sculptors, who could not earn a living because of a decline in demand for art, were hired by the Federal Arts Project. Among the 5,300 employed were easel painters and muralists. Artists painted 4,500 murals, more than 450,000 paintings, and made 19,000 sculptures. Like the FTP dramas, some art was critical of capitalism.

Federal subsidies had an impact on photography. Photographers documented the depression for the Farm Security Administration; they produced provocative work. Celebrated photographers, including Margaret Bourke-White, Dorothea Lange, Walker Evans, and Ben Shahn, photographed breadlines and Hoovervilles. Their work stood above the overall quality of WPA-financed art, which was mediocre. Employment, rather than quality, was the priority. Nevertheless, the WPA set a precedent for government aid to the arts.

Work for the Workers

Concern for workers led to the most enduring New Deal legacy: the Social Security Act of 1935, which established unemployment compensation, retirement pensions, and survivors' benefits. These were financed with taxes on employers and money withheld from employees' pay. Social Security laid a foundation for a federal social welfare system that would come after the New Deal.

The Resettlement Administration tried to transplant city dwellers and marginal farmers to suburban communities that blended the rural and urban lifestyles. Settlers were given tools, equipment, and training in subsistence agriculture. But the government resettled only 4,400 families.

A SAFETY NET FOR EVERYONE Americans learn about Social Security. (Franklin D. Roosevelt Presidential library)

"Greenbelt" towns proved so expensive that only three were built—near Washington, Milwaukee, and Cincinnati. In 1937 the Bankhead-Jones Farm Tenancy Act replaced the Resettlement Administration (FSA) with the Farm Security Administration, a source for low-interest loans that enabled tenants to purchase farmland.

Farmers also benefited from the Soil Conservation Service (SCS) and the Rural Electrification Administration (REA), both created in 1935. The former helped tame the dust storms by teaching farmers to control wind and water erosion. Commitment to soil conservation was strengthened in 1936 with the Soil Conservation and Domestic Allotment Act, adopted to replace the AAA after the Supreme Court nullified it. Under this law, farmers were paid to curb production of crops that depleted soil and to plant grasses and legumes that enriched land. Filling another need, the REA extended power lines to farmhouses where industry found it unprofitable.

When the program started in 1935, 90 percent of such families lacked electricity; by 1950, 90 percent had current.

The Public Utility Holding Company bill addressed the problem of monopolies. In 1932 the thirteen largest utility holding companies controlled 75 percent of the industry. The measure included a "death sentence" providing that any company that could not prove its usefulness to the public within five years would be dissolved. FDR's proposal aroused more antagonism from business than any previous New Deal measure.

The rich were angered by the Wealth Tax Act of 1935 that raised income, inheritance, and gift levies. Rates were increased on personal incomes above $50,000, peaking at 75 percent on incomes of more than $5 million, as well as on corporate incomes. Opponents condemned the statute as a scheme to win votes for Roosevelt from the envious masses. The legislation, paradoxically, raised little revenue and represented a deflationary strategy during economic contraction. Its chief impact was symbolic, allowing the president to portray himself as a champion of the poor and an enemy of the wealthy.

Roosevelt won political plaudits with the Banking Act and the Wagner Act. The first centralized the banking system and provided more government control, permitting the Federal Reserve Board to set discount rates and to determine the size of loans from federal banks. The Wagner Act encouraged labor's attempts to organize, outlawing some management practices, including company unions. It required employers to bargain with workers in good faith and created a strong National Labor Relations Board (NLRB) to oversee plant elections of bargaining agents and enforce labor laws. The Wagner Act was the most important pro-labor bill enacted.

Unionized labor increased its membership and organized new industries in the 1930s. A series of strikes erupted in 1934 by independent labor leaders demanding the right to represent workers. During the spring and summer strikes occurred among auto parts workers in Toledo, truck drivers in Minnesota, maritime laborers in San Francisco (escalating into a general strike), and textile workers in the South and New England. All but the textile workers won victories. The most significant transformation in organized labor, however, involved the American Federation of Labor (AFL), presumably outdated after the assembly line increased the demand for unskilled labor. Failure to organize the unskilled into unions that included all workers in a single industry ignited a rebellion against the AFL, led by John L. Lewis of the United Mine Workers (UMW). The AFL Council opposed industrial unions because organizing across work lines created jurisdictional disputes and dual unions. If workers in automobile plants, for example, were given the choice of joining a craft union or a union that included all auto workers, the competition might splinter the labor movement. Lewis countered that industrial unions were the only type practical in industries that made products such as autos, steel, and rubber. Industrial unions that combined under the Committee for Industrial Organization (CIO), which Lewis and his allies founded, would affiliate with the AFL, he promised. The council, claiming that the CIO violated the AFL constitution, ordered it to disband. After the CIO refused, the council expelled the ten CIO unions affiliated with the AFL in 1935. Three years later the CIO made the break final by transforming itself from a temporary committee into the Congress of Industrial Organizations.

The preeminent labor leader of the 1930s, Lewis began his organizing by forming the Steel Workers Organizing Committee, led by Philip Murray, the UMW vice president. In 1937 the Committee won a contract from the United States Steel Corporation that recognized it as the exclusive bargaining agent and provided a 10 percent wage increase, an easy victory over Big Steel. The smaller corporations, known collectively as Little Steel, resisted and the union struck, followed by months of industrial warfare. Roosevelt split with Lewis over tactics in the strike and condemned labor and management, calling for "a plague on both your houses." Eventually Little Steel capitulated after the NLRB ruled in favor of the union.

Automobile manufacturing was the largest unorganized industry. The CIO employed sit-down strikes for the first time to organize General Motors (GM). In sit-down strikes, the workers, instead of walking off the job, sat down at machines and refused to move, a tactic that prevented management from hiring strikebreakers—and provoked violent confrontations. Government officials, even those who sympathized with labor, doubted the legality of sit-down strikes because they might violate the right of private property. Sit-down strikers could halt production nationwide by seizing a key plant in an integrated industry. The United Automobile Workers (UAW), which shifted its affiliation from the AFL to the CIO in 1936, paralyzed the industry with a sit-down strike against GM at the Fisher Body plant in Flint, Michigan. Staying in the plant six weeks despite violence, the strikers helped win, in February 1937, concessions that gave the UAW an organizing monopoly for six months preceding an election (which the union won), and a 5 percent pay raise. The UAW also organized Chrysler after a sit-down strike. The Ford Motor Company proved more stubborn. Only after Henry Ford's wife threatened to leave him did Ford yield, approving a union contract that guaranteed the most generous terms in his industry. By the time of Pearl Harbor, the auto industry was unionized.

For all the gains labor made during the decade, there were setbacks. Organizing lagged in the South. The Supreme Court deprived unions of a weapon by ruling sit-down strikes illegal in 1939. The CIO, apparently dominant in the labor movement, had 71 percent of its membership in only six unions, and the largest pool of unorganized workers was among white-collar professionals, which favored the AFL. Some considered the CIO tainted because of its militant tactics and because communists had gained positions in the organization. Lewis was a villain to much of the public. In 1940 he vowed to destroy Roosevelt by endorsing his Republican foe, Wendell Willkie, pledging to resign as CIO president if FDR were reelected. When Roosevelt won, Lewis was forced out and Philip Murray succeeded him.

The Paradox of Minorities: Economic Help, Political Neglect

The New Deal ignited a revolution in the voting preferences of African Americans. Most of them backed the party of Abraham Lincoln until 1936, when they began to support Democrats. This trend continued for the rest of the century. For economic reasons, African Americans and other minorities became important allies of the New Deal. Not only did black people receive better jobs and housing through federal agencies than before, but they had advocates within the administration, including Harold Ickes, the interior secretary. A network of African Americans in government organized into a "Black Cabinet" under Mary McLeod Bethune, head of the NYA Division of Negro Affairs. Ickes had a firm ally in the first lady, teaming with her to arrange for the black singer Marian Anderson to perform at the Lincoln Memorial after she was barred from other Washington facilities. Eleanor Roosevelt made African Americans a priority, addressing interracial audiences, and inviting black entertainers to the White House.

Unlike his wife, FDR lacked African American friends and was not knowledgeable about their culture. Cautious, he paid little attention to the problems of black southerners because he feared alienating white southerners, especially members of Congress. The president appointed some advisers who were segregationists. In theory, the New Deal barred discrimination in its agencies, although it was practiced in some places. A bill to make lynching (murder by a mob, not limited to hanging) a federal crime, was introduced in the House and the Senate, only to be killed. FDR rejected his wife's pleas to back the legislation. Still, working-class African Americans, helped by jobs and relief, supported FDR despite his indifference to civil rights.

The legal system offered African Americans little hope, however, particularly in the South. A blatant injustice occurred after eight young black men were arrested in 1931 near Scottsboro, Alabama. Accused of raping

★ FATHER DIVINE: "GOD, HARLEM, U.S.A." ★

Father Divine has not simply made God black; he has made a black man God—and a humble American lynchable black man at that. [Marcus] Garvey had black devotees to worship his black God; Divine has white men to bow to his deified Black Man.

—WILLIAM PICKENS, NAACP

HEAVEN'S GATE
Father Divine's Peace Mission, New York City.
(Library of Congress)

ARGUABLY THE most charismatic mass black leader of the Era of Trial and Triumph was George Baker, a minister who called himself Father Divine and who said he was God. Little is known about his early life, although it is clear that he was a sharecropper's son who grew up in the rural South during the last quarter of the nineteenth century. The early 1900s found him in Baltimore, where he preached part time in a Baptist church and joined another preacher in a church, which broke up after a few years. Back in the South, he gained adherents of his own, only to run afoul of the law in Valdosta, Georgia, over his divine claims. Accused of causing a public nuisance, Baker was named in a lawsuit as "John Doe, alias God," and was ordered to leave the state or go to a mental hospital.

Northward he went again, finally settling in Sayville, New York, around 1918, calling himself the Reverend Major J. Devine and, later, simply Father Divine (as his followers referred to him). He became leader of what became known as the Peace Mission movement. His religious communes attracted disciples of all colors who rejected government aid and often gave all their possessions to the movement. They abstained from alcohol, tobacco, and sex. The movement offered religious guidance, help in finding jobs, and meals free of charge to anyone. The Missions provided nourishment for the body and soul that was welcomed during the Great Depression. "Because your god would not feed the people, I came and am feeding them," Divine told a skeptical mission guest. "Because your god kept such as you segregated and discriminated, I came and am unifying all nations together. That is why I came, because I did not believe in your god." The crowds Divine attracted so disturbed authorities that he was once more accused of being a public disturbance, convicted, and sentenced to a brief jail term. Days after the sentencing in 1932, the judge died of a heart attack, which Divine's flock took as further evidence of their God's power. "I hated to do it," he said.

One year later, Divine moved the Peace Mission to Harlem, and the movement began to grow rapidly, ultimately encompassing almost two hundred major centers, or "Heavens," mainly in New York City and Philadelphia. A letter arrived at Divine's door addressed to "God, Harlem, U.S.A." Membership statistics were not kept, yet the rolls likely numbered thousands, among them many well-off, educated whites in addition to poor blacks, brought together to banish the prejudice that kept people apart. The effort earned praise from no less than W. E. B. Du Bois, who observed that the movement was "interracial among people of the laboring and middle-class." In a more dramatic defiance of racial convention, as well as a contradiction of his own pronouncements against marriage and sex, Divine wed a white woman who was fifty years younger than he, Edna Rose Ritchings, in 1946, after the death of his first wife, Pininnah. Ritchings, or "Sweet Angel," became Mother Divine, who would inherit the leadership of the movement. Their marriage was a spiritual union and a means for Peninnah to live on in a new body, Father Divine assured his flock.

Divine's public voice was largely silent late in his life, as he remained secluded on his estate in suburban Philadelphia. His commitment to racial harmony, nonetheless, remained unshakable. A few months before his death in his eighties, in 1965, he commended President Lyndon Johnson for a speech urging passage of the Voting Rights Act, writing to Johnson, "It is with profound gratitude that I have witnessed this great ship of state being steered into a new world of unity and dignity for all mankind." The ship has yet to dock in that world, though Divine did much to point the vessel toward it. A national reform leader courted by politicians, "he had greater success in lifting followers from poverty and in breaking down the color line, in white suburbs and black ghettoes, than any other religious leader of the day," historian Robert Weisbrot wrote.

Divine's life was an example of the work of the hereafter accomplished in the present. "I would not give five cents for a God who could not help me here on the Earth, for such a God is not a God at hand. He is only an imagination," Divine said. "It is a false delusion—trying to make you think you had just as well go ahead and suffer and be enslaved and be lynched and everything else here, and after a while you are going to Heaven someplace. If God cannot prepare Heaven here for you, you are not going anywhere."

Sources: Robert Weisbrot's biography is *Father Divine* (1983). Also see Kenneth E. Burnham, *God Comes to America: Father Divine and the Peace Mission Movement* (1979).

two white women on a freight train, though there was no physical evidence of rape, an all-white jury convicted the "Scottsboro boys," and all but one were sentenced to die. The Supreme Court overturned the verdicts and a series of proceedings consumed eleven years and three more trials. The prejudice against the youths made their case notorious. The Communist Party exploited the injustice to promote anticapitalist propaganda. Ultimately, five defendants were convicted and sentenced to long terms. Charges against the others were dropped.

Communists worked diligently during the 1930s to recruit southern blacks, vowing to carve a black republic in the South. They did not gain many converts, but added martyrs to their cause. Angelo Herndon, a young black who became a recruiter for black labor unions in Birmingham, Alabama, was arrested in Atlanta for his ties to the Communist Party. While incarcerated, he was charged with inciting an insurrection. Convicted in 1933 and sentenced to twenty years of hard labor, Herndon failed at several appeals until the Supreme Court overturned the verdict in 1937. Communists' attempts to use the Herndon and Scottsboro injustices were reprimanded by W.E.B. Du Bois, who wrote of the Scottsboro tragedy, "American Negroes do not propose to be the shock troops of the Communist Revolution, driven out in front to death, cruelty and humiliation in order to win victories for white workers." Du Bois became alienated and controversial in the 1930s, resigning as editor of *Crisis* after quarreling with NAACP Executive Secretary Walter White, who advocated racial equality through integration. Du Bois himself argued for cultural and economic segregation. Late in the decade Du Bois became an apologist for Soviet and Japanese aggression, approving of the Hitler-Stalin Pact of 1939.

American Indians suffered during the depression as much as any minority group, but the Roosevelt administration produced an Indian New Deal led by John Collier, who had worked for improved conditions for Indians as commissioner of Indian affairs. Collier pumped federal funds into reservations to build schools, hospitals, and irrigation systems, improving tribal life and offering employment. The reforms also included the Indian Reorganization Act of 1934, intended to stop the sale of tribal lands to individuals and to return to Indians some control over their lives. Seventy-five percent of tribes voted to organize self-governing councils under the law, which slowed forced assimilation into white society. The measure also made the interior secretary the final authority over Indian affairs, a stipulation that harmed Indian interests when the sympathetic Ickes retired.

The prominence of Jews among New Dealers angered anti-Semites, whose hatred peaked during the 1930s. Gerald L. K. Smith, Elizabeth Dilling, Father Charles E. Coughlin, and other bigots blamed Jews for the depression, claimed Roosevelt was a Jew, denounced the "Jew Deal," and spread rumors of Jewish plots to control the world. Henry Ford lent his credibility to anti-Semitism, publishing anti-Jewish articles in his weekly newspaper, the Dearborn Independent. Organizations such as the Ku Klux Klan and pro-German groups proposed a solution to the "Jewish problem" in the United States that involved deporting or exterminating Jews. Jewish organizations, meanwhile, contributed to philanthropy, worked for racial justice, and for a foreign policy that would punish dictators.

Among Hispanics, immigration declined because of the depression; in fact, during the 1930s more Mexican Americans returned to Mexico than entered the United States. Most left for economic reasons. Hispanics learned that their language was a barrier to finding work, and most were limited to menial labor in city barrios or as migrant fruit and vegetable pickers. Hispanics rarely voted, so politicians ignored their interests.

The condition of the Japanese in America deteriorated in the 1930s. Those native to Japan clung to traditional ways, although their offspring, the Nisei, were inclined to adopt American culture. Many educated Japanese Americans experienced job discrimination, as Japanese militarism rose in the Far East. Chinese Americans, too, suffered from economic hardship. Yet white Americans viewed them as intelligent and admired their ability to survive destitution, to save, and to refuse government relief. They perceived the Chinese as victims of Japanese aggression and as potential allies in hostilities against Japan. Still, the Chinese could not become naturalized citizens until 1943.

In the workforce, the proportion of women increased marginally, from 24.3 percent in 1930 to 25.4 percent in 1940. Thirteen to 19 percent of WPA employees were women, most engaged in sewing, and eight thousand women worked in CCC camps, compared with 2.5 million men. Twenty percent of white women and 40 percent of black women worked outside the home, most due to economic necessity. Many African Americans were domestic servants; others were agricultural laborers. Some men resented the competition of women for scarce jobs, and 82 percent of men and women in a 1936 Gallup poll believed that wives should not work if their husbands had a job. Of professional women, three-quarters were teachers or nurses. Positions for female teachers, musicians, and doctors declined. Law and medical schools imposed quotas that restricted female students.

Women were prominent in the fight for racial equality. Lillian Smith and Paula Snelling, editors of literary journals, urged fellow southerners to cease using derogatory terms for blacks. Likewise, women admired Eleanor Roosevelt and played an active role in New Deal politics. Under the New Deal, more women were appointed to political jobs than in any previous administration, including the first woman cabinet member, ambassador, and appeals judge.

Opponents of the New Deal

As an advocate of gradual transformation, Roosevelt sought change to defend American values and institutions. "Reform if you would preserve," counseled FDR. Those who wanted radical change, and those who wanted no change at all, condemned him. Alone, none of these dissenters were formidable; in a disciplined coalition they might have posed a threat. Because they rejected the New Deal for different reasons, however, a coalition was unlikely. Foes on the Far Right believed that Roosevelt was part of a conspiracy of Jews, blacks, communists, and unions whose aim was to make the president world dictator, eradicate Christianity, and enshrine communism. The wealthy considered him a traitor to his class. On the Left, leaders such as the socialist Norman Thomas accused FDR of being a fascist.

Some of the opposition was personal. Roosevelt was accused of insanity, alcoholism, and of having contracted syphilis. Rumors circulated that Idaho Senator William Borah found the president cutting out paper dolls in the White House study. It was also rumored that maniacal laughter could be heard in the mansion and that Roosevelt's friends kept him in a straitjacket and put bars on the windows to prevent him from leaping out. Some argued that because his legs were disabled, the president's mind must be diabolical, a punishment from God. FDR was even accused of kidnapping the Lindbergh baby.

The main foe of the New Deal, the Republican Party, remained weak. The GOP was blamed for the depression and lacked competitive candidates to challenge Roosevelt. But foes of FDR found kindred minds in organizations created to battle the New Deal. The best known of these groups, the American Liberty League, included conservative businessmen but also former Democratic presidential nominees John W. Davis and Al Smith. Its membership peaked at 125,000 in 1936.

Communism, romanticized by a number of intellectuals as the wave of the future, should have grown in the United States during the depression, seemingly the fulfillment of Karl Marx's prophecy of the collapse of capitalism. Yet Communist Party membership grew slowly; not until 1938 did it surpass 60,000, its level in 1919. Communists denounced New Dealers as social fascists whose policies of limited reform would postpone a workers' revolution. This idea changed in 1935, however, at the direction of the Soviet Union. Deciding that fascism posed a greater danger than liberalism, the Soviet Party ordered its satellites to cooperate with liberal reformers in popular fronts. American communists worked to reelect Roosevelt in 1936. Under popular fronts, the Communist Party grew to almost 100,000 members in 1939. Then the Soviets twice ordered their parties in other countries to change course—in favor of an alliance with Germany in 1939, when the U.S.S.R. signed a treaty with Adolf Hitler, and against it in 1941, when the Fuhrer invaded the Soviet Union. The revelation that the party in the United States was a Kremlin puppet destroyed its credibility, and after 1939 it was never a mass movement.

Demagogues who promoted prescriptions for the economy represented the most serious challenge to the New Deal, none bigger than Louisiana senator Huey P. Long, the sole dissenter who was a professional politician with popular appeal. "There is no rule so sure as the one that the same mill that grinds out fortunes above a certain size at the top grinds out paupers at the bottom," said Long. His solution was to confiscate millionaires' property and redistribute it. Long wanted the government to take all yearly income above $1 million and all wealth in excess of $5 million, then use it to give every family a home, car, and radio, valuables worth at least $5,000. The Louisiana senator, known as "the Kingfish," would guarantee a yearly income of at least

SENATOR HUEY LONG
Shown here addressing the students of Louisiana State University in 1934.
(AP/Wide World Photos)

$2,500, old age pensions, a veterans bonus, public works, and free college educations. Though unworkable, the plan appealed to the poor. In 1934 Long organized a Share-Our-Wealth Society to publicize the scheme and hired Gerald L. K. Smith to promote the group nationwide. A more bombastic orator than Long, the minister was so successful that the organization had two hundred thousand adherents within a month, 3 million by the end of 1934, and 7.5 million by February 1935. Long hoped to launch a third-party candidacy for president in 1936, with the potential to win 11 percent of the vote, according to a poll Roosevelt commissioned. The Louisianan might decoy enough liberals' votes from FDR to elect a Republican, setting the stage for the Kingfish to win in 1940. Long was charismatic, had a genius-level IQ, and was a mesmerizing orator who spoke in the idiom of the common man. Possibly bipolar, he was gifted with enormous energy, a disarming sense of humor, and confidence verging on megalomania. He was single-minded, imaginative, and his energy fueled limitless ambition.

Yet Long and his Louisiana machine were vulnerable. Federal investigations discovered graft and tax evasion. Before federal officials could get to Long, an assassin's bullet beat them. Wounded by a gunman on September 8, 1935, the Kingfish died two days later, due in part to bungled surgery. On the state level, Long is remembered as one of the most powerful political bosses ever to dominate an American state. At the national level, the Kingfish is the subject of speculation about what he might have become.

Before Long's death, some journalists warned that he might consummate an alliance with Father Charles E. Coughlin, a Catholic priest in suburban Detroit who broadcast radio sermons about religion and politics. Coughlin became so popular that by 1932 he was addressing the largest audience in the world and receiving $500,000 per year in donations via mail. Turning from theology to politics, Coughlin supported Roosevelt in 1932, broke with him by late 1934, and founded a weekly newspaper. Less effective in advancing practical solutions than scapegoating, the priest identified an alleged conspiracy of Jews, bankers, FDR, and communists who had plotted the depression, as a prelude to world takeover. His feud with FDR intensified when the administration revealed that Coughlin had used listeners' donations to speculate in silver.

An unlikely ally of the demagogues of the depression, retired California physician Francis E. Townsend proposed a plan to give people over sixty a pension of $200 a month, on the conditions that they retire and spend each check before receiving the next one. In 1934 he and a friend founded a national organization that enlisted 10 million members within a year. The Townsend plan was introduced in Congress, where it was bluntly dismissed. Still, Townsend attracted the attention of Smith, who had left Louisiana after Long's death in search of another cause. Smith elbowed his way into the Townsend movement, trying to merge it with the Long and Coughlin organizations, and used his oratory to captivate Townsend's older audiences.

Trial and Triumph for Roosevelt

Roosevelt declared war on big business during the 1936 campaign, blaming greedy capitalists, in tandem with Hoover, for the economic calamity. He launched the first antitrust prosecution of his administration. Congress passed a windfall profits tax and a law to protect small businesses from chain store competition.

At the Democratic convention in Philadelphia, after Roosevelt and John Nance Garner were renominated by acclamation, Roosevelt summed up his crusade and contrasted his humane experimentation with the alleged indifferences of Hoover's administration. "Governments can err. Presidents do make mistakes, but the immortal Dante tells us that divine justice weighs the sins of the cold-blooded and the sins of the warm-hearted in different scales." FDR challenged the nation to meet the tests that it faced, referring to the depression, but, ironically, more appropriate to a war he did not know was coming. "There is a mysterious cycle in human events. To some generations much is given. Of other generations much is expected. This generation has a rendezvous with destiny."

The Republicans nominated Kansas Governor Alfred M. Landon for president and Chicago newspaper publisher Frank Knox for vice president. Simple, homespun, Landon was a moderate who favored New Deal relief and public works but denounced the bureaucracy, deficit spending, and Roosevelt's domination of Congress. Landon was barely known outside the Midwest, faced a popular incumbent who controlled patronage, and lacked an attractive alternative to the New Deal. An ineffectual campaigner, Landon gave speeches that included trivialities such as, "Everywhere I have gone in this country, I have found Americans."

The Communists nominated Earl Browder, who knew he had no chance of winning and wanted Roosevelt reelected. Calling other minority candidates stooges for Landon, Browder asked Communists to vote for FDR in states where the Communist ticket was not on the ballot. The Socialists nominated Norman Thomas, who assailed both the Communists and the president. Coughlin, Townsend, and Gerald L. K. Smith formed the Union Party and picked North Dakota Congressman William Lemke as its standard-bearer. The three demagogues, though, were more interested in their own programs than in electing Lemke. Coughlin seldom mentioned Lemke in his speeches. Townsend told his followers to vote for Landon where Lemke was not on the ballot. Lemke and Townsend condemned Gerald Smith as a fascist and broke with him a few weeks before the election.

In the most one-sided voting since 1820, the Democratic ticket won 60.7 percent of the popular vote, a share that would stand as a record for twenty-eight years, and 523 electoral votes to eight for the GOP. (Lemke polled 882,000 votes, Thomas 190,000, and Browder 80,000.) Roosevelt's party devastated the Republicans in congressional races, winding up with three-quarters of the House and almost four-fifths of the Senate. Economic issues dominated and the Democrats became the majority party.

The Supreme Court proved a more difficult obstacle for Roosevelt. Divided ideologically, with four conservatives, three liberals, and two moderates, the Court had knocked the props from under the New Deal in 1935 and 1936, nullifying the NIRA, the AAA, and a New York State minimum wage law. New Deal legislation, the justices ruled, granted excessive power to the chief executive, preempted states' rights by extension of the interstate commerce clause, and intruded in areas in which it had no regulatory authorization. Fearing that the Wagner Act and the Social Security Act would be overturned for similar reasons, Roosevelt condemned the Court for ruling on the wisdom of reform legislation rather than its constitutionality.

Without consulting Congress or his cabinet, FDR—who did not have the chance to appoint a justice in his first term—drew up a bill that would enable him to appoint enough justices to ensure a liberal majority. Introduced in February 1937, the measure authorized the president to appoint a justice whenever any justice with at least ten years of service did not retire within six months after turning seventy. Roosevelt said his objective was to inject youthful vigor into the legal system and allow it to dispose of cases promptly. His real purpose, as everyone knew, was to transform the Court, six of whose nine members were older than seventy, into a rubber stamp for the administration.

A firestorm of opposition ignited. Liberals and conservatives worried that Roosevelt's proposal would endanger the balance of power in the federal government. Even those who agreed with Roosevelt's goals disagreed with his methods and ridiculed the hypocrisy behind his public aim of making the judiciary more efficient. The Court counterattacked. Chief Justice Charles Evans Hughes predicted that more justices would require more conferences and discussions, prolonging hearings. Then the Court upheld a Washington State minimum wage law, the Wagner Act, and the Social Security Act—decisions called "the switch in time that saved nine." Also, conservative Justice Willis Van Devanter announced his retirement, convincing members of Congress that court-packing was unnecessary. Six months after his proposal was introduced, Roosevelt settled on a compromise that streamlined the judiciary without giving him additional appointments. And in the end he got his liberal court; vacancies permitted him to appoint seven justices in five years. The appointees included Hugo Black and William O. Douglas, who had long, distinguished tenures.

Roosevelt liked to say that he won the battle of wills with the court, if not with Congress, by intimidating the justices into sanctioning the constitutionality of the Second New Deal. If so, it came at the price of FDR acting like the village bully. Probably it was Roosevelt's awesome victory in the 1936 election, not the court-packing bill, that prodded the court to change direction. The defeat of his plan was the sharpest congressional rebuke Roosevelt suffered.

Economic decline followed the setback on court–packing. Concerned about the deficit, particularly the costs of the WPA and the PWA, Roosevelt slashed spending in the summer of 1937. He cut WPA employment by 59 percent and ordered Ickes to phase out the PWA. The economy slowed by August, unemployment rose by nearly 2 million people from September to December, and another 1 million people lost their jobs by Christmas. National income began to fall at nearly $800 million per month, steel production declined by three-fourths, and factory production sank to 1933 levels. By 1938 there were nearly as many unemployed as there were under Hoover—one of the great paradoxes of the New Deal, largely overlooked.

Roosevelt summoned a special session of Congress in November 1937, but it adjourned without enacting his recommendations. Ickes, Hopkins, and Perkins urged the administration to resume spending, and Roosevelt consulted with the British economist John Maynard Keynes, a leading advocate of deficit spending, who remarked afterward, "I don't think your president knows anything about economics." Roosevelt was unwilling to spend at the levels that Keynes proposed, yet in April 1938 he proposed a $3 billion package that Congress approved. The economy recovered by the summer of 1939.

Roosevelt never accepted a defeat without retaliating, a trait that belied his genial public persona. Livid when some senators deserted him during the court-packing debate, he stopped the flow of patronage to several conservatives, reasoned that only liberals would be faithful allies, and decided to transform the Democrats into the party of liberalism. In 1938 primary elections he campaigned against some conservative candidates of his own party in a fruitless effort. In November, Republicans made their first gains of the New Deal era, winning seventy-five House seats, seven Senate seats, and thirteen governorships. Democrats retained comfortable majorities in Congress, however, and even though conservatives could be effective in opposition, they could not enact a program. The result was a standoff that practically ended the New Deal.

Congress, nevertheless, approved a few important economic measures during Roosevelt's second term. In addition to the Bankhead-Jones Farm

Tenancy Act in 1937, there was the National Housing Act, which provided $500 million for public housing projects and clearing urban slums. The next year produced a more limited AAA and a Fair Labor Standards Act. The agriculture law, directed toward the continued farm surpluses and low prices, created procedures for curbing production of basic crops and allowed the government to extend loans to farmers and store their surpluses in warehouses until they could repay the loans and market their crops profitably. The labor act required a minimum hourly wage, a forty-hour workweek, and prohibition of child labor.

An Assessment of the New Deal

Debate over the New Deal long outlived Roosevelt. Leftists argued that it was too cautious and did not reach out to minorities. From the Right, writers criticized it for aggrandizing federal power and for introducing welfare dependency, a monstrous bureaucracy, and bloated deficits. To be sure, the New Deal failed to end the depression: it would take wartime spending to finish the job of recovery. More reasonably, the New Deal battled the Great Depression to a standstill.

Still, the quantity and quality of New Deal legislation are impressive, and it arrested the decline and brought hope to the masses. Roosevelt, by his activism, his oratory, and his optimistic personality, lifted the spirits of a nation whose problems were both economic and psychological. The president tapped the imaginations of brilliant academicians and intellectuals. Following his uncannily accurate intuition, he became perhaps the greatest party leader in American history. His New Deal was an improvement over the single-interest presidencies of the 1920s, paying attention to underrepresented groups and guaranteeing Americans a minimum of sustenance; and when recovery finally arrived, it can be argued, it was better based because of Roosevelt's contributions in the 1930s. Except for his affliction with polio, he led a charmed life, bold, fearless, nearly invulnerable in politics.

Roosevelt built a potent Democratic coalition of groups that supported the party though the end of the century. He established a clear ideological division between Democrats and Republicans, making his party the advocate of the "forgotten man." He and Eleanor Roosevelt, who set standards for activism by a first lady, were a synergism. During the Era of Trial and Triumph, the United States was fortunate to have them at the helm. Historians and public opinion polls of the twenty-first century continue to rank Franklin D. Roosevelt among the nation's three greatest presidents, in the company of George Washington and Abraham Lincoln.

CHAPTER TEN

Culture: Revolt and Retreat

P ARADOXICALLY, THE culture between the wars complemented the sizzle of prosperity and vented depression angst. Whether dancing to an upbeat tempo or soothing the beast of adversity, in the Era of Trial and Triumph the arts carried a message—a critical one, necessary for the nation's equilibrium. In the 1920s the arts dazzled; in the 1930s they helped provide a psychological safety net; in the 1940s they praised ammunition, the Almighty, and peace.

The 1920s and the 1930s

A nation of affluence and abundant leisure, the United States became the entertainment capital of the world in the 1920s. Industrial jobs aggravated nervousness, created a demand for amusements to fill time, and made Americans willing to pay billions to avoid boredom. The resulting popular culture homogenized a people once sharply defined by regional traits. Now, Americans listened to the same songs and news, danced the same dances, watched the same stars in movies and sports, read the same books, and practiced the same fads.

The 1920s, moreover, were a time of American adolescence, of cultural testing and innovation. When the decade ended, the United States and the rebels of the decade had grown up, sober and resigned. Like everyone who looks back at adolescence, the revolutionaries did so with regret, because the period had its wasted opportunities and dissipated energies; but they also looked back wistfully, as the decade had been enjoyable and they could not have matured without it. Part of the magic of youth is paradoxical—the failure to recognize its joys before they pass into memory.

In the depression-burdened 1930s, writers, artists, musicians, and actors—many of them unemployed—were in a struggle to survive amid adversity. Having fought for individualism in the 1920s, they changed course, experimenting with collectivism. Disillusionment with capitalism and sympathy with Marxism permeated their community. Once neglected, common people were portrayed as heroes. As the economy rebounded, the popularity of Marxism waned.

"The Lost Generation"

In the 1920s the insatiable curiosity about Charles Lindbergh illustrated the public's craving for heroes. Mass-market writing provided an escape from urbanization and industrialization. Few people read serious books. The best-selling writers were Geneva "Gene" Stratton-Porter, Harold Bell Wright, Zane Grey, and Edgar Rice Burroughs. Stratton-Porter emphasized optimism, love of nature, victory over adversity, and nostalgia. Rivaling her as a dispenser of optimism, Wright sold an average of 750,000 copies of each of his first twelve books. Grey, author of more than fifty Western novels that glorified self-reliance, sold 20 million books during the decade. Burroughs wrote more than forty novels, most about Tarzan's African adventures, reviving the frontier spirit.

The masses devoured periodicals such as newspapers, whose ownership was concentrated in chains, the largest belonging to William Randolph Hearst. Daily newspapers declined from 16,944 in 1914 to 10,176 in 1929, but total circulation increased. Tabloids that sensationalized news multiplied and passed older, traditional dailies in sales. Magazine reading increased, with publications that appealed to families having large circulations, among them the *Saturday Evening Post, Ladies' Home Journal,* and *Literary Digest.* Magazine advertising was so lucrative that an issue of the *Post* included one hundred pages of ads. Short-story magazines specialized in sports, romance, mysteries, and "true confessions." The prolific and acerbic journalist H. L. Mencken was an elitist and a conservative in politics, if not culture. The American people, he wrote, "constitute the most timorous, sniveling, poltroonish, ignominious mob of serfs and goosesteppers ever gathered under one flag since the end of the Middle Ages." Asked to explain why he lived in a country he criticized and satirized, he replied, "Why do men go to zoos?"

In the 1930s and 1940s, a generation in a hurry read more magazines than books, especially family-oriented periodicals with fiction that reinforced traditional values. Magazines and newspapers reflected the growing importance of political stories. The Washington press corps doubled, and foreign correspondents reported on the rise of European dictators. Political columnists Walter Lippmann, Arthur Krock, and Mark Sullivan were widely read, but so were humor writer Will Rogers, etiquette specialist Emily Post, and gossip columnist Walter Winchell.

In one of the paradoxes of the century, American literature and art in the 1920s enjoyed their greatest flowering since the mid-nineteenth century. The blooming was unexpected, as if someone intending to compose a grocery list ended up writing the great American novel. Americans who were ashamed of their literature at the decade's dawn could boast of it after 1929.

The artistic geniuses of this decade enlisted on the side of modernism against Victorian values. Because Victorian self-control was repressive, they strived to liberate spontaneity; modernists sought to inject passion into art. The best writers of the 1920s, called "the Lost Generation," rebelled against American society, against Puritanism, and against small towns. Historically original, members of the Lost Generation were frank, experimental, and daring. Seeking self-fulfillment, living for the moment, many of these marvelously naughty and incredibly witty authors were obsessed with sex. Some were unhappy, growing cynical before ceasing to be naive, drowning in drink or escaping in suicide. They fled the Midwest, seemingly a bland region that produced great writers, for Greenwich Village, Paris, Italy, and England, only to discover in their native land the themes they sought.

The representative figure of the decade and of the Lost Generation was F. Scott Fitzgerald, who amused, tantalized, and taunted with the brilliance of an exploding star. He broke through with *This Side of Paradise* (1920), an autobiographical book that described the collegiate experience in terms that appalled moralists and delighted young people. No mere chronicler of youthful rebellion, Fitzgerald and his wife, Zelda Sayre, lived it. Once Sayre called in a false fire alarm at a swank hotel; when firefighters arrived and asked about the source of the blaze, she pointed to her breasts and said, "Here!" Her spouse wrote one of the most enduring novels of American literature, *The Great Gatsby* (1925), the story of a poor man who lost a rich woman, became a wealthy bootlegger, and tried to win her again. Fame, however, did not bring contentment to Fitzgerald and Sayre. They burned themselves out in an endless round of parties. He became an alcoholic, and his productivity waned, while she suffered a nervous breakdown. Fitzgerald became a Hollywood screenwriter and died of a heart attack in 1940, at forty-four.

The most emulated writer was Ernest Hemingway, who joined the colony of expatriate American writers in Paris, the setting for his first noteworthy novel, *The Sun also Rises* (1926). He developed a lean, spare style, used few adjectives, and let the dialogue carry the story. Tough and realistic, Hemingway dealt with love, death, and stoicism in the face of tragedy. He was less productive after the 1920s, but *To Have and Have Not* (1937)

F. SCOTT FITZGERALD
1937. Photograph by
Carl Van Vechten.
(Library of Congress)

sold briskly, and *For Whom the Bell Tolls* (1940), set amid the Spanish Civil War, was an artistic success. Bipolar, he won the Nobel Prize for literature in 1954, seven years before taking his life.

Sinclair Lewis wrote merciless satires about the village (*Main Street*, 1920), the businessman (*Babbitt*, 1922), medical science (*Arrowsmith*, 1925), religious fundamentalism (*Elmer Gantry*, 1927), and politics (*The Man Who Knew Coolidge*, 1928). In 1930, the Nobel Prize committee made him the first American to win their honor for literature. Following his productive period in the 1920s, Lewis grew concerned by European fascists and American demagogues such as Huey Long and Father Charles E. Coughlin, anxiety that shaped the plot of *It Can't Happen Here* (1935). The title is ironic because in the novel fascism comes to the United States, under a totalitarian president who is toppled in a coup. By the conclusion, America is fighting a second civil war.

John Dos Passos, another social critic, established his reputation with *Three Soldiers* (1921) and *Manhattan Transfer* (1925), disdaining conventional capitalization and punctuation. Dos Passos raged against materialism in the 1930s and fed the revolutionary fervor of the depression era, until his faith in Marxism waned and he turned to conservative themes. Aspiring to write an autobiography of the United States in the twentieth century, he produced the most ambitious literary project of his generation, *U.S.A.*, a trilogy collected in 1938 after publication of the separate books *The 42nd Parallel* (1930), *1919* (1932), and *The Big Money* (1936).

Thomas Wolfe won fame with publication of *Look Homeward, Angel* in 1929. Perfecting the genre of autobiographical fiction, he sparkled briefly but brightly, writing three more novels, two issued posthumously. William Faulkner ranked Wolfe first among the writers of his generation. Some critics disagreed, placing Faulkner at the top. Setting his best fiction in Mississippi, his birthplace, Faulkner employed the stream-of-consciousness technique better than any American writer, shifting perspectives, mixing chronology, weaving bewilderingly complicated plots. Faulkner won the Nobel Prize in 1950, but his most productive period ran from the mid-1920s to the mid-1930s, during which he wrote *The Sound and the Fury* (1929), *As I Lay Dying* (1930), and *Absalom, Absalom!* (1936).

Although not comparable with Faulkner individually, southern writers known as the Fugitives, or the Agrarians, collectively exerted important influence. As students and teachers at Vanderbilt University, they founded a poetry magazine, *The Fugitive*, which published complex poems characterized by precise language. Later they addressed regional themes, publishing essays, novels, short stories, critical studies, and epic poems. In 1930 their group inspired *I'll Take My Stand*, a defense of southern agrarian culture. Another southerner, Ellen Glasgow, reached her apogee in the 1920s. In Dorinda Oakley, the protagonist of *Barren Ground* (1925), Glasgow created the most sharply crafted female character of the decade. Other women writers, including Willa Cather and Edith Wharton continued to write prolifically in the 1920s, having launched their careers in the previous decade.

Just as literature flourished among white southerners, it prospered in Harlem. The 1920s saw the Harlem Renaissance, when African American writers developed African themes. Protest and alienation inspired this renaissance. A participant in this ferment, critic Alain Locke, called the movement "a spiritual coming of age" that allowed the "New Negro" to change "social disillusionment to race pride." Versatile, the renaissance fostered jazz and blues, particularly at the Cotton Club, where musician Duke Ellington performed and Ethel Waters sang. James Weldon Johnson, successful as a high school principal, civil rights activist, consular official, and Tin Pan Alley songwriter, published a novel, a book of poetry, and a social history. Langston Hughes wrote poems, plays, fiction and nonfiction. African American culture blossomed in the works of Claude McKay,

Countee Cullen, W.E.B. Du Bois, Zora Neale Hunston, and Jean Toomer. In Harlem, where cafes, speakeasies, lounges, rib joints, and supper clubs catered to a largely white clientele, white and black people mingled. On Broadway, more than twenty black musicals opened from 1922 to 1929, singer Paul Robeson thrilled audiences, and Eugene O'Neill wrote plays about black themes.

Considered the greatest American dramatist, O'Neill won four Pulitzers and a Nobel Prize. From 1919 to 1934, he wrote twenty-five plays, almost two per year, opening four in 1924. Among his 1920s plays were *Anna Christie* (1921); *All God's Chillun Got Wings* (1924), about interracial marriage; and *Desire under the Elms* (1924). O'Neill's explorations of the dark side of the human psyche contrasted with the majority of popular plays, light musical comedies.

American poetry attracted serious attention between the wars. T. S. Eliot and Ezra Pound, still living in Europe, wrote intricate, pessimistic poetry that became staples of college anthologies and drew admiration from the elite. Hart Crane wrote the greatest epic poem with an American theme, *The Bridge* (1930), which used the Brooklyn Bridge as a metaphor for the United States. Edna St. Vincent Millay wrote the most-quoted verse of the decade, a stanza from the first poem in *A Few Figs from Thistles* (1920):

My candle burns at both ends,
It will not last the night;
But ah, my foes, and oh, my friends—
It gives a lovely light.

Millay won the Pulitzer in 1923 for her collection *The Harp-Weaver and Other Poems*. Another important poet, Marianne Moore, wrote of commonplace topics such as animals, baseball, and art objects in descriptive verse that incorporated quotations. Her poems were overlooked in her time, but she contributed to contemporary directions in American literature as a key critic and editor of the literary magazine *Dial*.

The Proletariat as Protagonist

The proletarian novel, concerned with the struggles of the laborer, developed during the 1930s. Tough-minded realism characterized the works, with profanity, violence, and sex animating the plots. Most of these novels were ephemeral because they were morals with stories rather than stories with morals, although some were great, lasting efforts. The most influen-

FLEEING THE DUST BOWL
Dust storm in Cimarron County, Oklahoma, 1936. Scenes like these
served as the inspiration for John Steinbeck's *Grapes of Wrath*.
(Franklin D. Roosevelt Presidential Library)

tial proletarian writer, John Steinbeck, set his best novels in the West, depicting migrant workers, ranch hands, and union organizers. Steinbeck's greatest work, *The Grapes of Wrath* (1939), described the migration of an Oklahoma farm family from the Dust Bowl to the fields of California. Other writers produced just a handful of works apiece, yet proved popular and enduring. Among them were Katherine Anne Porter, known for her exquisitely crafted short stories, and Nobel Prize winning Pearl Buck, whose novel *The Good Earth* (1931), set in China, was a best seller. Margaret Mitchell published her only novel, *Gone with the Wind*, in 1936 after ten years of writing. This epic of the Civil War and Reconstruction in Georgia sold 1 million copies in six months and became the most successful motion picture of the time.

Dramatists shared some of the sociopolitical tendencies of novelists, seeing the masses as prey of capitalist oppression. Most in tune with the radical tenor of the times, Clifford Odets wrote *Waiting for Lefty* (1935), the biggest hit of the decade. Audiences responded enthusiastically to the drama, based on a New York taxicab strike. Lillian Hellman was also a political leftist, but her plays did not reflect proletarian themes. Her first hit, *The Children's Hour* (1934), concerned false allegations of a lesbian relationship between two teachers at a boarding school; her second, *The Little Foxes* (1939), depicted a turn-of-the-century Southern family weakened by greed. Robert Sherwood, a speechwriter for President Franklin D. Roosevelt as well as a successful playwright, was another exception to the proletarian influence. He won Pulitzer Prizes for his plays, including *Abe Lincoln in Illinois* (1938) and the book *Roosevelt and Hopkins: An Intimate Story* (1948). Other hits included George Gershwin's *Porgy and Bess* (1935), Moss Hart's and George S. Kaufman's *You Can't Take It with You* (1936), and Thornton Wilder's *Our Town* (1938).

During World War II, authors profited from the largest mass market for books in U.S. history. The number of volumes published nearly doubled, and book sales increased more than 20 percent yearly. Bibles and dictionaries were in such demand that they had to be rationed. Writers were less alienated than in the 1920s and 1930s and more willing to explore themes of sentimentality, nostalgia, and religion. A dissenter was Richard Wright, who joined the Communist Party and established himself as the major black writer of the period with *Native Son* (1940), the story of a Chicago black man who accidentally killed his white employer's daughter. In 1945 Wright published the autobiographical *Black Boy*, expressing his rage at racism. Coming to believe that Communists exploited blacks for political purposes, he broke with the party in 1944.

Contrasting with Wright's passion, nonfiction grew more conservative. In 1943 Ayn Rand published *The Fountainhead*, which praised individualism over collectivism, sold steadily during and after the war, including millions of paperbacks. The favorite book of conservatives was *The Road to Serfdom* (1944), by an expatriate Austrian economist, Friedrich Hayek, who argued that modern liberalism was the path to tyranny. National planning would fail in the Soviet Union and the United States, he predicted.

Wartime produced few remarkable plays, although Arthur Miller and Tennessee Williams established themselves as top dramatists. Williams's *The Glass Menagerie* was produced on Broadway in 1944. Several successful musicals debuted during the war. Irving Berlin wrote the score for the popular *This Is the Army* (1942), and Richard Rodgers and Oscar Hammerstein II wrote *Oklahoma!* (1943), which played for more than 2,200 performances.

A BREAKTHROUGH ARTIST AND ENTERTAINER
Jazz musician Louis Armstrong.
(Library of Congress)

"All That Jazz"

Some of the most memorable popular music in U.S. history was first heard in the 1920s. The most important, jazz, was America's original contribution to music. Rooted in the blues, a genre that working-class African Americans created, jazz was born in New Orleans among black musicians who entertained in the opulent houses of prostitution. When the United States entered World War I, the War Department closed the district because New Orleans was a port of debarkation for troops. The musicians migrated to St. Louis, Chicago, New York, and the West Coast, where they played a music that was cathartic, a rebuttal to conformity and convention. Originally unwritten and improvised, yet intricate and sophisticated, emphasizing beat and accent rather than melody, jazz was designed to be listened and danced to, an urban art that thrived in crowded places. It was, a journalist wrote, "a perfect expression of the American city, with its restless bustle and motion, its multitude of unrelated details, and its underlying rhythmic progress toward a vague somewhere."

Early pioneers included Joe "King" Oliver, Ferdinand "Jelly Roll" Morton, and two men who became the leading jazz artists, Louis Armstrong and Duke Ellington. A pianist, bandleader, and prolific composer whose popularity soared in the 1920s, Ellington ranked as one of the greatest American musical geniuses. Another key figure, Paul Whiteman, was not Ellington's equal musically, but his more structured big-band music helped ensure the popularity of jazz among white people.

Because jazz was the "tom-tom of revolt," in Langston Hughes's term, traditionalists disliked it. Of the genre that a writer scorned as "music in the nude," one professor argued, "If we permit our boys and girls to be exposed indefinitely to this pernicious influence, the harm that will result may tear to pieces our whole social fabric." Perhaps the nation was beyond hope. One clergyman claimed that "in 1921–1922 jazz had caused the downfall of 1,000 girls in Chicago alone." Another foe complained that jazz had corrupted 70 percent of the women who became prostitutes in New York.

Popular melodic music concentrated in Tin Pan Alley, dominated by Irving Berlin. Among other talented composers were George Gershwin, whose "Rhapsody in Blue" was the most celebrated song of the 1920s, and Cole Porter. Bringing the composers' works to life was the job of singers including Rudy Vallee, whose soft crooning was the antithesis of jazz, and Al Jolson, whose life paralleled the role he played in the movie *The Jazz Singer* (1927). His father, a rabbi, wanted him to become a cantor, but Jolson turned to popular music and made more hit records than any singer of his time, popularizing "My Mammy," "April Showers," and "California Here I Come."

The 1920s were a boom time for Broadway musicals, giving rise to more than four hundred, twice as many as would open in the next decade. Jerome Kern was an accomplished composer and a pioneer in modernizing the musical theater. In addition to writing ten complete musicals, he scored *Show Boat*, the first musical in which music, dialogue, and dance were integral to the plot—previously a simplistic device used to introduce songs. Kern's lyricist was Oscar Hammerstein, one of the greatest songwriters of his era, who later collaborated with Richard Rodgers. The writer of fifteen scores for Broadway and London shows from 1925 to 1930, Rodgers worked with Lorenz Hart before joining Hammerstein. Musical comedies yielded hit songs, as did musical revues such as the *Ziegfeld Follies*.

When Americans were not watching musicals, whistling Tin Pan Alley tunes, or listening to jazz, they were likely to be dancing, performing steps as frenetic and uninhibited as the music of the 1920s. The first dance craze, which the voluptuous actress Mae West popularized, was the shimmy. The dancer stood in one place and, with little movement of the feet, shook the shoulders, torso, and pelvis. The shimmy gave way to the Charleston, a creation of black stevedores who worked in the harbor of Charleston, South Carolina, and moved north to take industrial jobs during World War I. Featuring rapid foot movements and relying on the hit song of the same name for its popularity, the Charleston receded in favor of the Black Bottom. The title referred to the muddy bottom of the Suwannee River because the dance suggested the dragging of feet through mud. More sedate, ballroom remained popular, and Arthur Murray earned millions teaching couples to dance.

Like jazz, dance critics warned of its effects on the social order. Clergy deplored the exhibitionism of the Charleston, saying it was sending people to hell. Some cities passed laws to inhibit dancers. A Cleveland ordinance stated, "Don't dance from the waist up; dance from the waist down." A law in Oshkosh, Wisconsin, must have been difficult to enforce, as it prohibited partners from "looking into each other's eyes while dancing." Some did carry dancing too far, participating in dance marathons, exhausting themselves and risking their health to win small prizes.

The marathons were one of the fads of the era. A classic paradox, a fad was an activity that began as a statement of noncomformity and became something that many people did. In 1923 the Chinese game of Mah-Jongg became a national craze, only to be supplanted one year later by a craze for crossword puzzles. The most exotic fad began in 1925, when Alvin "Shipwreck" Kelly became famous for flagpole sitting. On his perch, he slept with his thumbs anchored into a wooden seat and, during a sleet storm, used a hatchet to chip ice from his body. A young woman who became enamored of Kelly was hoisted up to meet him, and when he descended, they were married. In the depression decade of the 1930s, the times favored Monopoly, a board game that encouraged players to drive their rivals into bankruptcy, parodying the 1920s monopolies that facilitated the crash.

The 1930s music benefited from improvements in recording technology; sound movies, which made musicals possible, and the dissemination of songs via jukeboxes, and radio. Popular music never had a larger audience, a boon to leading composers, among them Irving Berlin, George and Ira Gershwin, Jerome Kern, Cole Porter, and Hoagy Carmichael, who extended their repertoire by writing Hollywood scores. When it came to performing, swing was king during the big band era. Although swing was rooted in black jazz styles, white bandleaders such as Tommy Dorsey, Artie Shaw, and Glenn Miller came to dominate it. Meanwhile, Bing Crosby, Frank Sinatra, and Billie Holiday crooned in a conversational manner.

During wartime, songs reflected the national mood about America's enemies. Some were bellicose or racist, including "You're a Sap, Mr. Jap," "We're Gonna Find a Feller Who is Yeller and Beat Him Red, White, and Blue,"

DANCE TO THE MUSIC
Dancing in a Harlem nightclub, late 1930s.
(Bettmann/Corbis)

"In the Fuehrer's Face," and "Praise the Lord and Pass the Ammunition."
Country music, too, began to boom, encouraged by feelings of nostalgia
for less complicated times and the mass migration of rural southerners to
the industrial centers of the North and the West.

The Radio

Without radio, jazz might not have spread beyond New Orleans, and the
denizens of Tin Pan Alley might have been limited to selling sheet music.
Initial broadcasts were confined to ships and the military, and people bought
radios as a novelty. The industry, consisting of one commercial radio station
in 1921, grew to thirty the next year, and exploded to 556 in 1923. The
Radio Corporation of America, which built the first station to promote the
sale of radios, organized the first network, the National Broadcasting
Company (NBC), in 1926. The Columbia Broadcasting System (CBS) followed in 1927, the Mutual Broadcasting System in 1934, and the American
Broadcasting Company (ABC) in 1943. Music dominated the airwaves,
although programs began to vary. In 1920 presidential election returns were

broadcast, and eight years later, candidates used radio to campaign. In 1921 the World Series was broadcast, pioneering coverage of sports. Soon there were comedy shows starring such performers as comedians Jack Benny and Fred Allen, dramatic programs such as *Buck Rogers* and *The Lone Ranger*, variety shows, soap operas, and quiz contests.

Sales of radios increased from $12.2 million in 1921 to $168.2 million in 1925 and $366 million in 1929. Almost half of American families owned radios by 1930, and there were more receiving sets in the United States than in all other countries combined. Advertisers recognized the potential of the medium, and by 1928 Henry Ford was paying $1,000 a minute for a chain of stations to advertise his cars. At first stations were so few they could broadcast ads at any frequency without overlapping. But as stations multiplied, Commerce Secretary Herbert Hoover negotiated voluntary agreements for transmission at different frequencies. In 1927 the Radio Act formalized federal oversight over broadcasting and created the Federal Radio Commission to license stations. The Federal Communications Commission assumed regulatory responsibilities in 1934.

Radio became pervasive in the 1930s. In 1929 there were 10,250,000 household radios in the United States, whereas by 1940 there were 28,040,000, and about 80 percent of all Americans had access to a radio. Technical aspects of broadcasting improved; radios became smaller; radios were installed in cars; and stations proliferated. Music dominated radio's menu. Politicians relied on broadcasts to promote themselves, most conspicuously President Franklin D. Roosevelt with his fireside chats. The volume of news programs doubled between 1932 and 1939.

Radio occupied a central role in family life. Daytime shows included soap operas, cooking shows, and programs on raising children. The evening offered heroes such as *Superman* and *Tarzan*; and quiz shows such as *Information Please*. Comedy fare included George Burns and Gracie Allen, and ventriloquist Edgar Bergen and his dummy, Charlie McCarthy. The most popular show was *Amos 'n' Andy*, on the air from 1928 to 1960. It was the creation of white comedians Freeman Gosden, who played Amos, and Charles Correll, who played Andy. First set in Chicago, then in Harlem, the show derived its humor from the misadventures of the owners of a taxi company with one cab.

Radio's credibility and power were so great that when Orson Welles broadcast H. G. Wells's "War of the Worlds" on Halloween eve in 1938, thousands fled their homes, thinking that stations were reporting an actual Martian invasion of Earth. A Pittsburgh man found his wife in their bathroom holding a bottle of poison and screaming, "I'd rather die this way than like that!"

Silence to Sound on Screen

For most of the 1920s, movie actors lacked the voices of their radio counterparts. When film producers realized there was a market for longer films, the silent industry expanded. There were twenty thousand theaters in the United States in 1920, when movies were the fifth-largest business, and some twenty-eight thousand in 1928. Among them were palaces such as the Roxy in New York, which seated 6,200, had 125 ushers, and boasted a 110-member orchestra. Attending the theater involved a full evening, beginning with a newsreel, followed by a short comedy, previews, an episode in a serial, and the feature presentation. By the mid-1920s major studios, notably Metro-Goldwyn-Mayer, Warner Brothers, Columbia, RKO, and United Artists, were churning out enough films to enable theater owners to change their offerings every other day.

If the early industry excelled in one genre, it was comedy, whose craftsmen raised pantomime to a level that has not been matched. Producer Mack Sennett assembled the finest stable of comedic talent in Hollywood history, and his Keystone Kops films elevated slapstick to an art. Other leading comedians were Harold Lloyd, Buster Keaton, W. C. Fields, and the team of Stan Laurel and Oliver Hardy. With brilliant producers and directors including D. W. Griffith and Cecil B. DeMille, the young industry continued to explore the genres of Westerns, love stories, and biblical epics. Early in the 1920s producers discovered that sex sold tickets, and roles went to sex symbols. Movies were given suggestive titles: *Married Flirts, Sinners in Silk, Rouged Lips*, and *The Queen of Sin*. The advertisement for *Flaming Youth* beckoned people to see "neckers, petters, white kisses, red kisses, pleasure-mad daughters, sensation-craving mothers, by an author who didn't dare sign his name; the truth, bold, naked, sensational." Worried about its image and fearing censorship, the industry hired Will Hays, President Warren G. Harding's postmaster general, to create and enforce a code assuring that movies had a moral ending and that on-screen sex and violence were limited.

The silent screen era started to ebb in 1926, when Warner Brothers introduced sound, first in several short films, then in *The Jazz Singer*. The first commercially successful movie with sound, it was more a "singie" than a "talkie," having six songs that Jolson lip-synched, only about five hundred spoken words, and subtitles for most of the dialogue. Despite its modest advances, *The Jazz Singer* inaugurated a trend, and before the decade was over, the silent picture was an anachronism.

Furnishing escape from the depression, movies became so important that families skimped on necessities to attend; seeing films was the most frequent dating activity. After a decline in movie attendance starting in 1929, theaters began cutting prices, and by 1933 attendance revived and stayed high the rest of the decade. Hollywood met the demand by turning out a large volume of cheap films, including gangster movies in the early 1930s. Gangsters were shown as financial successes, but morality required that they be killed at the end.

Among comedians, the greatest were the Marx brothers, who combined slapstick with puns. The brothers made five films from 1929 to 1933, including *Animal Crackers*, Paramount's most lucrative motion picture of 1930. W. C. Fields's persona was a braggart who drank excessively and hated children. Sometimes he was paired with the funny and seductive Mae West, who launched a genre of films about sexually aggressive women, one of which had her say, "When a girl goes wrong, men go right after her." West advanced the century's sexual revolution. Inspiring laughter, Frank Capra directed "screwball" comedies from 1931 to 1941. The most famous was *It Happened One Night* (1934), a romance starring Clark Gable and Claudette Colbert. Gable was one of the leading box-office attractions of the 1930s, thanks to his role in *Gone with the Wind* (1939). Following the movie, Gable was asked how it felt to be considered the world's greatest lover. "It's a living," he replied. Besides Gable, the motion picture industry was enriched by Walt Disney, who made the animated cartoon a fine art. Child star Shirley Temple was the top box office draw from 1935 to 1938 and the model for a line of dolls, clothes, and books. The era included musicals whose quality has never been surpassed, many of them starring Fred Astaire and Ginger Rogers.

During World War II, musicals, war films, spy films, and movies about resistance to Nazism were popular. Several classic movies appeared early in the 1940s: *The Grapes of Wrath* and *The Great Dictator* (both 1940), the latter an antifascist comedy in which Charlie Chaplin parodied Adolf Hitler. Other important films included the influential *Citizen Kane* (1941), featuring Welles as director and lead character, a newspaper publisher based on William Randolph Hearst; and *Casablanca* (1942) starring Humphrey Bogart. Alfred Hitchcock, the wizard of suspense and macabre humor, became the best-known director in the United States.

Visions of America

Visual art held up mirrors to the nation. During the decade of plenty a galaxy of art museums opened, among them the Museum of Modern Art in New York in 1929. Artists demanded high prices for their work, which was experimental and increasingly concerned with urban life. Joseph Stella found New York a rich environment, painting *Brooklyn Bridge* (1922) and a series entitled *New York Interpreted* that featured innovative use of light and shadow. Edward Hopper specialized in bleak city images—a lonely diner in an all-night restaurant, a tired usher in an empty movie theater—that elaborated on ideas the Ash Can school explored. Many realists, though, focused on the nation's rural and small town heritage and were dubbed Regionalists. Thomas Hart Benton, Grant Wood, and John Stuart Curry received popular and critical applause for painting the Midwest. The most enduring Regionalist image, Wood's *American Gothic* (1930), portrays a stern, pious farm couple symbolizing the stark Midwest.

Representative art remained popular with the public, but the avant garde was dominated by abstract styles pioneered in Europe. Modernist painters distorted reality, sometimes breaking it into cubes and triangles creating visual dissonance. Even artists who retained a regional emphasis began to revolt against the representational tradition. Georgia O'Keeffe, for instance, interpreted Western deserts by enlarging details so that objects lost their recognizable quality. Modernism in art existed during the 1920s in a symbiotic yet angry relationship with industrialization. The style was a paradox: progressive in an artistic sense, it was reactionary in its resistance to technological advancement, depicting machines that the artists considered dehumanizing. Modernist techniques and nonrepresentational experiments also influenced sculpture, but the public continued to prefer conventional forms. Gutzon Borglum carved busts into the sides of mountains in Georgia and South Dakota, Confederate army heroes in the former and presidents George Washington, Abraham Lincoln, Thomas Jefferson, and Theodore Roosevelt in the latter, at Mount Rushmore.

Like literature, painting was critical of capitalism in the 1930s. A furor arose when Diego Rivera, whom Nelson Rockefeller had paid $14,000 to paint a mural in Rockefeller Center, depicted V. I. Lenin scowling as American police beat strikers. Rockefeller fired Rivera and had the scene painted over. Other muralists depicted proletarian themes, and abstract art was enlisted in the struggle against capitalism. Then, in the World War II era, prosperity came to artists, whose sales soared, never to reach 1945 levels until 1960. Europeans driven from their native lands by the war, among them Marc Chagall, Salvador Dali, and Max Ernst, enriched American painting.

Photography continued its progress as a new art form in the 1930s and 1940s, finding markets in mass-circulation magazines. Architects found that work was plentiful in the 1940s, entire cities springing up around war plants. Walter Gropius and Ludwig Mies van der Rohe brought formal, structured, coherent theories of architecture to America after fleeing Europe. Frank Lloyd Wright, enjoying a revival in popularity, claimed that the box was the shape of fascism and disliked the coldness of much modern architecture. He endowed simple structures with warmth.

Education and the Intellectuals

The new art had a large audience of educated Americans. High school enrollment increased from 2.4 million to 4.2 million in the 1920s. When the decade started, there were more illiterates than college graduates, but the illiteracy rate dropped from 6 percent to 4.3 percent by 1930—from 23 percent to 16 percent among African Americans. Small schools were consolidated, allowing teachers to specialize, and they taught more vocational subjects and less Latin and Greek. Over the decade, college enrollment rose from 598,000 (4.7 percent of the college-age population) to 1,101,000 (7.2 percent, of which 43.7 percent were women), and the number of Ph.D.s awarded increased from 560 in 1920 to 2,071 in 1930. Many college students were preoccupied with extracurricular activities and were poorly informed; some freshmen at the University of Maine thought Martin Luther was the son of Moses, whom they described as a Roman emperor. College teaching became more professionalized, and the pressure to publish increased.

Veterans of academe, Frederick Jackson Turner and Charles A. Beard, remained among the outstanding historians in the decade, joined by Vernon Parrington, Carl Becker, and Arthur M. Schlesinger. Parrington was an obscure scholar until the first two volumes of his three-volume work *Main Currents in American Thought* appeared in 1927. He described the development of the idea of democracy in the lives and work of intellectuals from 1620 to the late nineteenth century. Becker challenged the belief that historians could write objectively about the past when present-day values shaped their assessments. Objectivity was an ideal for writers such as Schlesinger, whose chief contribution was to coedit the thirteen-volume *History of American Life.*

Beard became interested in historical relativism in the 1930s and concluded that objectivity was an illusion, arguing that a historian must begin research with a viewpoint. Most of his writing was devoted to keeping the United States out of war. Historians' social visions were not entirely liberal; William A. Dunning, Ulrich B. Phillips, William Dodd, and Frank Owsley focused on slavery, the Civil War, and Reconstruction from a pro-southern perspective. Professional historians and their debates, however, mattered little to lay readers, who were a market for popular history. Frederick Lewis Allen sold more than 1 million copies of his chronicle of the 1920s, *Only Yesterday* (1931). Douglas Southall Freeman and Allan Nevins, meticulous researchers and eloquent writers, captured broad audiences. Public attention was drawn to historic preservation.

In anthropology, Margaret Mead began fieldwork in the South Pacific in 1925 and published *Coming of Age in Samoa*, a milestone in the comparative study of cultures, three years later. Also pathbreaking, Robert and Helen Lynd produced the sociological study *Middletown* (1929), an examination of Muncie, Indiana, that provided a wealth of information on attitudes and lifestyles.

Refuge in Religion

Millions of Americans looked to religion for comfort during the depression. Attendance at fundamentalist churches rose fifty percent, whereas attendance at mainline Protestant churches declined 11 percent. Overall, religion lost ground to secularism during the Era of Trial and Triumph and did not regain it until World War II.

Catholics were enthusiastic about the New Deal, about 80 percent of them supporting the Roosevelt administration. Some thought the New Deal implemented the program that Pope Pius XI outlined in *Quadragesimo Anno* (1931), an encyclical that condemned laissez-faire capitalism, rejected unregulated competition, and insisted upon a living wage for workers and a new partnership between labor and capital. FDR appointed more Catholics than any previous president.

Many Protestant ministers were reformers; the most prominent was Reinhold Niebuhr, who revived interest in theology by making it relevant to contemporary life. Critical of both capitalism and Marxism, he argued that humanity could never achieve utopia because solutions to earthly problems were ephemeral. Still, people were obliged to strive for social justice. More optimistic, Norman Vincent Peale, the leading Protestant popularizer, promoted positive thinking, advising "You can if you think you can." Jews joined Protestants and Catholics in backing the New Deal, whose circle included young Jews such as Treasury Secretary Henry Morgenthau and Supreme Court Justice Felix Frankfurter.

The depression made it economically difficult for couples to marry. Weddings were postponed, and the average age at marriage was the oldest since before the turn of the century (26.7 years for men, 23.3 for women). Birth control was increasingly practiced. Women who married and had children compensated for declining family income by canning, baking, laundering, and sewing at home.

Sports: Cheering and Playing

Families could enjoy spectator sports, which basked in a golden age in the 1920s. Urban Americans no longer had the opportunity to participate in many sports, but they had the time to watch. Sports benefited from better equipment and places to play, radio broadcasts, and the demand for heroes. Sports appealed to fans largely because it was one of the last refuges of individualism and pure competition in an automated society.

Baseball was the most popular professional sport. By 1924, 27 million people were watching games, and attendance doubled from 1921 to 1930. Great players lured fans, none more than George Herman "Babe" Ruth. He specialized in the home run, which appeared more frequently in the 1920s, due to a livelier ball and rule changes. Ruth had excessive appetites for food, drink, sex, and gambling and, at 6 feet 2 inches and 215 pounds with a beer belly and spindly legs, did not look like an athlete. Still, he was good enough to break in as a pitcher with the Boston Red Sox and was moved to the outfield so he could bat daily. In 1920 the cash-strapped Red Sox sold Ruth to the New York Yankees, whom he helped set an attendance record in his first season. "The Sultan of Swat" and the Yankees enjoyed a spectacular season in 1927, when Ruth hit sixty home runs, a mark that would stand for thirty-four years, and led a powerful "Murderer's Row" lineup to the World Series championship.

The Yankees continued their dominance in the 1930s. Their first baseman and captain, Lou Gehrig, set a record by playing in 2,130 consecutive games and faced death with courage after contracting a fatal muscular disease. Late in the decade, Yankees centerfielder Joe DiMaggio, a star at the plate, in the field, and on the bases, started a memorable career. World War II sent more than four thousand players into the armed services, including Red Sox slugger Ted Williams. Women tried to fill the wartime void, and carve out a larger place for themselves in sports, by playing in their own professional baseball league.

Challenging baseball for fan loyalty, football was the centerpiece of college social life and attracted alumni donations and national name recognition. Yale, Stanford, Michigan, and Illinois built huge stadiums. Illinois had the best attraction, halfback Harold "Red" Grange, the "Galloping Ghost." In the first game in the new Illinois stadium in 1924, he returned "the opening kickoff ninety-five yards for a touchdown. Grange ran for four other touchdowns—three in the first quarter—completed several long passes, and gained 402 yards in total offense. On the sidelines, Knute Rockne of Notre Dame was a legendary coach. Unselfishness, teamwork, and dedication—values that Americans sensed were fading—characterized Rockne's teams, which won with speed, deception, cleverness, and finesse instead of brute force. Rockne was among the first coaches to use the forward pass and the single-wing formation, which made football more offense oriented.

Wartime brought fears of a Japanese attack, so the Rose Bowl was moved east from Pasadena, California, to Durham, North Carolina, for 1942. Professional football continued on a reduced scale; players who were not drafted worked in defense plants and played on weekends. College basketball lost fewer players because many were too tall for the military. An influx of tall centers early in the 1940s led to rules to limit the dominance of big players.

Perhaps the single greatest professional sporting event of the Era of Trial and Triumph was the rematch between boxers Jack Dempsey and Gene Tunney in 1927. Their first fight in 1926, in which Dempsey lost his heavyweight title, grossed $1.9 million. The next grossed $2.5 million, the two largest purses ever. Some 60 million people listened to the rematch on radio, the biggest radio audience for any event. In the seventh round Dempsey knocked Tunney down, but the referee delayed the count until Dempsey moved to a neutral corner, giving Tunney time to recover. Tunney knocked Dempsey down in the next round and, as his adversary tired, battered Dempsey and won a unanimous decision. In ath-

HEAVYWEIGHT CHAMPION
Boxer Joe Louis wins respect for African Americans. Photograph by Carl Van Vechten. (Library of Congress)

letics as in technology, raw power was yielding to technique, and future champions would emulate the faster, more sophisticated Tunney.

In golf, amateur Bobby Jones was the biggest star. Jones won the U.S. Amateur championship five times, the U.S. Open four times, and the British Open three times in the 1920s. Tennis was dominated by William "Big Bill" Tilden, who won the U.S. title in 1920 and went unbeaten from 1921 to 1928. Among women, Helen Wills, won three U.S. singles championships and eight Wimbledon singles titles. Swimming had stars in Johnny Weismuller, who set world records, then played Tarzan in the movies, and Gertrude Ederle. A gold medal winner in the 1924 Olympics at seventeen, Ederle became the first woman to swim the English Channel, beating the times of five men who had managed the feat, in 1926, when she held eighteen world records.

Sports was an avenue of achievement for minorities. African Americans, shut out of major league baseball late in the 1880s, formed Negro Leagues that remained popular through World War II and featured players whose greatness was recognized decades later. Rarely admitted into other professional sports, African Americans made strides, particularly in boxing, in which Joe Louis had a long reign as heavyweight champion. They starred in football, basketball, and track and field. In the 1932 Los Angeles Summer Olympic Games, Eddie Tolan and Ralph Metcalfe finished first and second, respectively, in the 100-meter dash; Tolan also won the 200-meter dash, making the sprints a sweep for the United States. Four years later at the Berlin Summer Games, Jesse Owens won the 100- and 200-meter dashes and the long jump, and anchored the winning 400-meter relay team.

Women's athletics was dominated by Mildred "Babe" Didrikson Zaharias, the greatest female athlete of all time and the most versatile athlete of either sex. In the 1932 Amateur Athletic Union national track meet, she won five events, tied for first in a sixth, and finished fourth in a seventh, single-handedly winning the team championship. In the 1936 Olympics, she won gold medals in the javelin and high hurdles and the silver medal in the high jump. Turning professional, Zaharias pitched for a women's baseball team; taking up golf, she was the top women's player in the 1940s. Not only did she run and jump, but she swam, shot at targets, rode horses, boxed, and excelled at tennis, basketball, polo, and billiards. Asked whether there was anything she did not play, she replied, "Yeah, dolls."

Riven with paradox, cultural transformation coexisted with prosperity, depression, and war. The land that produced unemployed millions, also produced millions who persevered. There burst forth from a seedbed of geniuses a blossoming of Americans who entertained, inspired, and awed with their passion, imagination, agility, and intellectual virtuosity.

★ CHAPTER ELEVEN ★

Interwar Diplomacy

THE INTERWAR era represented more trials than triumphs for American diplomacy and culminated in the greatest military conflagration of the century. Disillusioned after World War I and the failed Versailles peacemaking, Americans viewed European affairs like a child burned by touching a hot pan. They did not want to touch it again. Paradoxically, it touched them.

Nonintervention and Internationalism

The 1920s and 1930s have been termed a period of isolationism, or, more accurately, noninterventionism for American diplomacy. Americans conducted more world trade than ever, consummated a significant naval reduction treaty, and traveled abroad. American culture was influential worldwide, as were missionaries for Christianity. Some Americans were proud of their country's relative military isolation, or nonintervention, and determined to preserve it. Among them were such notables as William E. Borah of Idaho, chair of the Senate Foreign Relations Committee; William Randolph Hearst, the leading newspaper publisher; Robert McCormick, publisher of the *Chicago Tribune*, the largest midwestern daily; and Henry Ford.

The key to the American mind-set, however, was nationalism, as it was to many European countries and Japan. Ethnic minorities struggled to form nations and took pride in their heritage. In some European nations, nationalism was coupled with colonialism. Others, such as Germany and Italy, envied the greater colonial holdings of the British and the French. In the Soviet Union Stalin formally theoretically eschewed nationalism in his effort to build a classless world order, yet proved no different than the other colonial powers when his interests were at stake. Washington's international emphasis was on stability rather than democracy or economic equality worldwide.

The chief goal of American internationalists, like their counterparts, the isolationists, was to preserve world peace, a goal they shared with pacifists. They differed over how to achieve this goal. Internationalists believed collective solutions to wars could preempt them. Noninterventionists held that if wars erupted, the United States should remain above the fray. Pacifists did not believe in fighting, period. Yet Americans were major players on the world scene. By 1919, a debtor nation just five years before, the United States was a creditor. American technology in consumer products seized world leadership. Still, many Americans believed that Europeans constantly connived to involve them in another war. Presidents and secretaries of state reacted to events. President Warren Harding, ignorant of world affairs, told journalist Theodore Draper, "I don't know anything about European stuff." He delegated authority to Secretary of State Charles Evans Hughes. President Calvin Coolidge was not interested in foreign policy. President Herbert Hoover, in his career as a mining engineer, had lived and traveled abroad more than any twentieth-century president.

The United States technically remained at war with Germany, a consequence of not approving the Versailles Treaty, until Congress adopted a joint resolution ending hostilities and Harding signed it on July 2, 1921. Membership in the League of Nations continued unrealized, as Harding, Coolidge, and Hoover never advocated it. They favored American membership in the World Court, yet the 1926 congressional vote endorsing membership had reservations that were unacceptable to the other members, and Coolidge dropped the matter. The presidents continued Woodrow Wilson's policy of refusing to recognize the Soviet Union. Trade was not restrained, however. By 1928, one-fourth of all foreign investment there was American; one-third of all Ford-exported tractors went to the Soviets. In 1929 Ford agreed to help Soviets build cars and trucks. As commerce secretary, Hoover coordinated public and private relief efforts that sent $78 million worth of food to the famine-stricken Soviets and saved 10 million from starvation.

Postwar Payback: Debts and Reparations

During and after World War I the United States, with money from war bond sales at home, lent about $10.5 billion to the Allies and other European nations. Europeans argued that Washington should erase their debts because America had suffered neither the casualties nor the property damage they incurred. The United States from 1923 to 1930 renegotiated interest rates from an average of 5 percent to 1.6 percent, eliminating more than half the debt. Cancellation of the debts was unacceptable to Americans because it would have made the debts the responsibility of U.S. taxpayers who had bought war bonds. The United Sates also pointed out that the Allies were receiving reparations from Germany. An Allied commission had set reparations at $33 billion plus interest, payable in annual installments, but Germany fell behind and defaulted in December 1922. French and Belgian troops occupied the industrialized Ruhr Valley to compel payment; Germans resorted to passive resistance, and their economy collapsed. Whereas before the war one American dollar was worth 4.2 German Marks, by 1924 it took 4 trillion Marks to equal a dollar. Inflation destroyed the savings of the German middle class, inciting resentment and provoking demands for an authoritarian regime to exact revenge.

In 1924 a League of Nations commission under Charles G. Dawes, formerly Harding's budget director, developed a plan that pared reparations and provided Germany with a $200 million loan, half from the United States, to stabilize its currency. After the Germans accepted the proposal, the Ruhr occupation ended, payments resumed, and Dawes won the Nobel Peace Prize. Germany fell behind, and in 1929 another commission reduced reparations to $8.8 billion plus 5.5 percent interest yearly. It set a graduated scale of payments over fifty-nine years, an agreement that shipwrecked on the rocks of the Great Depression. In 1932 President Hoover called for a one-year moratorium on all intergovernmental debt, hoping the move would enable private creditors to collect obligations and save American banks that had invested in European securities. That June, Germany's creditors agreed to forgive nine-tenths of reparations owed them if the United States would cancel the war debts. Washington declined, but after 1932 few reparations or debts were paid.

Campaigns for World Peace

During the 1920s a movement for peace and disarmament flourished in the United States. Ernest Hemingway, John Dos Passos, and William Faulkner wrote antiwar novels. With their recently won right to vote, women devoted themselves to the peace crusade, constituting two-thirds of the activists. They formed groups such as the Women's International League for Peace and Freedom, led by Jane Addams, whose work brought her the 1931 Nobel Peace Prize. The Women's Peace Union tried but failed to get a constitutional amendment to outlaw war passed in each Congress from 1926 to 1939. Still, the women's peace movement was a factor behind a naval disarmament conference that met from late 1921 to early 1922 in Washington. Money also was a motive. The cost of constructing a battleship increased from $5 million in 1900 to $40 million in

1920. Britain had an aging fleet that would be expensive to replace; and Japan knew that it could not compete with American wealth in an arms race. Limiting naval competition required settlement of issues in the Far East, a crucial area of competition. At London's suggestion, Hughes invited nations with an interest in the region to participate.

Three complementary covenants emerged. The Four Power Treaty bound the United States, Britain, France, and Japan to respect each other's Pacific possessions and to consult if disputes arose. The Nine Power Treaty sought to curb competition among foreign powers in China and opened all of China to international trade. Under the Five Power Treaty, the parties agreed not to fortify their Pacific colonies as well as to scrap some battleships and to construct none for ten years. Tonnage ceilings were established, with each nation given a ratio. For every 5 ships allowed to the United States and Britain, Japan could have 3 and France and Italy 1.67 each. Aircraft carriers were included in the ceilings, but no bounds were set on planes, submarines, destroyers, or cruisers. This provision proved a major shortcoming, as was the failure to invite Germany and the Soviet Union. The agreements were the most significant diplomatic achievements between the world wars. The Five Power Treaty was the first major arms limitation accord in the history of the modern world.

Later attempts to curb arms were less successful. In 1927 Coolidge initiated a conference in Geneva to limit smaller warships, yet France and Italy refused to take part. After the conference adjourned without an agreement, American peace leaders refocused on a project long under consideration, to make war illegal. Even in the absence of sanctions, peace activists thought, the stigma of world opinion would deter potential aggressors. Also, they could be tried in an international court for waging offensive wars. Borah had introduced such a resolution in the Senate in 1923, with no result. Then, in 1927, James T. Shotwell, an official with the Carnegie Endowment for International Peace, asked French Foreign Minister Aristide Briand to propose a treaty outlawing war between the United States and France. Secretary of State Frank Kellogg resisted because it would effectively ally the two nations. He countered with a proposal asking all countries to adhere. Outmaneuvered, Briand agreed, and sixty-four nations, among them future war makers, signed the Pact of Paris, or the Kellogg-Briand Treaty, in August 1928. Kellogg won the Nobel Peace Prize. Some dismissed the treaty as hopelessly idealistic because there was no way of enforcing it. One senator mocked the pact as an "international kiss."

Hoover tried to limit arms at conferences in 1930 at London and in 1932 at Geneva. At London, the United States, Britain, and Japan promised to apply the 5:5:3 ratio to smaller ships. In addition, the Japanese were granted parity in submarines, the moratorium on capital ship construction was extended to 1936, and rules for submarine warfare were codified. The Geneva meeting was a failure. Hoover proposed the elimination of offensive weapons, reduction of total weaponry by 30 percent, and limitation of armies. His plans were doomed when, during a recess, Adolf Hitler's militaristic Nazi Party won a plurality in German's parliamentary election.

Japanese Aggression

The major foreign crisis of Hoover's administration began with Japanese aggression against China in Manchuria. Japan, whose army defied its civilian government and intimidated its prime minister, expanded into Manchuria after World War I to exploit timber, coal, and iron. The move triggered competition with the Soviet Union and China, in which Tokyo gained the upper hand by wresting control of key railroads. By the early 1930s, nearly 90 percent of Japanese foreign investment was in Manchuria; however, rising Chinese nationalism jeopardized control of the colony. China had been in turmoil since the overthrow of the Manchu dynasty in 1911. Subsequent civil wars broke out between Sun Yat-sen and regional warlords, but Sun's successor, Jiang Jieshe (Chiang Kai-Shek), leader of the Nationalist Guomindang (Kuomintang) Party, appeared on the brink of adding Manchuria to his conquests. To justify its dominance of the province, the Japanese army staged an incident on September 18, 1931, setting off an explosion on the South Manchurian Railway near Mukden and blaming the Chinese for sabotage. Retaliating, Japan seized Mukden and surrounding territory, violating international law. The Japanese compounded their aggression by bombing civilians in Shanghai. The League of Nations, despite the obligation to defend Chinese territory, only investigated the affair.

As the Hoover cabinet debated options, Secretary of State Henry L. Stimson and the president stalled for nearly four months. Hoover was no pacifist; his philosophy reflected the nickname of the football team in his hometown of West Branch, Iowa, "the Fighting Quakers." But no American official advocated military intervention because U.S. forces were too weak and American interests were not directly at stake. "The American people don't give a hoot in a rain barrel who controls North China," the *Philadelphia Record* declared. Stimson favored economic sanctions against Japan, yet Hoover disagreed, fearing they might lead to war. Early in 1932, the Stimson Doctrine was announced, amounting to moral condemnation unaccompanied by sanctions. The secretary of state informed Japan and China that the United States would not recognize conquests that violated international law. Japan, undeterred, declared a puppet state, Manchukuo, independent of China. The United States and the League withheld recognition without taking additional action. Tokyo left the League, and aggressors in Europe scorned the weak reaction.

Possessor of the most powerful armed forces in the world at the conclusion of World War I, the United States permitted its army and navy to atrophy during the Great Depression. Under the Hoover administration, not a single warship was constructed, and the country did not build to the limits allowed under the Washington and London naval treaties. The army totaled only 136,000 troops and the air corps was impotent. Leader of army aviators in World War I, General Billy Mitchell advocated air power throughout the 1920s. He proved its potential when his planes sank obsolete battleships during practice runs. Because he stridently opposed his superiors' neglect of air power, Mitchell was court-martialed, and he quit the army. In 1942, the Pearl Harbor attack having vindicated his views, Congress removed the stigma of the court-martial and promoted Mitchell, posthumously.

The "Good Neighbor"

In dealing with Latin America, the United States faced dilemmas. Washington preferred friendly, democratic governments, yet stability was its main objective, partly to protect American business and American lives. If the United States refrained from intervening, dictators might proliferate throughout the Western Hemisphere. Yet intervening seemed like bullying, and it was easier to go in than to get out. When Harding took office, the United States had troops in Panama, Cuba, the Dominican Republic, Haiti, and Nicaragua, but by the end of the Hoover administration, nearly all of them had been removed. Harding, Coolidge, and Hoover made a transition from the interventionism of Theodore Roosevelt, William Howard Taft, and Woodrow Wilson to the disengagement of the New Deal.

Mexico presented the most urgent controversy. The 1917 Mexican constitution stated that natural resources belonged to Mexicans and that property owned by foreigners was subject to expropriation. This policy angered American businessmen, who by 1920 held 40 percent of Mexican land and almost 60 percent of oil reserves. Harding and Coolidge would not recognize the government of Alvaro Obregon, who enforced the constitution, seized Catholic Church property, and suppressed religious schools. Also, they demanded the repeal of laws banning foreign ownership. In 1923 the countries concluded the Bucareli Agreement, which exempted land developed before 1917 from confiscation and allowed land obtained after then to be expropriated, with compensation in Mexican bonds. Though American property owners remained unhappy, the United States recognized Obregon's rule and allowed loans to Mexico. However, Obregon's successor, Plutarco Elias Calles, repudiated the agreement, inflaming a crisis. Calles signed legislation limiting foreign ownership of property bought before 1917 to fifty years and specifying that foreigners who owned Mexican land could not appeal to their governments. To avert an American-Mexican war, in 1927 Coolidge sent banker Dwight Morrow to Mexico to arrange a compromise. Deferential to the Mexicans, Morrow negotiated a solution that saved face for both nations. Calles, in turn, persuaded the Mexican Supreme Court to invalidate the legislation.

Trouble emerged in Nicaragua in 1925, after Coolidge removed troops who had occupied the country since 1912. Civil war erupted, and four presidents were sworn in within thirteen months. Coolidge returned the soldiers in 1926 and sent Stimson to seek an accord the next year. Not all Nicaraguans accepted the deal, and the troops remained to supervise elections in 1928, 1930, and 1932. They withdrew shortly before Roosevelt took office. Indeed, the Good Neighbor policy in the region, usually associated with FDR, started during the Hoover administration. Hoover carried the policy of military disengagement further than did his predecessors. As president-elect, he toured Latin America and announced, "We have a desire to maintain not only the cordial relations of governments with each other but the relations of good neighbors." Later, Hoover said the United States would intervene militarily only if an outside power threatened to take over a hemispheric nation. He also refused to send soldiers during revolutions and began the phased withdrawal of troops that Roosevelt completed.

Franklin Roosevelt was a relatively cosmopolitan president, at least superficially. European governesses tutored him in German and French; he studied European history at Groton and Harvard. From 1900 to 1912 he toured Europe three times and the Caribbean twice. Still, he came to the White House with few principles to guide his foreign policy. So FDR improvised as the situation dictated. He made no speeches on foreign affairs during the 1932 campaign and, upon taking office, reduced appropriations for the small, underequipped army and used the money for domestic priorities.

In his first inaugural address, Roosevelt said, "In the field of foreign policy, I would dedicate this nation to the policy of the good neighbor." Reporters isolated "good neighbor" and applied it to his policy of nonintervention in the Western Hemisphere. If the term and the policy really originated with Hoover, however, FDR went further than the Republican by translating it into action. In 1934 Roosevelt negotiated a treaty abrogating the Platt Amendment, by which the United States asserted a right to intervene in Cuba. Before the year was over, all American troops had been withdrawn from Haiti. Two years later America concluded a treaty with Panama, relinquishing the right to intervene there.

The United States also loosened the reins on its major colony, the Philippines. In 1934 FDR signed into law the Tydings-McDuffie Act, providing for independence in 1946. In the interim the Philippines would have dominion status and would be given self-rule gradually. Roosevelt was one of the first Western leaders to recognize that the epoch of colonialism was ending, and the United States was one of the first nations to relinquish a colony voluntarily. His policies toward the Philippines and Latin America were meant to give America an anticolonial record, in contrast with the European dictatorships, and unite the hemisphere into an alliance against external threats, codified in the Declaration of Lima (1938) and the Act of Havana (1940). During World War II every nation in the hemisphere except Argentina cooperated with the Allies.

In Latin America Roosevelt neither rebuilt the economies nor reformed the politics of America's neighbors. Yet he proved more tolerant of their independence than were previous U.S. presidents. For example, in 1938, when Mexico nationalized foreign property, including oil, he accepted compensation to owners on terms favorable to Mexico. In another departure from previous chief executives, FDR extended diplomatic recognition to the Soviet Union in 1933, hoping closer relations would stimulate trade.

Hitler's Rise to Power

Depression and the sting of defeat in World War I paved Adolf Hitler's rise to power in Germany. A charismatic zealot, he believed in the triumph of will and violence. Hitler defined Germans, or Aryans, as a superior race destined to rule the world. Germany must conquer the inferior peoples of Eastern Europe and the Soviet Union, he said, liquidating the old, the ill, and Jews. Paranoid of Jews, Hitler said: "The heaviest blow ever struck humanity was the coming of Christianity. Bolshevism is Christianity's illegitimate child. Both are inventions of the Jews." Americans were a mongrel race incapable of thwarting him. At first they made no attempt to stop him, like the British and the French, and within six years of coming to power Hitler had overturned the European order. The United States, meanwhile, was grappling with the depression, and Britain was struggling to retain its empire. France was constructing the Maginot Line, concrete pillboxes and artillery emplacements near the German border.

Hitler removed Germany from the League of Nations in 1933, began rearmament in 1934, and introduced conscription in 1935, defying the

Versailles Treaty. In March 1936 he violated the treaty again when his army marched into the Rhineland, a demilitarized zone. Hitler was bluffing; if the French Army resisted, his generals had orders to withdraw. Seven months later Hitler signed an alliance with Benito Mussolini, the ruler of Italy, who described the future of Europe as revolving around a Rome-Berlin axis, coining the term, "Axis alliance." Mussolini felt he needed colonies to brandish Italian might. The dictator attacked Ethiopia in 1935. Emperor Haile Selassie appealed to the League of Nations to save his country; but the League responded with no more than weak economic sanctions that did not include coal or oil. America took no tangible action at all.

Rather, noninterventionists prevailed. Some of the isolationists in Congress were to the Left of Roosevelt on economic issues. Among them were the Republicans William E. Borah, Gerald P. Nye, and Arthur H. Vandenberg; the progressives George W. Norris and Robert M. La Follette Jr.; and the Democrat Burton K. Wheeler, all in the Senate. Outside the Capitol the isolationists' Far-Right fringe groups were led by demagogues such as Father Charles E. Coughlin, Gerald L. K. Smith, and Elizabeth Dilling.

In 1934 the Johnson Act prohibited loans to any foreign government in default to the United States, a ban that applied to most of Europe. Around the same time, a Senate committee under Nye began an investigation into the role of arms manufacturers in seducing the country into involvement in World War I. The inquiry concluded in 1936 that the United States went to war as a result of a conspiracy of those manufacturers. Books about the arms industry added strength to the conspiracy theory. The isolationist impulse crested in January 1935, when Congress, intimidated by a coalition including Louisiana Senator Huey Long, Coughlin, and Hearst, defeated a proposal for American membership on the World Court. Lawmakers also stymied FDR's hope for an arms embargo against Italy in retaliation for its Ethiopian invasion. FDR wanted Congress to authorize him to distinguish aggressors from victims in implementing such embargoes. Instead, Congress passed an embargo against all belligerents. Worrying about the fate of New Deal measures if he resisted, the president reluctantly approved the embargo contained in the Neutrality Act. The law favored the well-armed Italians over the poorly armed Ethiopians.

European events hurtled out of control in 1936. In July, Spanish General Francisco Franco led a revolt against the republican, or Loyalist, government. Many Americans supported the Loyalists. Four thousand of them fought in a volunteer brigade. The Soviet Union backed the republic, but Germany and Italy favored Franco, supplying nearly 40 percent of his troops and almost all his arms. They helped him win a civil war that lasted three years and killed more than 1 million. Roosevelt's priority was to contain war, not save Spanish democracy. In keeping with that priority, Congress approved, in January 1937, a joint resolution applying the Neutrality Act to civil wars. On May 1, FDR signed a new, two-year Neutrality Act that gave the president discretion to certify whether a state of war existed; if he did, an arms embargo would be declared against both sides. Commodities other than weapons could be sold to belligerents only on a cash-and-carry basis.

Outbreak of War

In March 1938 German soldiers marched into Austria, and Hitler proclaimed the Anschluss, the union of Austria and Germany, claiming that it was the will of the Austrians. Britain and France protested mildly and the United States did nothing, although the Versailles Treaty barred the Anschluss. Next Hitler began making demands upon Czechoslovakia, insisting that the Sudetenland, a Czech region with a large German population, be annexed to Germany. Whenever the Czechs yielded to a German demand, the Fuhrer raised the ante. With war seeming imminent, Hitler, Mussolini, British Prime Minister Neville Chamberlain, and French Prime Minister Edouard Daladier met at Munich, Germany, to seek a compromise. The British and the French decided to appease Hitler by giving him the Sudetenland. Hitler declared, "This is the last territorial demand I have to make in Europe." Chamberlain announced that he had achieved "peace with honor . . . peace in our time," an assessment with which Winston Churchill, his chief political foe in Britain, disagreed. "Do not suppose that this is the end," Churchill warned. "This is only the beginning of the reckoning."

If Hitler's ambition had been limited to rectifying injustices, appeasement might have worked at the expense of neighbors bordering Germany. Yet he had an insatiable appetite for territory, and by refusing to commit themselves to containing him, the other European nations and the United States invited further aggression. The Fuhrer planned to bring other lands under his heel, and to exterminate Jews. There were only 500,000 Jews among the 85 million inhabitants of Germany, yet Hitler blamed them for all German afflictions, including the defeat in World War I. Jews' civil rights already had been restricted before a fateful incident in 1938. A young Polish Jew assassinated a minor German official in Paris, triggering Kristallnacht, or "the Night of Broken Glass." Nazi soldiers and civilians beat Jews, arrested them, burned their synagogues, destroyed their businesses, and compelled them to pay huge sums in damages to their own property. New regulations barred Jews from engaging in retail trade, attending college, using public libraries, and driving cars. Most ominous, twenty-five thousand Jews were sent to concentration camps, where many were murdered. Jews attempting to flee Germany, sadly, could find no country to accept them. The United States would not relax immigration laws, not even to allow twenty thousand Jewish children to be admitted outside quotas. A ship carrying 930 Jewish refugees en route from Hamburg to Cuba was not allowed to dock.

Hitler's intention to dominate all Europe became clear on March 15, 1939, when German troops invaded the rest of Czechoslovakia. He plotted to take Poland next, a move that necessitated neutralizing the Soviet Union. Joseph Stalin, eager for a slice of Poland, distrusting the British and the French, and naively trusting Hitler, obliged by negotiating a neutrality pact with Germany that made world war inevitable. Even as he completed the treaty, the Fuhrer planned to turn on the Soviets once he had extinguished his enemies in the West. Announcement of the treaty, signed on August 23, shocked the world, for communists and fascists were arch-enemies. Then Hitler made demands on Poland and escalated them beyond reason. Finally realizing the futility of appeasement, Britain declared that it would defend Poland. On September 1, Hitler invaded Poland, and two days later London and Paris declared war on Germany

Stalin emulated his cynical ally by seizing the eastern half of Poland, annexing the Baltic republics of Estonia, Latvia, and Lithuania, and demanding extravagant territorial concessions from neighboring Finland. When the Finns refused, he invaded, taking their country only after his Red Army suffered embarrassing casualties against a vastly smaller military. Albania, which Mussolini attacked in April 1939, also was under Axis control. At Roosevelt's suggestion, Congress repealed the arms embargo in November and adopted yet another Neutrality Act. This one allowed the Allies to buy arms and civilian goods from the United States on a cash-and-carry basis.

Hitler took Poland with a Blitzkrieg, or lightning war, featuring rapid penetration with tanks, planes, and personnel carriers. He did not attempt additional conquests during the winter of 1939–1940, inactivity that military experts called the Sitzkrieg, or phony war. But in April 1940 Hitler burst out of his defensive positions to seize Norway and Denmark, and in May he added Belgium, the Netherlands, and Luxembourg. Then, outflanking the Maginot Line to the north, he invaded France. His forces pushed the French and British armies toward the sea, where more than three hundred thousand troops were rescued in an evacuation at Dunkirk. Less than ten days later, German forces entered Paris. On June 22 the humiliated French signed a surrender in the railway car in the Compiegne forest in which Germany had surrendered in 1918. In the unoccupied south of France, General Henri Petain established the Vichy government that collaborated with the Nazis.

Only Britain, which no longer had an army on the continent, remained free, protected from invasion across the English Channel because its fleet still controlled the North Sea. Hoping to avoid an invasion, Hitler tried to bomb the British into submission with his Luftwaffe, but failed. The much smaller Royal Air Force, with the aid of radar and the incentive of self-preservation, won the Battle of Britain. Frustrated, the Fuhrer shifted his air attacks from air bases to cities and the bombing of civilian populations, only to fail again. Far from breaking the British spirit, the bombing stiffened their will to resist. Britain then bombed Berlin, making the conflict a total war in which civilians on both sides became targets.

FDR'S Third Term

In 1940, as France collapsed and Britain struggled to survive Hitler's attacks, Americans hoped the Allies would win the war and grappled with questions about their own country. If Britain fell, would the United States be next? Would the great moats—the Atlantic and Pacific oceans—insure immunity from attack? There was also a presidential election. The great riddle was whether Roosevelt would break the two-term tradition set by George Washington. FDR vacillated for months before the Chicago convention. Then he decided the Axis threat justified another term, a decision that alienated some of his close advisers. To overcome tradition, FDR felt he must appear to be drafted. Hence he publicly disavowed third-term ambitions and privately plotted a convention demonstration for himself that would look spontaneous. In addition, he stole some GOP thunder by appointing two prominent Republicans to his cabinet, Henry L. Stimson as war secretary and Frank Knox as navy secretary.

The Republicans at Philadelphia turned to an eleventh-hour entrant, Wendell Willkie, a utility executive and political novice. Handsome, an internationalist, and a supporter of many New Deal reforms, he became a Roosevelt foe when the Tennessee Valley Authority overwhelmed his company. To broaden the geographic and ideological appeal of their ticket, Republicans made progressive Oregon Senator Charles McNary Willkie's running mate. Roosevelt chose Henry Wallace, his controversial secretary of agriculture, having broken with Garner over the third term issue.

Willkie initially attacked the New Deal and Roosevelt for power-mongering. FDR said the war crisis mandated tested leadership. Though Willkie supported preparedness measures, late in the campaign, finding himself far behind in the polls, he began to brand the president a warmonger.

Roosevelt retorted: "I have said this before, but I shall say it again and again. Your boys are not going to be sent into any foreign wars." Willkie replied scathingly that if FDR's pledge "is no better than his promise to balance the budget, they're almost on the transports!" But every new danger in Europe or Asia enhanced Roosevelt's chances. FDR received 27 million popular votes and 449 electoral votes to 22 million and 82 for Willkie, the smallest plurality of any candidate since 1916.

Roosevelt had to overcome mounting opposition from anti-interventionists. With his encouragement, internationalists had created the Committee to Defend America by Aiding the Allies and a smaller, more militant group, Fight for Freedom Inc. Still, the isolationist organizations were more formidable and better financed. In July 1940 midwestern businessmen helped form the America First Committee, supported by leaders such as Hearst, Ford, Colonel Robert McCormick, and Charles Lindbergh. Boasting 850,000 members at its peak, the committee argued that the United States weakened its defenses by shipping to Britain weapons that American forces needed. Lindbergh was the most effective critic of Roosevelt's policies and the most influential isolationist. He traveled to Germany several times, mostly to inspect the Luftwaffe, was impressed by German might, and accepted and kept a top civilian medal that government gave him. Worse, he described Jews as a threat to America because of their alleged dominance over foreign policy, the radio, the press, and the motion picture industry. The anti-Semitic overtones of Lindbergh and others, including some German Americans and groups implicitly sympathetic to Hitler, embarrassed America First. Such elements constrained Roosevelt's ability to check aggression, due to their allying themselves with respectable anti-interventionists and pacifists.

"A Date Which Will Live in Infamy"

The British, rapidly depleting their financial resources by buying weapons and food abroad, faced a crisis. To overcome it, Roosevelt agreed in September 1940 to transfer fifty destroyers used in World War I to Britain in exchange for leases on British air and naval bases in the Western Hemisphere. He also signed a conscription bill. Then, in January 1941, FDR proposed the Lend-Lease Bill to let London purchase arms on credit or to borrow them for the remainder of the war. If the home of one's neighbor caught fire, one would not try to sell the neighbor a hose, but lend it to him and get it back after the fire was out, he said. The logic of Roosevelt's analogy did not impress isolationists. Elizabeth Dilling brought six hundred mothers to Washington to demonstrate against the measure.

Senator Robert A. Taft quipped: "Lending war equipment is a good deal like lending chewing gum. You don't want it back." Wheeler was more vicious in denouncing Lend-Lease as a perverse form of the Agricultural Adjustment Administration—the "New Deal's triple-A foreign policy" he said would "plow under every fourth American boy." Roosevelt replied, "That is really the rottenest thing that has ever been said in public life in my generation." To charges that the bill would inspire Hitler to attack the United States, FDR said: "Such aid is not an act of war. When the dictators are ready to make war on us, they will not wait for an act of war on our part. They did not wait for Norway or Belgium or the Netherlands to commit an act of war." Also, he had said that aiding Britain was the best way to protect the Western Hemisphere. "We must be the great arsenal of democracy," he announced. After heated debate, Congress passed Lend-Lease, and Roosevelt signed the legislation in March.

The British, however, needed an ally more desperately than supplies and received one from an unexpected quarter in the summer of 1941. On June 22 Hitler sent waves of troops into the Soviet Union, driving Stalin into the allied camp. Some Americans on the Far Right preferred a German triumph to a Soviet one. Others hoped the two great armies would grind each other down. Missouri Senator Harry S Truman suggested, "If we see that Germany is winning, we ought to help Russia, and if Russia is winning, we ought to help Germany." By contrast, Churchill, who had succeeded Chamberlain as prime minister, considered the Soviets expedient allies, "If Hitler invaded Hell, I would at least make a favorable reference to the Devil in the House of Commons," he said. American Communists, once foes of Hitler, then his friends, became enemies once again. With the world crisis peaking, the army was concerned that it would have to release one-year draftees. The administration wanted to extend the term of service for the duration of the war, but the Senate substituted an eighteen-month extension, which passed easily in that chamber but barely won a House vote, 203 to 202, evidence of the strength of isolationism.

London laid the grounds for a significant alliance in the secret Churchill-Roosevelt meeting on August 9, 1941, off the coast of Argentia, Newfoundland. The talks marked the start of a warm friendship between the prime minister and the president, Churchill told FDR, "It is fun to be in the same decade with you." Their chief objective, the stipulation of war aims, was expressed in the Atlantic Charter which upheld democracy. By fall, the American road to war reached another intersection. The United States, which had begun convoying British ships, was fighting an undeclared war in the Atlantic. On September 4 the destroyer *Greer* exchanged shots with a German submarine it had been stalking. Roosevelt called the incident an unprovoked German attack. On October 16, eleven crewmen died when a German torpedo struck the destroyer *Kearny*, and two weeks later 115 sailors went down with the destroyer *Reuben James*, the first American warship sunk by a U-boat. In November, Congress responded by revising the Neutrality Act to let merchant ships arm and to deliver cargoes to belligerent ports.

Yet for the United States, war did not break out in the Atlantic, where everyone anticipated it, but in the Pacific, from Japan, holder of a Far East empire seized while Americans were focused on Hitler. Japan lacked resources and sought to expand to become a great power in the Pacific by excluding the only potential competitor for regional dominance, the United States. In 1937, Tokyo expanded the fighting over China beyond Manchuria: Japan seized major Chinese cities. Jiang Jieshe retreated to the interior, and communists waged guerrilla combat against the invaders. Roosevelt did not proclaim a state of war, under the pretense that Japan had not declared war, and America rushed arms to China. His mind on the conflict, the president delivered his first major foreign policy speech on October 5, 1937. "War must be quarantined like an epidemic disease," the commander in chief said, although he offered no proposals and did not follow up. On December 12, Japanese planes sank the American gunboat *Panay* on the Yangtze River, killing three people and wounding seventy-four. Anti-interventionists questioned the stationing of a warship in such dangerous waters, and few Americans demanded war against Japan. The Japanese Empire apologized and paid an indemnity. A day after the sinking, a constitutional amendment requiring a national referendum before the United States could go to war (unless attacked) was brought to the House floor, where it was defeated, 209 to 188.

In September 1940, emboldened by the dazzling German victories, the Japanese formulating plans for an empire that included China, French Indochina, Thailand, British Malaya, British Borneo, the Dutch East Indies, Burma, Australia, New Zealand, and possibly India and the Philippines. That month, Japan occupied northern Indochina and signed the Tripartite Pact, an alliance with Germany and Italy. In response, the United States placed embargoes on aviation gasoline, lubricating oil, and scrap metal. The next spring Japan signed a nonaggression treaty with the Soviet Union. Stalin freed Tokyo to attack the United States. Then, in July 1941, Japan moved into southern Indochina despite warnings from Washington. FDR froze Japanese assets in America. Also, Roosevelt closed the Panama Canal to Japanese shipping and recalled General Douglas MacArthur from retirement to command American forces in the Far East. The State Department placed an embargo on oil, the most important commodity for Japan's navy.

THE PACIFIC FLEET IN FLAMES
Pearl Harbor, December 7, 1941.
(Franklin D. Roosevelt Presidential Library)

With the embargo tightening, Prime Minister Fumimaro Konoye proposed, in August, a summit to settle differences. Stalling for time while he dealt with Hitler, Roosevelt feared a conference would bring a showdown too quickly. Also, the Japanese might use a failed meeting as an excuse for war. FDR thus refused to meet Konoye, whose cabinet fell on October 18. His successor was the militarist war minister, Hideki Tojo. Throughout the fall, though, Japanese Ambassador Kichisaburo Nomura negotiated with Secretary of State Cordell Hull. China kept the two sides apart. Washington demanded that Japan withdraw, and Tokyo demanded that the United States stop sending arms to China.

Japan had a brief period in which an attack on the United States would be feasible. With no more than a six-month oil supply, it was close to losing its naval superiority to the American construction program (it did in 1942). Weather conditions and the supreme command favored an attack by early December 1941. Afterward, conditions would not be suitable until spring and the oil shortage would be crippling. The Japanese objective was an American base 3,900 miles from the home islands, Pearl Harbor in Hawaii. Contemplation of an attack on a nation so much larger, with more natural resources, seems mad, but Tokyo, realizing that it would be defeated in a protracted war, planned a knockout blow against the American Pacific fleet. The empire believed the United States would concede in the Pacific to focus resources against Hitler. Therefore, on November 25, 1941, a task force including six aircraft carriers, two battleships, and nine destroyers started for Hawaii on a route far to the north of usual shipping channels.

Since late 1940 American cryptanalysts had been able to read the most secure Japanese diplomatic code, called "Magic." On November 22, 1941, they decoded a message to Nomura and his associate ordering them to seek an agreement by November 29 because later "things are automatically going to happen." On November 26 navy experts decoded a long message that seemed to indicate an attack was being planned. Among the mass of messages intercepted, some pointed to Pearl Harbor, yet many appeared to suggest that the Philippines or Singapore would be targeted. Rumors abounded, one that a dog on an Oahu beach was "barking in Morse Code to [a] Japanese sub offshore." Roosevelt wrote to Emperor Hirohito on December 6, urging him to withdraw from Indochina. The note never reached him, for the Japanese war cabinet intercepted it.

That evening, FDR read the final message from Tokyo to its envoys in Washington and said, "This means war." He had expected war, but did not instigate it; his primary concern at the time was Germany. If there was no plot in the United States to provoke war, however, there was plenty of incompetence. The Pearl Harbor commander responded to a War Department warning by alerting his troops for sabotage, not for attack. Planes were parked wingtip to wingtip so they could be guarded from saboteurs; it would have taken four hours to launch them. Antiaircraft ammunition was stored and locked. No patrols were operating north of Oahu. Radar was in use only on an experimental basis. Reports of airplanes approaching were dismissed.

At daybreak on December 7, dive-bombers and torpedo planes roared in. By 10:00 A.M., battleship row was a smoldering ruin. The Japanese sank or damaged 8 battleships, 3 light cruisers, 3 destroyers, and 188 planes. The United States suffered 3,345 casualties, Japan less than one hundred. The defeat, paradoxically, was not so massive as it seemed: the battleship, the ultimate weapon in World War I, had been rendered obsolete by air power, and the American aircraft carriers were in port or at sea. Japan, nevertheless, had silenced the anti-interventionists, united Americans or war, and started a fight that it could not win. "I fear we have awakened a sleeping

WAR AGAINST JAPAN
Franklin Roosevelt
signs the Declaration
of War with Japan.
(Library of Congress)

giant," Admiral Isoroku Yamamoto, the planner of the attack, said soberly. The next day, Roosevelt appeared before Congress, and called December 7 "a date which will live in infamy." He requested a declaration of war that was swiftly adopted. On December 11 Germany and Italy declared war on the United States. Washington returned the compliment one day later. Hitler, who was not obliged to fight America because he was not consulted about the Pearl Harbor attack, thought victory was certain. Had he been imaginative, he might have declared war on Japan rather than on the United States, placing Americans in an untenable position.

Twenty-three years and twenty-six days after the armistice of 1918, America was at war again. The "rendezvous with destiny" which FDR predicted in his 1936 acceptance speech had arrived. Ironically, in 1936 Roosevelt was talking about the Great Depression.

CHAPTER TWELVE

World War II: Home Front and Battlefront, 1941–1945

I N THE Era of Trial and Triumph, World War II was the greatest trial and the greatest triumph. Paradoxically, it separated families, required sacrifice, and killed hundreds of thousands, yet it unified the nation, ended the Great Depression, and healed the nation. World War II is the story of people who marched out of 1941 and into 1942 bewildered by the planet exploding around them and were remade. War required the federal government to dominate Americans through massive spending and intervention in people's lives—a course that would be unpopular in peacetime. Changes on the domestic front in wartime surpassed those of any other period in the Time of Paradox.

Transformation

Facing their greatest challenge, Americans shared a purpose. Those who did not go abroad to fight wanted to contribute, donating blood, buying bonds, planting Victory Gardens, and collecting newspapers and tin cans for recycling. When the War Production Board asked for 4 million tons of scrap metal in two months, people responded with 5 million in three weeks; one town with 207 residents collected 225 tons. Women volunteered to work in hospitals, day care centers, and schools.

Sacrifices were required. Industrial accidents killed some three hundred thousand workers. More Americans relocated than at any time in history. To conserve resources, the country limited consumer access to new cars, tires, electrical appliances, and nylon stockings; ten major items were rationed, among them meat, shoes, sugar, and gasoline.

Military bases and war industries transformed communities and regions. The West Coast, once isolated, became the fastest growing part of the country, producing 20 percent of war goods despite having 10 percent of the population. Industrial growth anticipated to take fifty years occurred in four. People traveled less for pleasure, entertained in their homes, got to know their neighbors, and dressed informally. Circulation of library books increased. Parlor games, especially checkers, gained popularity, but hunting and fishing were banned. The government forbade the manufacture of tennis and golf balls to conserve raw materials.

Paradoxically, teen crime, delinquency, illegitimacy, prostitution, and venereal disease soared. Teenagers called "Victory Girls" crowded bus depots in cities, saying they wanted to meet soldiers for sex to help military morale. Overall crime declined, however, and medical and dental care improved. The army provided some people with the best diets they ever had. When the American Medical Association dropped its opposition to prepaid insurance, Blue Cross and Blue Shield enrolled tens of millions. Despite the war, the death rate dropped to a record low and life expectancy increased.

The United States became more of a middle-class nation. Personal income more than doubled, and it was more fairly distributed than ever: the share of the national income that the wealthiest 5 percent controlled declined from 23.7 percent in 1939 to 16.8 percent in 1944. The portion of national income going to interest and rent dropped 20 percent during the conflict. It took more than twenty years of postwar prosperity for income to increase comparably. "The more cheerful side of this tale is that the underprivileged third of America's population undoubtedly lived better during the war and for some time afterward than they had ever lived before," an economist wrote. Even the prosperity of the 1920s was eclipsed in terms of gross national product, retail sales, new investment, and national income. The war brought full employment. By 1945, in addition to the 11.4 million people in the armed forces, 52.8 million were employed at home, up from 45.7 million in 1939.

Mobilizing the Economy

The war was won as much on the assembly lines as on the front lines. Not only did the United States possess far more natural and human resources than the Axis powers, but it used them more efficiently. Six months after Pearl Harbor, American factory production exceeded the Axis nations combined, and before the end of the war, the United States was producing twice as much as the enemy. During the conflict, Americans built 88,410 tanks, 299,293 airplanes, 6,500,000 million rifles, 1,566 military vessels, and 5,777 merchant ships.

The war facilitated a reconciliation of government and big business. Honored throughout much of the 1920s and demonized during the depression, businessmen again were venerated. Some executives took leaves from their jobs to run government agencies. The government provided low-interest loans and tax deductions to enlarge plants and to retool factories for war production, relaxed enforcement of antitrust laws, and offered contracts that guaranteed a profit.

The auto industry ceased making new cars after January 31, 1942, and built planes and tanks. The most dramatic increase in productivity, though, was in shipbuilding, as merchant vessels were built more rapidly than anyone thought possible. Production was imperiled when the United States' supply of raw rubber from the Dutch East Indies was cut off, a problem addressed when industrialist Bernard Baruch devised a program of conservation and synthetic rubber production. The government spent $700 million to build fifty-one synthetic rubber plants and leased them to private companies, helping increase production one hundred times from 1941 to 1944.

To coordinate war production, Franklin D. Roosevelt created the War Production Board in 1942. Policies of war agencies were coordinated under James F. Byrnes, who resigned from the Supreme Court to lead the Office of Economic Stabilization and then the Office of War Mobilization in 1943. Coordination was also the goal of the Office of Defense Transportation (ODT), created in 1941, and the War Manpower Commission (WMC), formed in 1942. The ODT operated truck lines, buses, and railroads as an integrated system. Railroads remained privately held and doubled the amount of freight carried. The Big Inch pipeline was laid to transport oil from Texas to Pennsylvania, reducing the number of oil tankers sunk in coastal waters. By contrast, the WMC was charged with moving not goods but people, into jobs vital to the war effort.

For agriculture, the war was a bonanza. Farmers' income rose 250 percent from 1939 to 1945. Civilian food consumption was the highest in history, and one-quarter of agricultural goods went to feed the armed forces and the Allies. Although the farm population declined 20 percent and the number of tenant farmers and sharecroppers fell 33 percent, farm productivity increased 28 percent, thanks to mechanization, longer hours, fertilizers, hybrid crops, and pesticides. The federal government encouraged agriculture by exempting farm workers from the draft.

Overseas, the United States killed some 500,000 enemy troops at a cost of more than $360 billion and paid a high price for the property its military destroyed; metaphorically it would have cost less simply to buy the property. From 1940 to 1945 the country spent nearly twice as much as in the previous 150 years. The yearly budget was more than ten times that of prewar years, $100 billion in 1945 alone, and the national debt sky-rocketed from $43 billion in 1940 to $269 billion in 1946. Borrowing financed about 54 percent of the outlays; taxes paid the rest. Individual and corporate income taxes, which had provided 30 percent of government revenue in 1933, furnished 76 percent by 1944. The Revenue Act of 1942 raised income taxes to their highest rates ever, 81 percent in the top bracket, and reduced exemptions, so levies were made on lower-income groups for the first time. Forty-two million people paid income taxes in 1944, up from 17 million in 1942 and 4 million people in 1939. In 1943 another Revenue Act introduced payroll deductions for income taxes, and the next year Congress approved a tax increase, though less than Roosevelt had requested. Increased corporate and excise taxes took much of industry's profits, so few industrialists and investors grew rich from the war. Bonds, an additional source of money for the government, were sold not only to borrow funds but to soak up money available for consumer goods. This policy helped control inflation and gave people a sense of patriotic participation in the war. About $200 billion of war bonds were sold to 85 million people in eight loan drives. Schoolchildren bought $1 billion of bonds and war stamps.

Labor union membership rose from 9 million in 1942 to 15 million in 1945, and more Americans belonged to unions than worked on farms, a historic first. To handle labor disagreements, FDR created the National Defense Mediation Board in 1941; the next year the agency gave way to the National War Labor Board (NWLB), on which labor, business, and the public were represented equally. The NWLB applied "the Little Steel formula," so called because it had been worked out in a dispute concerning the smaller steel mills. Because the cost of living had increased 15 percent in 1942, the board permitted wages to go up as much as 15 percent excluding overtime, a move that helped check inflation. The NWLB handled 17,650 disputes involving 12 million workers, yet in forty cases Roosevelt seized plants to ensure production. When a nationwide railroad strike loomed in 1944, the government took over the railroads, only to return them in three weeks, after the president arbitrated the dispute. Work interruptions amounted to just one day per worker for the duration of the war. John L. Lewis, who returned as head of the United Mine Workers, became a villain for leading his members on strikes in 1941 and 1943 and gaining higher wages.

While they were winning labor peace, Americans were winning the war in laboratories. Scientists developed or perfected the bazooka, which could pierce a tank; the radio proximity fuse, which exploded according to nearness to the target; napalm flamethrowers; amphibious vehicles for landing on beaches; medical treatments for the wounded, including new drugs; insect repellents; improved navigational aids; and radar and sonar. Most consequential, revolutionary advances in physics made possible the atom bomb—presenting the deadliest paradoxes of the century. In 1939 several scientists aware of German progress in nuclear physics persuaded Albert Einstein to sign a letter to Roosevelt calling attention to the possibility of producing bombs from uranium. Little headway was made until the summer of 1941 when Vannevar Bush, FDR's top science adviser, told him a bomb appeared feasible, and in 1942 the first controlled nuclear reaction took place at the University of Chicago. One year later, a new unit of the Army Corps of Engineers, the Manhattan District, took over research, leading to a breakthrough in which scientists under J. Robert Oppenheimer at Los Alamos, New Mexico, brought together fissionable material to produce an explosion in July 1945. The entire project, costing about $2 billion, was unknown to most in Congress, even to Vice President Harry S Truman.

Defeating the enemy required the work of journalists and advertising executives as well. Poet and Librarian of Congress Archibald MacLeish and journalist Elmer Davis contributed by heading the Office of Facts and Figures and the Office of War Information, respectively. MacLeish's organization was charged with disseminating information about the war to the press and the public before Davis's agency took over the task. The Office of Censorship banned publication of weather forecasts that might aid enemy bombers and excised sensitive information from soldiers' letters home. Hollywood produced films to stimulate patriotism, some depicting individual Americans overcoming swarms of Germans and Japanese. Comic books, which reached millions, were sent abroad, showing superheroes single-handedly winning battles.

Civil Liberties and Racial Tension

Whatever the propagandists proclaimed, not all Americans welcomed the opportunity to inflict pain and death. Most conscientious objectors were allowed to fill noncombat roles in the military or to perform essential civilian work. But more than 5,500 were jailed for refusing to serve, more than three-fourths of them Jehovah's Witnesses who requested exemptions on the ground that all were ministers. They were denied status as conscientious objectors because they did not oppose all wars.

Prosecutions for sedition were rare, although in July 1942 a federal grand jury indicted twenty-eight native fascists on suspicion of undermining military morale. A mistrial was declared after the judge died, and the

JAPANESE CIVILIANS ARE SENT TO CAMPS
Newly arrived Japanese-Americans at an internment camp
in San Bruno, California, 1942. Photograph by Dorothea Lange.
(National Archives)

indictments were dropped after the war. The most serious breech of civil liberties was perpetrated upon 117,000 Japanese Americans, two-thirds of whom were U.S. citizens. They were rounded up, incarcerated in camps, forced to dispose of their property at a fraction of its value, and branded as disloyal. They were vulnerable because they belonged to a people who had inflicted a succession of defeats on the United States. They were easier to detain than German and Italian Americans, whose numbers were greater but were not as geographically concentrated. Attitudes changed over time. Early in 1943 the army began accepting recruits for a combat unit of Nisei, the American-born offspring of the Japanese. About twelve hundred fought in the 442nd Combat Team, which earned fame for bravery in the Italian campaign. By 1945 most of the Japanese Americans had been allowed to return home. The Supreme Court seemed of two minds about the episode, ruling in one case that the United States had the right to order the internment and in another that the government could not detain anyone whose loyalty had been established. Not until 1988 did

Congress apologize to Japanese Americans and agree to pay compensation to each surviving internee.

African Americans made significant economic progress because of the demand for labor. More than 1 million moved from the South to the North to take jobs in war industries; those who stayed in the South migrated from rural areas to cities for employment. More unions were open to them. The number of African Americans in manufacturing rose from .5 to 1.2 million and in government jobs from 50,000 to 200,000. After the war, 250,000 black veterans attended college with government benefits. Some white people resented competition from African Americans, who were not hired in war industries until the labor shortage became acute. Incensed when several war industries refused to hire African Americans, A. Philip Randolph threatened a massive protest march on Washington. Fearing racial violence, FDR agreed to declare an end to job discrimination in defense industries and government employment but refused to desegregate the armed forces. In June 1942 Roosevelt issued an executive order creating the Fair Employment Practices Committee to prevent discrimination in work, and Randolph canceled the march.

Recognizing the paradox of fighting for democracy outside the United States while denying it to black Americans, many white people felt that racial discrimination was immoral, a belief underscored by Gunnar Myrdal's findings in the comprehensive study *An American Dilemma* (1944). Eradicating it completely was not likely in a country where deadly race riots broke out in major cities. The worst started in June 1943 in Detroit, as fights erupted between black and white people at Belle Isle Park; looting and burning raged before federal troops quelled violence that left twenty-five African Americans and nine white Americans dead. Two months later Harlem erupted after a confrontation between a white police officer and a black soldier; six African Americans perished and three hundred people were injured. In meeting rooms and government halls, the struggle against segregation nonetheless made only modest gains, although it gathered momentum for postwar years. The NAACP grew from 50,000 members and 335 branches in 1940 to nearly 500,000 and 1,000 in 1945; the Congress of Racial Equality was founded in Chicago. Also, in 1944 the Supreme Court held in *Smith v. Allwright* that the Texas Democratic Party could not exclude black people from voting in primary elections.

Racial unrest was intense in California. Mexican American teens sporting ducktail haircuts and flashy, broad-shouldered zoot suits with thigh-length jackets allegedly attacked sailors who dated Hispanic women, triggering a wave of beatings by white soldiers and sailors in May and June 1943 in Oakland and Los Angeles. Indians in California sued the federal government for $100 million to pay for land that was taken from them in the 1850s. Roosevelt vetoed a compensation bill, saying the government had "a duty to the future, not the past." Litigation continued for thirty-five years until a deal was struck to pay tribes 47 cents per acre. Other changes for Native Americans were swifter: many left reservations to work in war plants, never to return. Those who did return brought the benefits of technology. Chinese Americans elicited sympathy because China was an ally of the United States. In 1943 Congress repealed the 1882 Chinese Exclusion Act. Four years later the War Brides Act allowed Chinese brides of American men to enter the country. Moreover, Congress granted all Chinese immigrants the long-denied right to become naturalized citizens.

The chief concern of American Jews was the rescue of their European kin from Adolf Hitler's Holocaust. Some 982 were admitted, but immigration quotas remained in place. FDR sought a haven for Jews outside the United States, only to encounter resistance. Even when information reached his administration about the Führer's gassing of Jews, Roosevelt found such

WOMEN AND THE WAR EFFORT
Building boats for the Marines, 1941.
(Franklin D. Roosevelt Presidential Library)

reports unbelievable. He rejected pleas to bomb gas chambers, crematoriums, and rail lines leading to death camps, arguing that doing so would divert air power from military targets and prolong the war. The administration pointed out that bombing death camps would kill inmates, and rail lines, a small target, could be quickly repaired. The public, although mainly ignorant of the Holocaust, did not consider stopping persecution of the Jews a priority. America did pluck some 200,000 Jews from harm's way by ransom, false passports, and other subterfuges under the War Refugee Board, established in January 1944. Millions could have been spared had the nation acted sooner.

As employment rose among racial and ethnic minorities due to the scarcity of workers, so it grew for women. The fictional "Rosie the Riveter" was a symbol. The female labor force increased 50 percent from 1940 to 1945. Employment rose in every field save domestic service, the most spectacular increases occurring in factory work, particularly defense industries. The federal government hired nearly 1 million, many as clerical workers in the nation's capital. Black women moved out of farm and domestic labor into service and manufacturing. Women's share of the labor movement climbed from 9.4 percent of union members to 21.8 percent in four years. Wages increased in absolute terms and in relation to men's, aided by a few state equal-wage laws and a NWLB decision ordering equal pay for women who did the same jobs as men. Advances for women were not limited to employment: their numbers also grew in college enrollment and political participation. At home there was revolution as well; a higher percentage of women married in the 1940s than ever before. Hasty marriages led to higher divorce rates and, starting in 1946, a baby boom that would prove one of the most important developments of the second half of the century. Many women used contraception, and abortions were common, if illegal; the rate of out-of-wedlock births increased nevertheless. More married women, mothers, and older women took jobs, and for the first time married women outnumbered single ones in the workforce. The government and some employers provided childcare, but most women used relatives. The war advanced the sexual revolution in ways that went beyond sexuality and included work and parenting roles, family structure, birth control, and a population explosion.

Integration came more slowly to the armed forces, than to civilian society. At the time of Pearl Harbor, only 5,000 soldiers in an army of 230,000 were African American. Many draft boards considered African Americans unfit for combat and were reluctant to conscript them; the Marines had no black personnel; the navy accepted blacks only as mess attendants and cooks. Attitudes changed when the government realized that discrimination wasted human resources. By September 1944, when the size of the armed forces peaked, 702,000 African Americans served in the army, 165,000 in the navy, 17,000 as Marines, and 5,000 in the Coast Guard. They were usually trained in segregated facilities and assigned to separate units under white officers for labor such as building roads and unloading ships. When assigned to combat units, African Americans fought capably. The 99 Pursuit Squadron, an Army Air Corps unit known as the Tuskegee Airmen, fought effectively in North Africa, Italy, and Germany.

There was less discrimination against Hispanics and Indians. Nearly 300,000 Spanish-speaking troops served in the military, and Mexican Americans were overrepresented, considering their share of the general population. They volunteered for dangerous missions, valor recognized with Congressional Medals of Honor for eleven Spanish speakers. Indians in large numbers sought military duty. Many were decorated for bravery. In communication units, they used codes based upon their languages to confuse enemy interpreters.

That warfare had grown increasingly technical, and that 10 percent of all armed forces personnel were administrative and technical, expedited the employment of women, who were hired for office, communications, and health care work. Around 140,000 women served in the Women's Army Corps (WAC), and 44,000 in the navy's Women Accepted for Voluntary Emergency Service (WAVES). Some 23,000 joined the Marine Women's Reserve, and 13,000 enlisted in the Coast Guard. Some performed risky tasks, such as test piloting, although they were not allowed in combat. Traditionalists feared that war would harden women and cost them their femininity or that female soldiers would encourage promiscuity in the armed forces—fears that were not realized. The rate of venereal disease was lower for servicewomen than for the general population. Some female soldiers served abroad. On most foreign bases they lived in barbed wire compounds and could leave only in groups under armed escort, believed necessary to protect them from sex-starved male troops.

The United States at War

Roosevelt inspired Americans and gave them confidence. No contingency plans were made for defeat or compromise. The president did not participate in tactical decisions, as did Winston Churchill, nor did he hire and fire generals, as had Abraham Lincoln. Complementing Roosevelt's skills was the dominant personality among top military leaders, General George C. Marshall, a statesman who selected able subordinates. The supreme Allied commander in Europe was General Dwight D. Eisenhower, who helped soothe difficulties between the Americans and the other Allies.

The Allies decided that defeating Hitler would take priority over subduing Japan because Germany appeared the more dangerous foe and because German scientists might develop weapons of mass destruction. Most of the army's forces and equipment were assigned to Europe, while most of the navy and almost all the Marines were concentrated in the Pacific. Control of the Atlantic, where the first American-German conflicts had taken place, was necessary for victory in Europe. In that ocean, the navy had to protect shipping, support amphibious landings, and shell invasion targets. The German surface fleet was never a major factor, despite some attacks on convoys to the Soviet Union, because it was no match for the British.

Germany's 150 submarines constituted their chief threat in the Battle of the Atlantic in 1941. The United States initially was ill equipped to combat submarines, which took a terrible toll, sinking 360 merchant ships in the first half of 1942. The U-boats operated in wolf packs in the mid-Atlantic, following convoys into nightfall before converging to attack. Allied technology and techniques improved and by May 1943 the battle was virtually won. Ships were grouped in convoys protected by planes and destroyers. Sonar was improved, and by 1943 miniature units were placed in planes and on small boats. Finally, the Americans' ability to build ships faster than the Germans could sink them was critical. The battle was costly on both sides. The Allies lost 2,828 merchant ships, 187 warships, and 40,000 men; the Germans lost two-thirds of their submarines and practically suspended naval warfare by late 1943, due to heavy losses.

Two weeks after Pearl Harbor, Churchill met Roosevelt in Washington for the Arcadia Conference and declared that American ground troops would be used first in North Africa. The decision angered Stalin, whose soldiers were fighting Germans alone on the Eastern Front and needed relief that only an invasion in Western Europe could bring. North Africa was of limited strategic importance, yet it was the only place where the British were fighting the Germans on land, and FDR was determined to give Americans a sense of participation. Britain had moved soldiers to the upper Mediterranean coast to defend Egypt and the Suez Canal, opposed at first by Italians, guarding their colonies. Vichy France was a presence, too, nominally in control of Morocco and Algeria. Eisenhower led the Allied invasion of North Africa, where the major questions were whether the French would resist, whether the campaign could be kept secret, and whether Germany might sink the invading fleet.

But the fleet approached undetected and, with air support from escort carriers and bombers based in England, landed at Casablanca, Oran, and Algiers on November 8, 1942. French resistance was light and ceased after the Germans occupied Vichy France on November 11. Almost simultane-ously, the British launched an offensive from the East. General Bernard Montgomery defeated German General Erwin Rommel at El Alamein, Libya, in late October and early November, then began advancing west-ward to link with Eisenhower's forces. Germany rushed reinforcements to Tunisia, only slowing the Allies, and by May 11, 1943, Axis opposition in North Africa had been broken. Germany and Italy lost almost 1 million soldiers killed or taken prisoner.

At the Casablanca Conference in January 1943, Roosevelt and Churchill chose to follow the North African offensive with an invasion of Sicily. This offensive made the easiest logistical use of troops in North Africa and might divert some Axis troops from the Soviet front. Like the North African campaign, the effort in Sicily was not of great strategic impact, how-ever, it postponed British-based troops from invading France. Early on July 10, 1943, the U.S. Seventh Army under General George S. Patton and the British Eighth Army under Montgomery landed in Sicily. Stormy weather and the lack of a preinvasion bombardment helped preserve the surprise. By the end of the second day, the Allies had put ashore eighty thousand men, in addition to support vehicles, landing craft, and tanks, many of which had bogged down in the beaches or were grounded on sandbars. Whatever their problems, their forces commanded air and sea and with-stood furious counterattacks. Montgomery was to advance up the south-east coast to capture Messina, the city at the tip of Sicily separated from Italy by the Strait of Messina. Patton was to move from the southwest, offering support to Montgomery and preventing the Axis from blocking the capture of Messina, but he decided to take Messina himself, arriving there one day ahead of Montgomery. The Axis lost 164,000, killed or cap-tured, although most escaped across the strait to Italy.

The conquest of Sicily precipitated the fall of Benito Mussolini and the collapse of the Italian war effort. Italians had grown disillusioned with the conflict, and their army had little incentive to fight. Adolf Hitler dom-inated the Axis, making Italians realize they had as much to fear from a German victory as from a German defeat. Two weeks after the Allied land-ing in Sicily, the fascist Grand Council voted no-confidence in Mussolini, and King Victor Emmanuel ordered his arrest. Italy negotiated a surren-der and capitulated secretly to the Allies on September 3, 1944. Hitler rushed troops to Italy to disarm the army and rescue Mussolini from a mountain prison in a daring commando raid; then Der Führer installed Il Duce as ruler of a small German puppet state in northern Italy.

The invasion of Italy had started on September 9, 1943, when American soldiers landed at Salerno. Meeting little resistance at the beachhead, the troops, with air and naval support, repelled a strong German counterattack on September 12. On October 1, the Allies captured Naples and hoped to reach Rome by Christmas—an estimate that was too optimistic by a year. Few regions were less conducive to ground operations than the mountainous Italian peninsula, traversed by streams and rugged terrain that made tanks useless. Mountain fighting favored the defenders. Germans blocked the Allied advance at Monte Cassino, site of a fourteen-hundred-year-old Benedictine monastery, proving so formidable that the Allies decided to outflank it with an amphibious assault at Anzio. The landing surprised the Germans, and conditions were favorable for pushing in from the beach to the lightly defended countryside. Instead, the commander built up forces and supplies at the beachhead, awaiting a counterattack. When the counterattack came, it nearly drove the Americans into the sea. Anzio was the only amphibious invasion of the war in which U.S. forces failed to expand out of a beachhead.

Simultaneous with the Anzio invasion was an offensive at Monte Cassino, also a failure. Reluctantly, the Allies bombed the monastery. The war in Italy became a bloody impasse, with the longest-lasting static front in Europe. Finally French soldiers broke through German lines and opened the road to Rome. Allied forces captured Rome on June 4, 1944, two days before invading France.

Some American planners hoped that air power could crush Germany, without an invasion of France, yet military leaders differed over whether to use it to support ground operations or to wreck German industry and transportation. The British Royal Air Force, carrying the load early in the war, concluded that daylight raids cost too many bombers and resorted to night operations. By mid-1943, though, bombing was taking place around the clock, the British by night, the Americans by day. The chief American bombers, the B-17 Flying Fortress and the B-24 Liberator, were more heavily armed with defensive machine guns than the British planes and had accurate bombsights that made precision bombing during daylight feasible. Americans thought their operations were accurate enough to knock out specific targets such as airplane factories, in contrast to the British preference for saturation bombing. Allied research would conclude, however, that 65 percent of all bombs failed to come within five miles of their targets, and the United States grew skeptical of its ability to bomb accurately anything smaller than a city. By the end of the war, fire-bombing had replaced precision bombing.

Bombing raids set back the Nazi war effort. Germany was compelled to divert resources to combat the air offensive. By 1943, 1 million troops were assigned to antiaircraft duty, and it took a labor force of 1.5 million men to repair damage. Further, the air war disabled the Luftwaffe, depriving ground troops of tactical support. The Luftwaffe, the Allies initially discovered, was more lethal to bombers than antiaircraft fire. Bombers sustained costly losses when fighter escorts did not accompany them. By early 1944, the range of the P-51 Mustang and the P-47 Thunderbolt had been extended, and the Luftwaffe was ineffective in defending cities. Airpower did not destroy Germany, but it was instrumental in winning the war. It deterred an invasion of England, ensured the success of the Normandy invasion, and sank battleships and submarines in the Battle of the Atlantic.

As the war turned in favor of the Allies, Hitler invented new weapons. The first pilotless flying bombs, or V-1s, appeared over London in June 1944, a menace that killed 6,000 British civilians and wounded 17,000. Three months later, Germany launched the first V-2 supersonic rockets at London, leaving 3,000 dead and 6,500 hurt before the weapons' base was captured. Such arms heralded a new age in warfare and had a profound psychological effect on their victims, although fewer people died than from a single conventional air raid. Another German breakthrough, jet fighters, vastly superior to Allied planes, were used in July 1944, but there were not many and few pilots could fly them. The war ended before the impact of German science could be brought to bear, justifying the Allied decision to make Germany their first priority.

D-Day: The Great Invasion

In November 1943 Roosevelt met Churchill and Jiang Jieshe at two conferences in Cairo, Egypt, sandwiched around a parley with Joseph Stalin and Churchill at Tehran. Few strategic decisions were made at the Cairo meetings. At Tehran, the first gathering of the Big Three, one of the most important decisions of the war was made: the invasion of France was scheduled for the spring or summer of 1944. Stalin agreed to coordinate an offensive to complement the invasion. Since 1941 his armies had carried the burden of fighting on land, defeating Germany in the battles of Stalingrad and Leningrad in 1943 to check Hitler on the Eastern Front. Stalingrad, a turning point in the war, assured that the Soviets would survive and roll back the Nazis. By 1944 Hitler's armies were on the verge of being crushed between the jaws of a massive vise of two great armies advancing from the East and the West.

Elaborate efforts confused the Germans about the site for the Normandy invasion, the largest undertaking in the history of warfare. The Allies prevented Germany from conducting aerial surveillance of their control of the

ADDRESSING THE TROOPS
Dwight D. Eisenhower with paratroopers before D-Day.
(Library of Congress)

air. Planes dropped foil strips and the Allies launched barrage balloons to fool German radar into predicting that an invasion lay at the Pas-de-Calais, north of the objective. The allies broadcast simulated fake traffic and bombed more heavily near Calais than near Normandy. The English Channel was narrower and calmer at Calais, an obvious site for an invasion. Success in outmaneuvering the Germans came partly from the Allies' ability to read German codes. Hitler believed he had the most secure enciphering system ever developed, based on a machine known as Enigma. Confounding him, British cryptanalysts built their own Enigma and could decipher most messages within hours. The material that became known as Ultra was indispensable to the deception surrounding the Normandy invasion.

Other preparations proved effective. The air command bombed transportation facilities, and the French resistance sabotaged its rail system.

Practically every bridge west of the Seine was destroyed, making it impossible for the Germans to reinforce rapidly. Naval commandos landed by night to inspect German obstructions at the beaches. On the evening before the invasion, minesweepers began clearing the ocean. Tanks were designed to operate on soft, wet beaches and detonate land mines ahead of them. Because heavy equipment could not be loaded directly onto the beach, the Allies constructed two artificial harbors, which they towed across the channel, then sunk obsolete ships to create breakwaters.

Weather was critical. Ideal tidal conditions occurred on only three days per month. Surface winds could not exceed eighteen miles per hour, and paratroopers required moonlight for night landings. On the day the invasion was scheduled, Eisenhower's meteorologist predicted thunderstorms at Normandy, so Eisenhower postponed it until the next day. Conditions were not perfect then, either, but the rainy, windy weather added to the element of surprise. As dawn broke on June 6, Germans found the horizon filled with nearly three thousand ships, which launched an intense bombardment before the first of 155,000 troops landed at beaches, where 9,000 became casualties. Once the forces established a beachhead, their task was to break out into countryside that was not conducive to tank operations because of the thick hedges and mounds of earth that farmers used to fence livestock. Still, by the end of the month, the Allies had the Germans near collapse in Normandy and began to advance more swiftly than anyone expected. On August 25, French and American forces liberated Paris.

Some German generals, realizing the war was lost, tried to assassinate Der Führer. In the spring of 1943, a bomb placed on Hitler's plane had failed to explode. Then, motivated by the Normandy invasion, on July 20, 1944, a colonel planted a time bomb in his briefcase and carried it into a conference with Hitler; the blast killed four men, but Hitler escaped. Der Führer reacted by purging the army and government of everyone suspected of participating in the assassination scheme. He executed five thousand and sent ten thousand to concentration camps. Rommel, who knew of the plot, was given a choice: suicide or trial and execution. He chose death by cyanide.

Reeling from D-Day, the German military was exposed to a new threat when American and French forces invaded the French Riviera on August 15, 1944. Meeting little resistance, they captured fifty-seven thousand Nazi troops within two weeks. Preparing to strike another blow, Eisenhower directed Montgomery's army group to sweep northward toward the Ruhr as U.S. General Omar Bradley's moved east toward the Saar. They advanced so quickly that by late August they had outrun their supplies and competed for scarce gasoline. Each general claimed that if given all the gasoline, he could envelop the retreating Germans and bring the war in Europe to an end. Instead, Eisenhower settled on a slower offensive along a broad front, fearing that too swift of an advance by tanks would leave them without gasoline. Early in September, Montgomery proposed a daring move that Eisenhower accepted: airborne troops dropped behind German lines would take bridges over the Rhine in Holland intact, then Allied armor would close the gap. The operation, which began on September 10, marked the first daylight paratroop drop of the war but fell short of Montgomery's hopes and incurred heavy casualties. In December allied expectations were thwarted once more when Hitler's troops struck at the lightly defended line in the Ardennes Forest creating a bulge in Allies' lines. Hitler had ordered the audacious Panzer tank offensive, with the port of Antwerp in Belgium his objective. However, his army could not sustain an offensive, and the overly ambitious attack would, paradoxically, hastened his defeat.

With fog grounding the Allied aircraft, the Germans, striking in bitter cold and six inches of snow, penetrated sixty miles in the Battle of the Bulge. On December 22 they surrounded the crucial road-junction city of Bastogne and sent an ultimatum to the Allied commander to surrender. Brigadier General Anthony McAuliffe replied, "Nuts!" The skies cleared the next day, and fighter-bombers pounded German tank columns as the Panzers sputtered for lack of gasoline. Three days later, the Allies relieved Bastogne, then gradually pinched in the top and bottom of the bulge, squashing the offensive. The battle, the biggest ever fought on the ground by American arms, involved 600,000 U.S. troops and left 19,000 of them dead out of 70,000 casualties. The Germans, who could not replace their losses, had 100,000 casualties, contributing to the attrition of their army. The Battle of the Bulge delayed the Allied offensive in the west for a few weeks; the Soviets surged toward Berlin from the east.

1944: Wartime Election

During wartime the federal bureaucracy, which expanded by 60 percent under the New Deal, mushroomed by 300 percent; the president became more active, and Congress delegated immense authority to him. Nevertheless, the electorate seemed wary of Roosevelt. As prosperity returned, voters, who had more to conserve, became more conservative. In the 1942 congressional elections low turnout hurt the Democrats, whose majorities in both houses were pared. A combination of Republicans and conservative southern Democrats won the upper hand in Congress and terminated the Works Progress Administration, the Civilian Conservation Corps, and the National Youth Administration. With a war on FDR had no qualms about seeking the 1944 Democratic nomination, and no one challenged him. The chief suspense at the Chicago convention was about the vice presidential nomination, particularly because Roosevelt's health was failing. Willing to replace Vice President Henry Wallace, who was unpopular with conservatives, FDR privately endorsed a compromise choice, Missouri Senator Harry S Truman, chair of a committee that exposed incompetence and corruption in defense production. Delegates ratified his selection.

Wendell Willkie was a contender for the Republican nomination again, but after failing in the Wisconsin primary he withdrew, and New York District Attorney Thomas E. Dewey won the prize. Isolationist Ohio Governor John Bricker was tapped for the second spot. Dewey, whose only hope was for the war to end before election day, tried to make FDR's health an issue. He denounced Roosevelt for accepting the backing of the Congress of Industrial Organizations, and accused the administration of being influenced by communists and radicals. Roosevelt, who benefited from his role as commander in chief and American battle successes, condemned the GOP for isolationism and blamed it again for the Great Depression. Both parties endorsed membership in a postwar United Nations, a goal Willkie promoted in his book *One World*. The Senate would endorse the UN charter in late July 1945.

Roosevelt won 36 states and 432 electoral votes to Dewey's 12 and 99, gaining 53.4 percent of the popular vote (25.6 million ballots). Ominously FDR, sixty-two, had aged dramatically. He had grown frail and thin, his hands trembled, and he had dark circles under his eyes. Finding him suffering from heart disease and hypertension, and, without telling him how serious his condition was, his doctors told him to cut down on cigarettes and prescribed heart medications and at least ten hours of sleep nightly. "He has a great and terrible job to do, and he's got to do it even if it kills him," Labor Secretary Frances Perkins said.

End of the Third Reich

With combat in Europe raging in 1944 and 1945, the Allies held a series of diplomatic meetings to plan the postwar world. In July 1944 Treasury Secretary Henry Morgenthau led a conference at Bretton Woods, New Hampshire, to outline economic recovery; establishment of an International Monetary Fund and an International Bank for Reconstruction and Development were recommended. Two months afterward FDR and Churchill met in Quebec in an atmosphere of imminent victory and preliminarily approved a plan to dismember Germany, destroy its industrial

THE BIG THREE'S FINAL MEETING
Churchill, Roosevelt, and Stalin at Yalta, February 1945.
(Franklin D. Roosevelt Presidential Library)

base, and make it an agrarian nation. This scheme of Morgenthau's was scrapped. Meanwhile, representatives of the United States, Britain, China, and the Soviet Union gathered at Dumbarton Oaks, a Washington estate, to discuss the UN charter.

The Big Three met for the last time at Yalta, in the Russian Crimea, in February 1945. Roosevelt, though ill and frail, dominated the talks. The main issues were Poland, the UN, and the war against Japan. Churchill feared the Soviets would install puppet governments in Poland and other Eastern European countries the Red Army occupied. Stalin agreed to hold democratic elections in Poland, but argued that the country was in the Soviet sphere of influence and insisted on a friendly government. With his army occupying Poland, there was little the British or the Americans could do to stop Stalin from imposing a government. Such territorial conflicts, arising during the last months of European fighting, helped sow the seeds for a Cold War between the United States and the U.S.S.R.

In his other objectives, Roosevelt was more successful. Stalin assented to UN participation and to join the war on Japan within three months after the war in Europe ended. In return, the Soviet Union received three votes in the UN General Assembly and Far East territorial concessions. It was agreed that the Red Army would liberate Berlin, a controversial decision. Churchill wanted to beat the Soviets to the German capital, yet FDR deferred to Eisenhower, who did not consider it an important military objective.

First the Western armies had to cross the Rhine. Continuing to advance along a broad front, the Allies reached the Rhine at Dusseldorf, Germany, on March 2, 1945, to find bridges destroyed. On March 7 an American division took the bridge at Remagen intact, and the U.S. First Army, capitalizing on the breakthrough, sped eight thousand soldiers across the span in twenty-four hours. A German counterattack failed, as American troops poured in until the bridge collapsed on March 17. By that time pontoons spanned the Rhine. Patton's troops crossed the river on March 23, with Montgomery's following the next day. When April arrived, the Germans were near total defeat, losing two thousand prisoners daily to each Allied division. On April 4 Patton's men liberated the Ohrdruf-Nord concentration camp, confirming the most malignant side of Nazism: the slaughter of Jews, Gypsies, Soviets, and homosexuals. The battle-hardened Patton vomited when he saw the prisoners, and the mayor of Ohrdruf and his wife, after being forced to tour the camp, hanged themselves. At the liberation of another camp, an American sergeant observed, "It was like stepping into the Dark Ages."

The war was also coming to an end in Italy, where the Allies opened their final offensive April 9, 1945. On April 28 Italian partisans murdered Mussolini and his mistress, brought the bodies to Milan, and strung them up by their heels. German forces in the country surrendered on May 2, the day the Allies captured Berlin. Suited neither by temperament nor resources to fight a long war, Hitler could win campaigns but not a protracted war against the two mightiest powers on earth—the United States and the Soviet Union. Unable to face the ramifications of his malevolence, Hitler poisoned his wife and then himself. Fearing the poison might fail, he shot himself in his bunker underneath Berlin, two days after Mussolini died. On May 7, Germany surrendered and May 7 was Victory in Europe Day—an outcome that Roosevelt did not see.

Sitting for a portrait on April 12, 1945, at Warm Springs, Roosevelt suddenly raised his left hand to his temple, said, "I have a terrific headache," and slumped in his chair. He never regained consciousness and died of a stroke. Millions were shocked by the death of the only president they had ever known, a man who, according to many historians, was the greatest chief executive of the century. Roosevelt was by no means without flaws, but he helped free his office from the inhibitions of the past, his country from depression, and his world from tyranny.

The War Turns against Japan

In the Pacific, the decisive factor was naval airpower, in which ships and planes were closely coordinated. The Pacific fleet was organized into task forces centered on aircraft carriers, including the cruisers and destroyers that accompanied them. Battleships, too slow to keep up with the task forces, were more useful for shelling islands before an invasion. Submarines were used for scouting and preying on merchant and military vessels. Japanese aviators who had been fighting in Asia were more experienced than American pilots. Until the introduction of the F6F Hellcat, the navy had no plane as maneuverable as the Zero. But Japan could not replace lost pilots, planes, and ships as quickly as could the Americans.

American troops and their equipment had to be transported across thousands of ocean miles to land on hostile shores and face Japanese soldiers who fought tenaciously in the tropical jungles. Considering surrender a disgrace, the Japanese adopted suicidal tactics and had more casualties than their enemy in each island engagement. Their plan was to seize, fortify, and defend Pacific islands and archipelagos within thousands of miles of Japan, making the price to take them too costly for the Americans. Like the Germans, they did not consider Americans a match for them and believed they could hold a sphere of influence if they discouraged their foe from fighting a prolonged war. They misjudged the American intention, which was to fight the war to a conclusion, not a stalemate. Planners decided that they did not have to oust Japan from all islands, many of them small, sparsely populated, and relatively worthless except for their military value. Rather, they would frustrate the Japanese by leapfrogging—fighting to capture key islands, build airfields and naval bases and, with control of the air and sea assured, hop over strong defensive positions.

In the immediate aftermath of Pearl Harbor, the Japanese scored conquests comparable to the Blitzkrieg. As bombers were striking Pearl Harbor, air raids were mounted on Midway Island, Wake Island, Guam, Hong Kong, southern Thailand, northern Malaya, and the Philippines, all of which Tokyo claimed within six months. Rangoon and Singapore likewise fell. Worse, the Allies were beaten in the Battle of the Java Sea, the first noteworthy fleet action, in January 1942. On the other hand, the campaign for the Philippines was the longest and most arduous for Japan. After destroying the U.S. Air Force on the ground on December 7, 1941, the main Japanese force landed on Luzon on December 22. Under General Douglas MacArthur, the Americans retreated to the mountainous Bataan Peninsula jungle following two weeks of heavy fighting and, short of food and drugs, suffered more casualties from starvation and disease than combat. MacArthur set up command on the isle of Corregidor in Manila Harbor, but in February was ordered to go to Australia and fled through Japanese lines in a PT boat. Americans on Bataan surrendered on April 9, and the Japanese took Corregidor on May 6. Captured soldiers were forced to walk sixty-five miles in blistering heat without food or water—the infamous Bataan Death March that killed ten thousand American and Filipino troops (and, after the war, led to war-crimes trials for Japanese commanders). Survivors were taken to Japan as slave labor. On one ship, prisoners in a hold without air went mad with thirst and slashed each other's throats and wrists in an effort to suck blood. Many of the boats were sunk by American planes or submarines whose crews did not realize they were killing comrades.

In April 1942, a Japanese fleet set out to invade Port Moresby on New Guinea to put Japan within range to bomb Australia. The United States clashed with the Japanese in the Battle of the Coral Sea, sinking one carrier and losing one, a tactical draw that was a setback for Japan because it was compelled to cancel invasion plans. Fought entirely by carrier-based planes, it was the first naval battle in which surface fleets never made visual contact. That same month, American aviators, starved for a psychological victory, staged a daring raid on Tokyo. Sixteen B-25 bombers lifted off from the carrier *Hornet* some 650 miles offshore. Lacking sufficient gasoline to return, and unable to land bombers on an aircraft carrier, the planes were to fly on to friendly airfields in China. Most made it, yet eight fliers landed in enemy territory. Three were executed for bombing residential areas. The raid raised American morale, although it inflicted small damage.

With Japanese strategists seeking a decisive battle to smash the American fleet, Admiral Isoroku Yamamoto took most of his navy to attack Midway in June 1942, after a diversionary strike at the Aleutians. Aware of the scheme because of their ability to read Japanese codes, American planners set a trap, sending forces to await Yamamoto north of Midway. When Yamamoto's planes attacked, leaving their aircraft carriers unprotected, American pilots decimated his fleet, sinking four carriers to offset the loss of one carrier. Paradoxically, the decisive battle that Yamamoto sought was a devastating defeat. The Battle of Midway marked the end of Japanese expansion. American intelligence scored another coup that month. Cryptanalysts learned of Yamamoto's planned tour of the Solomons, allowing fighters to shoot down his plane, killing him and robbing Japan of its best admiral. The Solomons also figured in the first American offensive in the Pacific, at Guadalcanal in August. After Marines invaded, a series of naval engagements ensued while both sides attempted to reinforce troops. Ground fighting raged until the Japanese evacuated in February 1943. Guadalcanal marked another watershed in the war, for, henceforth, Japan was on the defensive and the United States did not lose a battle.

By the fall of 1943 the American offensive was proceeding rapidly, bolstered by six new Hellcat-stocked carriers for Pacific duty. Admiral Chester W. Nimitz was set to fight toward Japan through a line of islands including the Gilberts, the Marshalls, and the Marianas, as General Douglas MacArthur was to wage an offensive in the Southwest Pacific. On November 20 the navy attacked Tarawa in the Gilberts, preceding a landing of Marines, who subdued the island in three days. Nimitz next assaulted the Marshalls and took them by February 3, 1944, after stiff resistance. The next campaign, the most ambitious to date, focused in June 1944 on the Marianas, control of which was critical because B-29 bombers based there could attack the Japanese home islands. Saipan, the largest of the island group, was the scene of the bloodiest campaign and another serious defeat for Japan. The Americans lost 29 planes and 14,000 casualties. The Japanese lost 273 of the 373 planes that attacked the invading task force, 3 aircraft carriers, and 30,000 dead. About 50,000 Japanese were killed defending the Marianas. The United States constructed air bases there and a key harbor at Guam.

MacArthur, when forced to flee the Philippines, had vowed to return, a promise he insisted on redeeming. On October 20, 1944, as Marines landed on Leyte, MacArthur waded ashore to announce, "People of the Philippines, I have returned." The Marines seized the island, but not before the Battle of Leyte Gulf, the biggest naval engagement in the history of warfare and the last in World War II. For the first time the Japanese used kamikazes, planes loaded with explosives and flown into American ships by pilots on suicide missions, yet their navy was devastated, losing its four remaining carriers, three battleships, nine cruisers, and twelve destroyers. On January 9, 1945, Marines reached Luzon, the major Philippine island, and began fighting that took the lives of almost all the 260,000 Japanese defenders. In Manila, house-to-house fighting killed 100,000 civilians, but Americans captured the capital. Corregidor surrendered on March 2, and resistance ended by June 30, though fighting persisted in outlying islands.

The fighting for Iwo Jima, a small volcanic island, featured a moment that would be forever frozen in the American mind. Planes bombed the island for seventy-four days before 60,000 soldiers invaded on February 19, 1945, although the Japanese, who had constructed a maze of underground caves and tunnels, largely survived the bombardment and fought to the death. Mount Suribachi, dominating Iwo Jima, was honeycombed with caves, pillboxes, and bunkers that the Japanese defended ferociously, directing artillery fire from its peak toward the beaches. Nevertheless, Marines gradually fought their way up Suribachi, using flame throwers and explosives, and on the third day of combat three were photographed raising the American flag on the mountain, a photo that won the Pulitzer Prize and became the most famous picture of the war. Of the 23,000 defenders, 20,000 died; the United States lost nearly 6,000 dead.

The final American target before the planned invasion of the home islands was Okinawa, a sixty-mile-long island 350 miles southwest of Japan. Preliminary bombardment began on October 10, 1944, with the invasion getting under way on April 1, 1945. Seventy-seven thousand defended Okinawa against 183,000 American troops, the Japanese losing ten dead for each American killed and holding out more than eighty-three days, making planners in the United States fearful of the cost of invading Japan. There was apprehension despite faith in airpower. By early 1944 the Allies had the B-29 bomber, which flew at higher altitudes and had a longer range than the lighter, slower B-17, for an effort that wreaked havoc in Japan. At first, the director of the campaign, Major General Curtis LeMay, whose forces were based first in China and then in the Marianas, sought to cripple Japanese aircraft production. Soon, he shifted to area bombing, with incendiary bombs that ignited firestorms in cities built largely of wood and paper. A raid of 344 bombers on Tokyo on March 9, 1945, killed 84,000, wounded 41,000, and left more than 1 million homeless. Excluding nuclear bombs, the air raids destroyed 43 percent of sixty-three major Japanese cities, eliminated 42 percent of Japanese industrial capacity, and slew, injured, or left homeless 22 million.

If warfare in the Pacific turned from frustration to fruition for the Americans, it was unlike the war in China. The United States had few troops in China, yet a group of volunteers under retired Colonel Claire Chennault, the Flying Tigers, had been fighting in the air since 1940. Chennault's hopes that an air offensive against Japan by China-based planes would end the war proved unfounded. On the ground, aid from Washington was tangible in the person of Lieutenant General Joseph Stilwell, designated to represent Americans in China and to serve as chief of staff for Jiang Jieshe. Jiang's army was corrupt, demoralized, and ineffective, and Jiang was reluctant to fight. He wanted to conserve his army for the civil war against the communists that he knew would follow the defeat of Japan. His refusal to wage war aggressively, and the inability of his forces to recapture Burma, angered the irascible Stilwell, who quarreled constantly with the arrogant and secretive Generalissmo. In 1944 Roosevelt

★ PAUL TIBBETS: A FATEFUL FLIGHT ★

There is no morality in warfare. You kill children. You kill women. You kill old men. You don't seek them out, but they die. That's what happens in war.
—PAUL W. TIBBETS JR.

DEADLY CARGO
Paul Tibbets Jr. dropped
the first atom bomb.
(National Archives)

BOTH CARRIED a deadly cargo. In his coverall pocket, the pilot had a small box with twelve cyanide capsules; if their aircraft appeared to be in trouble, he and his eleven crewmen could choose suicide by poison or gun, to escape capture and torture by the enemy. In its bay, the plane bore the atomic bomb that was to be dropped on Hiroshima, Japan, on the morning of August 6, 1945.

Just before the runway ended near a cliff, Colonel Paul W. Tibbets Jr. lifted the *Enola Gay*, named for his mother, into the sky. He had led an 1,800-man force at Wendover, Utah, nearly a year in secret preparation. It was not until a few hours after takeoff that he told his crew the kind of bomb in the bay. Doubts about the righteousness of the mission did not trouble him. "Our crew did not do the bombing in anger," Tibbets said more than fifty years later. "We did it because we were determined to stop the killing, stop the war. I would have done anything to get to Japan and stop the killing."

Six hours and two thousand miles after takeoff, the moment came. Seventeen seconds past 8:15 A.M., the bomb bay opened and the weapon plummeted toward Hiroshima. Abruptly 9,700 pounds lighter, the plane bolted up ten feet and Tibbets pushed it into a sharp, diving right turn so it would not be directly above the blast. Forty-three seconds after it was dropped, the bomb detonated. Its flash blinded everyone aboard, and its rising shock wave battered the *Enola Gay* twice, jolting the crew. Then the air calmed, and the tail gunner saw flames and smoke on the ground, with a mushroom cloud billowing upward.

It was beyond compare, beyond comprehension. For the tape recording of the crew members' reactions, the thirty-year-old Tibbets confessed that he had expected to see a big explosion, but not of the magnitude he actually observed. Decades later, he recalled, "I looked at that city—and there was no city, there was nothing but the fringes of where the city used to be. There had been a city when we were making our approach, but now there was no humanity there."

The aftermath for Tibbets was often harsh, in the United States and overseas. Sent to a post in India in the 1960s, he was branded "the world's greatest killer" in procommunist newspapers and assigned a bodyguard. Eventually, the hostile press compelled the State Department to recall Tibbets and close the mission. Quitting the armed services following a distinguished thirty-year stint, he was sure that he was a victim of public opinion that blamed him for the bombing. He was, nevertheless, unapologetic. Asked whether he could sleep at night, Tibbets said in an interview published in 1999, "I sleep so well because I know how many people got to live full lives because of what we did."

And he added: "If you could fix me up so that I could do the same things in an airplane now that I could do in 1945? If you could do that and this country was in trouble, I would jump in there to beat hell."

Sources: For insight on Paul Tibbets and his mission, see Bob Greene's columns in the *Chicago Tribune* on January 10–13, 1999. Other good accounts of the mission are Gordon Thomas and Max Morgan Witts, *Enola Gay* (1977), and Peter Wyden, *Day One: Before Hiroshima and After* (1984).

sent a personal emissary, Major General Patrick J. Hurley, to resolve the Stilwell-Jiang dispute. After Hurley sided with Jiang, FDR recalled Stilwell and replaced him with Major General Albert C. Wedemeyer, who was no more successful in getting the Chinese to fight. Roosevelt's attempt to treat China as a great power was unrealistic, and to the Americans, the China campaign turned out to be one of the most vexing of the war. The main contribution of the Allied forces in China was to tie down Japanese troops.

The Atomic Age Begins

In the last seven weeks of the war, American planes, aircraft carriers, and surface vessels participated in the bombing of Japan, as the United States tightened a naval blockade of the islands. The deadliest bombs would be dropped last.

In July 1945, the Allies held their final wartime summit at Potsdam, Germany, at which Stalin alone remained of the Big Three. Truman had replaced the deceased Roosevelt as president, and during the conference Clement R. Attlee took over for Churchill, whom he had defeated in British elections. The conference settled few issues, and the Americans and the British were shocked when Stalin demanded huge reparations from Germany, a sign that the Grand Alliance was breaking up. At the gathering, Truman was informed of the first successful detonation of the atomic bomb on July 16, 1945, in a New Mexico desert. The United States, Britain, and China issued the Potsdam Declaration, urging Japan to surrender or face annihilation (although the bomb was not mentioned). Truman told Stalin of the powerful weapon, without revealing that it was an atomic bomb. Tokyo would not yield, so on August 6, three B-29s headed to drop a deadly payload on Hiroshima, chosen because it had been spared from heavy bombing and had no prisoner-of-war camps. The bomb caused 140,000 deaths and destroyed more than 80 percent of the city. A few hours later, the White House announced the existence of the bomb and warned the Japanese that unless they surrendered, "they may expect a rain of ruin from the air, the like of which has never been seen on this earth."

Forecasts of bad weather advanced the date for use of the second atomic bomb, sparing the primary target, Kokura, and condemning Nagasaki to destruction. No presidential decision was involved in the timing of the second bomb; that was left to the military, which was instructed to delude the Japanese into thinking that the United States had a large arsenal of atomic bombs when there were only two. Ultimately, some 70,000 would die from the bomb dropped August 9 at Nagasaki. The Soviet Union declared war on Japan on August 10, helping convince the Japanese that their cause was doomed. Humanity had unlocked and unleashed the secret of the atom, a breakthrough fraught with paradox that held, and would fulfill, much promise for good, but also would leave the world in fear of nuclear destruction. Even after the Nagasaki bombing, though, Tokyo was slow to surrender. To Allied demands for unconditional surrender, Japan responded by asking for the right to retain Emperor Hirohito. The Allies agreed, provided that he was to be a figurehead subject to their command. Japanese dislike of the condition aside, Hirohito agreed and announced the surrender, after an unsuccessful military coup attempt, on August 15. The official treaty of surrender was signed in Tokyo Bay aboard the battleship *Missouri* on September 2, 1945.

In later years, use of the bomb incurred recriminations in the United States, with debate over whether the war could have been ended without resort to the weapon. Some scientists and historians argued that the bomb was unnecessary, inhumane, immoral, ill-timed, petty vengeance for Pearl Harbor, and even racist. But it is difficult to imagine Japan giving up without the effects of the atomic bombs supplemented by the Soviet declaration of war. The alternatives were worse. Continued nonatomic bombing would have cost more lives than atomic bombing, and an invasion would have meant terrible losses on both sides, including Japanese civilians. Destruction of the home islands in hand-to-hand combat, instead of swift, comparatively limited death from above, would likely have left more bitterness among the survivors. Moreover, there is no question that the atomic bomb would have been used against the Germans had it been ready, nor is

JAPAN SURRENDERS
Douglas MacArthur signs for the United States on Tokyo Bay, September 2, 1945.
(National Archives)

there any doubt that Germany and Japan, both of which had nuclear programs, would have used the weapon against their opponents. And in the long run, the destruction and revulsion from the bomb made future military use of nuclear weapons unlikely. The atomic genie was never again freed from its bottle in the twentieth century.

The war exacted a horrific price: 20 million dead from the Soviet Union; 10.45 million from China; 5.5 million from Germany; 5.8 million from Poland, most of them Holocaust victims; 1.9 million from Japan; 430,000 from Britain; and more than 400,000 from the United States. Among American servicemen, just one in ten was ever exposed to combat, and with an overall death rate of five per one thousand, the military was, paradoxically, safer than the industrial home front, where the death rate was twice as high. The American contribution to the war was essential, involving millions of troops over vast distances and massive amounts of supplies to allies. Still, it was the Soviets who made the most important contribution to defeating Hitler in Europe. While the United States relied primarily on technology to overcome the Germans far from its soil, the Red Army wore them down with brute force, incurring horrible losses on Soviet land.

World War II wreaked unprecedented destruction and environmental damage that would affect generations. It set colonialism on a course toward extinction, required massive spending, accelerated scientific development, helped discredit racism, precipitated substantial (if sometimes temporary) changes in women's roles, and effected major changes in the economy and society. It ended the Great Depression and was a greater factor in redistributing income than any social program in American history. Like the conflagration, the era from 1920 to 1945 was cathartic, shaping the United States to a degree matched in few periods of comparable length. The country showed bravery that most generations could not equal and, with victory over the Axis, reached the apogee of its influence as a global power—but it could not banish the many tensions that loomed. Never before or since did the future seem so promising, or so perilous, as it did in the summer of 1945.

The American Economy, 1929–1945

Percent of civilian Labor force[1] (Unemployment rate)		Gross National Product in billions [2]		Summary of the Federal Government Finances (as of 12/31 each year)** Total Gross Debt in Millions	
1929	3.2	1929	104.4	1929	16.9
1930	8.7	1930	95.1	1930	16.1
1931	15.9	1931	89.5	1931	16.8
1932	23.6	1932	76.4	1932	19.4
1933	24.9	1933	74.2	1933	22.5
1934	21.7	1934	80.8	1934	57.0
1935	20.1	1935	91.4	1935	28.7
1936	19.9	1936	100.9	1936	33.7
1937	14.3	1937	109.1	1937	36.4
1938	19.0	1938	103.2	1938	37.1
1939	17.2	1939	111.0	1939	40.4
1940	14.6	1940	121.0	1940	42.9
1941	9.9	1941	138.7	1941	48.9
1942	4.7	1942	154.7	1942	72.4
1943	1.9	1943	170.2	1943	136.6
1944	1.2	1944	183.6	1944	201.0
1945	1.9	1945	180.9	1945	258.6

*From the *Historical Statistics of the United States: Colonial Times to 1970 (Bicentennial Edition).* September 1975. U.S. Department of Commerce, Bureau of the Census.

[2]**From the *Historical Statistics of the United States: Colonial Times to 1957 (A Statistical Abstract Supplement).* 1961. U.S. Department of Commerce, Bureau of the Census.

Bibliographic Essay

General Works

General histories of the interwar period include Glen Jeansonne, *Transformation and Reaction: America, 1921–1945* (2004); David M. Kennedy, *Freedom from Fear: The American People in Depression and War, 1929–1945* (1999); Michael Parrish, *Anxious Decades: America in Prosperity and Depression, 1929–1941* (1992); Page Smith, *Redeeming the Time: A People's History of the 1920s and the New Deal* (1987), especially strong on the conflict between capital and labor; and Sean Dennis Cashman, *America in the Twenties and Thirties: The Olympian Age of Franklin D. Roosevelt* (1989).

Histories of the 1920s include Ellis W. Hawley, *The Great War and the Search for a Modern Order: A History of the American People and Their Institutions, 1917–1933* (1979); Goeffrey Perrett, *America in the Twenties: A History* (1982), detailed and well-written; David J. Goldberg, *Discounted America: The United States in the 1920s* (1999); Arthur M. Schlesinger Jr., *The Age of Roosevelt*, vol. 1, *The Crisis of the Old Order, 1919–1933* (1958), by an author noted for his erudite style; and Paul A. Carter's succinct *The Twenties in America* (1975), and *Another Part of the Twenties* (1977). For a general history of the 1930s, see Gerald D. Nash, *The Crucial Era: The Great Depression and World War II, 1929–1945* (1992).

On women, works include Glenna Matthews, *"Just a Housewife": The Rise and Fall of Domesticity in America* (1987); Alice Kessler-Harris, *Out to Work: A History of Wage-Earning Women in the United States* (1982); Lois Scharf and Joan M. Jensen, eds., *Decades of Discontent: The Women's Movement, 1920–1940* (1983); and Robin Muncy, *Creating a Female Dominion in American Reform, 1890–1935* (1991). On African Americans, Native Americans, and immigrants, Leonard Dinnerstein et al., *Natives and Strangers: Blacks, Indians, and Immigrants in America* (1990), is a sweeping survey. Among the better histories of African Americans are John Hope Franklin, *From Slavery to Freedom: A History of American Negroes* (1967); Herbert Aptheker, *Afro-American History: The Modern Era* (1971); and Nicholas Lemann, *The Promised Land: The Great Black Migration and How It Changed America* (1991). On Mexican Americans, see David Guitierrez, *Walls and Mirrors* (1995). On Asian Americans, see Roger Daniels, *Asian-Americans* (1988). On the Italians and the Sacco-Vanzetti case, see Louis Joughlin and Edmond Morgan, *Postmortem: New Evidence in the Case of Sacco and Vanzetti* (1985), and Paul Avrich, *Sacco and Vanzetti: The Anarchist Persuasion* (1991). The Ku Klux Klan is examined in Wyn Craig Wade, *The Fiery Cross: The Ku Klux Klan in America* (1987); Richard K. Tucker, *The Dragon and the Cross: The Rise and Fall of the Ku Klux Klan in Middle America* (1991); Kathleen M. Blee, *Women of the Klan: Racism and Gender in the 1920s* (1991); and Nancy MacLean, *Behind the Mask of Chivalry: The Making of the Second Ku Klux Klan* (1994). Regarding labor, the best study is Irving Bernstein, *The Lean Years: A History of the American Worker, 1920–1933* (1960). Also helpful are Robert H. Zieger, *American Workers, American Unions, 1920–1985* (1986); David Brody, *Workers in Industrial America* (1980); and James R. Green, *The World of the Worker: Labor in Twentieth-Century America* (1980). Among the many studies of business are James M. Cortada, *Before the Computer: IBM, NCR, Borroughs, Remington, and the Industry They Created, 1865–1956* (1993), a fine history that focuses on technology; and James W. Prothro, *Dollar Decade: Business Ideas in the 1920s* (1985). On the automobile, which transformed business and society, see James J. Fink, *The Automobile Age (1988)*; and Lois Scharf, *Taking the Wheel: Women and the Coming of the Motor Age* (1991).

Presidents, Prosperity, and Depression

On the Republican reign of the 1920s, see John D. Hicks, *Republican Ascendancy, 1921–1933* (1958), which is dated but remains a solid political history. On Warren G. Harding, the best biography is Francis Russell, *The Shadow of Blooming Grove* (1968); also useful are Eugene P. Trani and David L. Wilson, *The Presidency of Warren G. Harding* (1977); Robert K. Murray, *The Harding Era: Warren G. Harding and His Administration* (1969); the highly critical Andrew Sinclair, *The Available Man* (1975); and Robert H. Ferrell, *The Strange Deaths of President Harding* (1996). The most recent biography of Harding, John W. Dean, *Warren G. Harding* (2004), considers Harding an underrated politician. On Calvin Coolidge, the most balanced book by far is Robert H. Ferrell, *The Presidency of*

Calvin Coolidge (1998). Other biographies include Robert Sobel, *Coolidge: An American Enigma* (1998), and Claude M. Fuess, *Calvin Coolidge: The Man from Vermont* (1981). There are numerous biographies of Herbert Hoover and accounts of his administration. David Burner, *Herbert Hoover: A Public Life* (1979), finds Hoover's personality flawed but his presidential policies constructive; Albert U. Romasco argues in *The Poverty of Abundance: Hoover, the Nation, the Depression* (1965), that his policies were a failure; and Joan Hoff-Wilson, *Herbert Hoover: Forgotten Progressive* (1975), considers him a Progressive out of his element. The most detailed account of Hoover's policies is Martin Fausold, *The Presidency of Herbert Hoover* (1985).

The stock market is treated in Robert Sobel, *The Great Bull Market: Wall Street in the 1920s* (1968), and John Kenneth Galbraith, *The Great Crash, 1929* (1961). Accounts of the depression include John A. Garraty, *The Great Depression* (1986), which provides a worldwide perspective; Edward Robb Ellis, *A Nation in Torment: The Great American Depression, 1929–1939* (1970); Gerald D. Nash, *The Great Depression and World War II: Organizing America, 1933–1945* (1979), a general account; Robert S. McElvaine, *The Great Depression: America, 1929–1941* (1984); and T. H. Watkins, *Great Depression: America in the 1930s* (1993), and *Hungry Years: A Narrative History of the Great Depression in America* (1999).

Franklin D. Roosevelt and the New Deal have generated an enormous literature. The best synthesis of the New Deal era remains James MacGregor Burns, *Roosevelt: The Lion and the Fox* (1956). Frank Friedel has written a comprehensive study, *Franklin D. Roosevelt*, 4 vols. (1952–1973), and a one-volume study, *Franklin D. Roosevelt: A Rendezvous with Destiny* (1990). Other single-volume works include George McJimsey, *The Presidency of Franklin Delano Roosevelt* (2000). Blanche Wiesen Cook has written a virtually definitive biography of the best-known first lady, *Eleanor Roosevelt*, vols. 1 and 2 (1992, 1999). General histories of the New Deal include Arthur M. Schlesinger Jr.'s three-volume *Age of Roosevelt*; William E. Leuchtenburg, *Franklin D. Roosevelt and the New Deal, 1932–1940* (1963), and *The FDR Years: On Roosevelt and his Legacy* (1995); and Alan Brinkley, *The End of Reform: New Deal Liberalism in Recession and War* (1995).

On FDR's opponents, see Albert Fried, *FDR and His Enemies* (1999); T. Harry Williams, *Huey Long* (1969); William Ivy Hair, *The Kingfish and His Realm: The Life and Times of Huey P. Long* (1991); Glen Jeansonne, *Messiah of the Masses: Huey P. Long and the Great Depression* (1993), a critical interpretation; Alan Brinkley, *Voices of Protest: Huey Long, Father Coughlin, and the Great Depression* (1982), elegantly written; Glen Jeansonne, *Gerald L. K. Smith: Minister of Hate* (1997); and

Leo P. Ribuffo, *The Old Christian Right: The Protestant Far Right from the Great Depression to the Cold War* (1983). Communism in 1930s America is the subject of Harvey Klehr, *The Heyday of American Communism: The Depression Decade* (1984); see also Mark Naison, *Communists in Harlem during the Depression* (1983). More general studies include Donald R. McCoy, *Angry Voices: Left of Center Politics in the New Deal Era* (1958); Kate Weigand, *Red Feminism: American Communism and the Making of Women's Liberation* (2000); and Richard H. Pells, *Radical Visions and American Dreams: Culture and Social Thought in the Depression Years* (1998).

Culture

General works include Ethan Mordden, *That Jazz! An Idiosyncratic Social History of the American Twenties* (1978); Barbara H. Solomon, ed., *Ain't We Got Fun? Essays, Lyrics, and Stories of the Twenties* (1980); Paula S. Fass, *The Damned and the Beautiful: American Youth in the 1920s* (1972); Alice Goldfarb Marquis, *Hopes and Ashes: The Birth of Modern Times, 1929–1939* (1986); the classic sociological study by Robert S. and Helen M. Lynd, *Middletown: A Study in Contemporary American Culture* (1929), and the sequel, *Middletown in Transition* (1937). On the greatest popular hero of the age, the best study is A. Scott Berg, *Lindbergh* (1998); see also Von Hardesty, *Lindbergh: Flight's Enigmatic Hero* (2002). On literature, see Frederick Hoffman, *The Twenties: American Writing in the Postwar Decade* (1965); Daniel Joseph Singal, *The War within: From Victorian to Modernist Thought in the South, 1919–1945* (1988); Nathan I. Huggins, *Harlem Renaissance* (1971); and Addison Gayle Jr., *The Way of the New World: The Black Novel in America* (1976). On the visual arts and architecture, see William S. Lieberman, ed., *Art of the Twenties* (1979); Abraham A. Davidson, *Early American Modernist Painting, 1910–1935* (1981); and Brendan Gill, *Many Masks: A Life of Frank Lloyd Wright* (1987). New Deal contributions to the arts are covered in Richard D. McKinzie, *The New Deal for Artists* (1973); and Francis V. O'Connor, *Federal Art Patronage, 1933–1943* (1966). On music and dance, among the best studies are Arnold Shaw, *The Jazz Age: Popular Music in the 1920s* (1987); Burton W. Peretti, *The Creation of Jazz: Music, Race, and Culture in Urban America* (1994); and Tony Thomas, *That's Dancing* (1984). On radio, see Eric F. Barnouw, *A Tower in Babel: A History of Broadcasting in the United States*, vol. 1, *To 1933* (1966), and *The Golden Web: A History of Broadcasting in the United States*, vol. 2, *To 1948* (1968). For motion pictures, see Andrew

Bergman, *We're in the Money: Depression America and Its Films* (1971), and Edward Wagenknecht, *The Movies in the Age of Innocence* (1962).

The literature on religious history is rich. The standard work on fundamentalism is George N. Marsden, *Fundamentalism and American Culture: The Shaping of Twentieth-Century Evangelism, 1870–1925* (1980). On the Scopes trial, the best book is Edward J. Larson, *Summer for the Gods: The Scopes Trial and America's Continuing Debate over Science and Religion* (1997). Also see Bernard Weisberger, *They Gathered at the River: The Story of the Great Revivalists and Their Impact on Religion in America* (1958); Florence M. Szasz, *The Divided Mind of Protestant America, 1880–1939* (1982); Joseph L. Blau, *Judaism in America: From Curiosity to Third Faith* (1976); and William M. Halsey, *The Survival of American Innocence: Catholicism in a Era of Disillusionment, 1920–1940* (1980).

For sports, turn to Elliot J. Gorn and Warren Goldstein, *A Brief History of American Sports* (1993); Benjamin G. Rader, *American Sports: From the Age of Folk Games to the Age of Televised Sports* (1999); Donn Rogosin, *Invisible Men* (1995), about black baseball before integration; and John M. Carroll, *Red Grange and the Rise of Modern Football* (1999).

Diplomacy and War

Warren I. Cohen has written the best short account of foreign policy in the 1920s, *Empire without Tears: American Foreign Relations, 1921–1933* (1987). Foster Rhea Dulles, *America's Rise to World Power, 1894–1954* (1963), is a reliable survey. Akira Iriye, *After Imperialism: The Search for a New Order in the Far East, 1921–1931* (1965), examines policy in the Pacific. Peace movements between the world wars are covered in Charles DeBenedetti, *Origins of the Modern American Peace Movement, 1915–1929* (1978), and Harriet Hyman Alonso, *The Women's Peace Union and the Outlawry of War, 1921–1942* (1989).

FDR's diplomacy is discussed succinctly in Robert A. Divine, *Roosevelt and World War II* (1971), and in more detail in Robert Dallek, *Franklin D. Roosevelt and American Foreign Policy, 1932–1945* (1979). Attempts to aid the Allies are included in Warren F. Kimball, *The Most Unsordid Act: Lend-Lease, 1939–1941* (1969), and Waldo Heinrichs, *Threshold of War: Franklin D. Roosevelt and American Entry into World War II* (1988). Isolationists are covered in Wayne S. Cole, *Roosevelt and the Isolationists, 1932–1945* (1983), and *America First: The Battle against Intervention, 1940–1941* (1953), and Bill Kauffman, *America First! Its History, Culture, and Politics* (1995). Glen Jeansonne, *Women of the Far Right: The Mothers'*

Movement and World War II (1996), describes a movement that sympathized with Adolf Hitler and opposed the American war against fascism. On the coming of World War II, two of the best works, though dated and overly detailed, are William L. Langer and S. Everett Gleason, *The Challenge to Isolation, 1937–1940* (1952), and *The Undeclared War, 1940–1941* (1953). For a Pacific study, see Akira Iriye, *The Origins of the Second World War in Asia and the Pacific* (1987). On Pearl Harbor, see Gordon W. Prange, *At Dawn We Slept: The Untold Story of Pearl Harbor* (1981).

General works on the war and the American role include H. P. Willmott, *The Great Crusade: A New Complete History of the Second World War* (1989); John Keegan, *The Second World War* (1989); Gerhard Weinberg, *A World at Arms: A Global History of World War II* (1994); Geoffrey Perrett, *There's a War To Be Won: The United States Army in World War II* (1991); William L. O'Neill, *A Democracy at War: America's Fight at Home and Abroad in World War II* (1993); and Charles B. MacDonald, *The Mighty Endeavor: The American War in Europe* (1986). For other aspects of the war, see Samuel Eliot Morison, *The Two-Ocean War* (1963), a masterful account of naval warfare; Rick Atkinson, *An Army at Dawn: The War in Africa, 1942–1943* (2002), an acclaimed study of the first joint military operation conducted by the Allies; Dan Van Der Vat, *The Atlantic Campaign* (1988); Stephen E. Ambrose, *The Supreme Commander: The War Years of Dwight D. Eisenhower* (1970); Ronald H. Spector, *Eagle against the Sun: The American War with Japan* (1985); and two riveting biographies, William Manchester, *American Caesar: Douglas MacArthur, 1880–1964* (1973); and Barbara Tuchman, *Stilwell and the American Experience in China* (1975).

On Roosevelt's role, the best is James MacGregor Burns, *Roosevelt: Soldier of Freedom* (1970). Also consult Eric Larrabee, *Commander in Chief: Franklin Delano Roosevelt, His Lieutenants and Their War* (1987); Kenneth Davis, *FDR: The War President, 1940–1943* (2000), and Doris Kearns Goodwin, *Franklin and Eleanor Roosevelt: The Home Front in World War II* (1994). Michael Beschloss, *The Conquerors: Roosevelt, Truman, and the Destruction of Hitler's Germany* (2002) describes Roosevelt's and Truman's efforts to make certain that Germany would never threaten the world again. Accounts of genocide in Europe are included in Henry L. Feingold, *The Politics of Rescue: The Roosevelt Administration and the Holocaust, 1938–1945* (1970); David S. Wyman, *The Abandonment of the Jews: America and the Holocaust, 1941–1945* (1984); Richard Breitman and Alan Kraut, *American Refugee Policy and American Jewry, 1933–1945* (1987); and Richard Breitman, *Official Secrets: What the Nazis Planned, What the British and Americans Knew* (1998).

The development of the atomic bomb is well chronicled in Richard Rhodes, *The Making of the Atomic Bomb* (1986). Use of the bomb is studied in Martin J. Sherwin, *A World Destroyed: The Atomic Bomb and the Grand Alliance* (1975), and Gar Alperovitz, *The Decision To Use the Atomic Bomb and the Architecture of an American Myth* (1995).

On the war at home, the best general histories are Geoffrey Perrett, *Days of Sadness, Years of Triumph, 1939–1945* (1973), and John Morton Blum, *V Was for Victory: Politics and American Culture during World War II* (1976). Also see Lewis A. Erenberg and Susan E. Hirsch, *The War in American Culture: Society and Consciousness during World War II* (1998); Richard Polenberg, *War and Society: The United States, 1941–1945* (1972); Nelson Lichtenstein, *Labor's War at Home: The CIO in World War II* (1982); and Joel Seidman, *American Labor from Defense to Reconversion* (1982). For the internment of Japanese-Americans, see Roger Daniels, *Prisoners without Trial: Japanese Americans in World War II* (1993), and Tetsuden Kashima, *Judgment without Trial: Japanese-American Imprisonment during World War II* (2003). On the roles of women and blacks, see D'Ann Campbell, *Women at War with America* (1984); Margaret Paton-Walsh, *Our War Too: American Women against the Axis* (2002); Neil Wynn, *The Afro-American and the Second World War* (1976); and Richard N. Dalfiume, *Desegregation of the U.S. Armed Forces, 1939–1953* (1969).

"To be or not to be? That is the question."

—Shakespeare, *Hamlet*

IN THE PERIOD from 1890 to 1945 Americans reveled in the fountain of their youth. Yet like youths, we stumbled, fell, got up, and went on. In many cases, we learned from our mistakes. The epoch was a time of euphoria, tragedy, reason, and chaos, a time of contradiction and confusion, as well as time of confidence and high purpose—a time of paradox. Americans struggled, with mixed success, to prove themselves, simultaneously, kind and gentle, and tough and smart. We overcame challenges and emerged to encounter new ones. The epoch was a time of great adventure, of loss, grief, and trauma, to be sure, but also a time of learning, maturing, and finding wisdom.

Three events dominated the period: World War I, the Great Depression, and World War II. These events defined and toughened Americans, and made them the world's leaders in industrial and military might, diplomacy, and finance. Americans wore the crown of their achievements uneasily. For much of the period we ran scared.

Spurred by advances in transportation and communication, culture underwent a more rapid transformation than at any previous time in history. The rate of change accelerated in the second half of the twentieth century. Many changes resulted from necessity. Writers, musicians, painters, and playwrights were compelled to shape new modes of expression to articulate the experience of living in a world where older values were called into question.

Images raced across the globe through the transmission of photographs. Motion pictures held audiences spellbound in darkened cinemas at every corner of the nation. The technology to bring moving, talking pictures into every home already existed in the 1930s, but not until after World War II would this new technology be fully exploited. Television would build on the social effects of radio and movies.

Many creative artists struggled to find fulfillment within the American system. Even as capitalism lurched and stumbled during the Great Depression, the economic system survived intact, and breathed new life at the end of World War II. During the first half of the twentieth century popular entertainment reached audiences of unprecedented size, yet it was also a period of experimentation. Modernism in art and architecture communicated in simpler geometry and greater verbal directness. The prose of Ernest Hemingway struck to the point without lavish displays of literary formality. The era's representational painters worked in simpler lines than their predecessors in a hurried effort to grasp the essence of their subjects. The increasing pace of life left cultural artifacts that might be appreciated at a glance, even if they only revealed their full meaning upon reflection.

Perhaps the largest enigma of the age was its greatest president, Franklin Delano Roosevelt, a man with many superficial acquaintances, but few, if any, intimate friends. Unlike Theodore Roosevelt, Franklin wrote very little and expressed himself solely in the spoken word—and then guardedly. He sealed himself off emotionally from his wife, his family, and his political allies. No one knew his religious and philosophic beliefs. Despite his wit, he did not say much. Despite his friendliness, he was manipulative and relished power. He might have been a less compassionate person than the publicly despised Herbert Hoover. Both were stubborn and sensitive to criticism, though Hoover, a poor politician, betrayed his bitterness openly. Yet Roosevelt worked diligently to destroy political opponents, including Hoover, and usually succeeded.

The epoch's greatest paradox might be that its greatest president could not be elected in the twenty-first century. When I was a small boy, I asked my father, "Does the Army accept disabled people?"

"Well, the Commander-in-Chief was confined to a wheel chair."

I was astonished to learn that FDR could not stand unaided, much less walk. Yet he concealed this successfully from much of the public and persuaded reporters not to photograph him in his wheelchair. The great president, like the great nation he represented, was, paradoxically, both extraordinarily strong and extraordinarily vulnerable.

If Roosevelt were to seek the presidency today he would have to run in fifty primaries and caucuses stretching over about two years, and appear personally to deliver hundreds of speeches to raise the millions of dollars necessary for a modern campaign. Television would magnify his handicap, especially if he had to participate in a series of televised debates. The press would probe his private life and find infidelity. Even more important, in the context of today's investigative reporting it would not have been easy to conceal that in 1944 FDR was a dying man.

If we seek guidance from the great leaders of the past, we must seek it in their ideals rather than in their wisdom about specific problems, for our problems are quite different. Hindsight is not 20/20 or historians would always agree, and of course we do not. Just as history delights in surprise, historians can be idiosyncratic. What is one to think of a historian, such as the current one, who admires both Herbert Hoover and Franklin Roosevelt?

There are other paradoxes, some specific to the period, others universal:

- The paradox that tough diplomacy in the Pacific invited war whereas tougher diplomacy in Europe might have short-circuited Hitler's expansion
- The paradox that our memories of the past are sometimes mellower than living through it was
- The paradox that the solution to some problems is the incubator of others, as victory in World War II incubated the Cold War
- The paradox that to ordinary Americans the microcosm is often more important than the macrocosm. During the greatest periods of trial, many Americans found fulfillment in love, work, and family
- The paradox that we only learn from failure. We are lucky, indeed, if we make our mistakes early enough to correct them.
- The paradox that the only constant is change
- The paradox that history can correct the record but it cannot correct the past
- The paradox that the more fleeting a pleasure, the more delicious it is
- The paradox that we sometimes complain the most in the best of times and pull together in the worst of times

Americans wondered whether the first half of the century marked the end of an era, or the beginning, of a new, more dangerous one. It was both. In the period after 1945 Americans would not be allowed to rest in peace, but would be required to be constantly vigilant in a world made more terrible by liberating the atomic genie. Although Hitler's armies had marched across Europe and the Japanese had bombed American soil, the weapons of the postwar period were the most potent ever designed by humans. The choice of Americans and their adversaries would be to live in an uneasy peace or to commit mutual suicide. In the words of Hamlet, "To be, or not to be?"

Index

About the Author

GLEN JEANSONNE has taught twentieth-century American history at the University of Louisiana–Lafayette, Williams College, and the University of Wisconsin–Milwaukee. *A Time of Paradox* is his ninth book, which include *Leander Perez* (1977), *Gerald L. K. Smith* (1988), *Huey Long* (1993), *Transformation and Reaction* (1994), and *Women of the Far Right* (1997). Jeansonne received his B.A. in history from the University of Louisiana–Lafayette, where he graduated salutatorian in 1968, and his Ph.D. from Florida State University in 1973.

DAVID LUHRSSEN has lectured at Marquette University, Beloit College, and the Milwaukee Institute of Art and Design. He has written extensively on music, film, and culture.